CREATIVE COACHING

A Support Group for Children with ADHD

With Curriculum-Based Activities

2nd Edition

by Nancy McDougall & Janet Roper

ISBN # 1-889636-40-1
LCCN # 2001088729

Although the authors and publishers have made every effort to ensure the accuracy and completeness of information contained in this book, we assume no responsibility for errors, inaccuracies, omissions, or any inconsistencies herein. Any slights of people, places or organizations are unintentional.

Cover Design & Book Layout - Elizabeth Madden, Elaine Callahan
Project Editors - Melissa White and Lisa Nordlund

10 9 8 7 6 5 4 3 2 1
Printed in the United States of America

What Professionals & Parents Say About Creative Coaching

"Attention Deficit Hyperactivity Disorder (ADHD) is a common childhood condition affecting 5% of the school age population. Dealing with these children in the classroom can be very stressful. Medications can help the problem greatly, but we often ask ourselves if we can do more. Children spend so much of their time in school, it is no wonder that teachers and counselors can have a big impact."

"This curriculum is put together by two highly experienced school counselors. These dedicated educators have worked with many of my patients and I have been very impressed by their persistence and skill at working with kids. This curriculum is a valuable compendium of their long experience, filled with practical tips and down-to-earth suggestions for dealing with ADHD children."

"I think this curriculum will make you feel much more comfortable dealing with the ADHD child in your school. Untreated ADHD is a major risk factor for drug abuse, school drop outs, and juvenile delinquency. Through intervention, you have a real chance of steering your ADHD students clear of these hazards."

☆ Steven R. Pliszka, M.D., Chief of Child & Adolescent Psychiatry, University of Texas Health Science Center, San Antonio

"I have reviewed *Creative Coaching* and find it to be the most helpful tool for counselors that I have seen in my 20 years of working with ADD children."

☆ James S. Wicoff, M.D., Child/Adolescent/Adult Psychiatry

"*Creative Coaching* is a 'must have' resource for the elementary school counselor striving to assist these students. It is well organized, straightforward, full of examples, and presented in a language (coaching) that is readily recognized by all ages. It is a gold mine of ideas and strategies that will capture the attention of these students. *Creative Coachings* is a marvelous program which will help students be successful and counselors be rewarded."

☆ Randall V. Sellers, M.D., Child, Adolescent & Adult Psychiatry

"ADHD affects 5% of children, making it, perhaps, the most common medical problem seen in schools. If untreated, it often affects learning, grades, self-confidence, self-esteem, mood, anxiety, and even conduct. All too often the treatment is limited to medication only. As effective as medicines are, many symptoms and differences remain in the ADHD child. *Creative Coaching* as a curriculum-based support group for ADHD children is a comprehensive, effective, and fun approach that any elementary counselor can use to help their ADHD students. The cookbook approach makes it easy to use. My advice to school counselors is to stop reinventing the wheel and use *Creative Coaching* as your guide to helping your ADHD students."

☆ John C. Burnside, M.D. Child & Adolescent Psychiatry

Creative Coaching is a comprehensive, user-friendly guide to enable any educator or therapist to begin running a social skills group for school-age children with ADHD. This manual is crammed with useful, practical information from the most recent research on ADHD to specific guidelines to address children's questions in a way they will understand. *Creative Coaching* is a 'must' for any professional working with ADHD clients, whether in a classroom, group, or individually."

☆ Mel Cohen, M.D. Child & Adolescent Psychiatry

"*Creative Coaching* is a spectacular collection of truly useful perspectives, strategies, and tool. I highly recommend it!"
   ☆ Thom Hartmann, Author of *ADD Success Stories* & co-editor of *Think Fast*.

"I just wanted to let you know how much having *Creative Coaching* has helped in working with my students. It is very interesting to see how parents participate with their children with the home practice activities. Students love it when parents' compliments were read aloud in group! So many activities for each skill will help to personalize what can be done with different children and age groups. Having all these well planned, skill appropriate and FUN activities at my fingertips is a Godsend."
   ☆ Teri Myers, Elementary School Counselor (2 years)

"As I reflect back over these past weeks, I think what a wonderful opportunity it's been to use your ideas. For me, having lots of options and activities to choose from is very important. The message is key, but the method has to be good!"
   ☆ Sandra Foster, Elementary School Counselor (15 years)

"I am continuing to incorporate some of your topics and activities with my already existing curriculum depending on the concept being taught that session. I find your activities and play options help to flesh out my lesson and make for a more exciting session altogether."
   ☆ Shawn Langford, M.A., LPC in private practice

"*Creative Coaching* is right on target with many of the students' interest in sports. The students came up with wonderful ideas on how they help themselves pay attention. For these children, who often hear that they aren't good at paying attention, it was fun to feel like experts. One of the best features of this program is that the preparation time for the counselor is minimal! I can read through the objectives, game plan, and discussion questions in 10 minutes and I am completely prepared for a very effective group."
   ☆ Cathy Ortiz, Elementary School Counselor (1st year)

"The athletic boys in group really related to the coaching theme; the kids really seemed to understand the Connecting to the Real World. They love to 'huddle up' for objectives and enjoy the physical activity."
   ☆ Melanie Vaughan, Elementary School Counselor (4 years)

"We saw improved listening skills - specifically looking at the person who talks. The introductory parent meeting was beneficial as it helped us to understand that it (ADHD) is a condition correctable through medication; the descriptions of the different medications and potential side effects was reassuring."
   ☆ Parents of a 3rd grader

"Our child benefited from learning to listen more efficiently and express herself at an appropriate time. She absolutely loved the group sessions and wishes she could still come." A compliment this parent wrote to her child reads: "I have noticed a big change in the way you listen better & pay more attention while someone else is talking. You are much more calm these days. We are proud of you!"
   ☆ Mother of a 1st grader

Dedication

Dedicated to our husbands Doug Roper and
Michael McDougall, whose deep, abiding
and patient love has sustained,
encouraged and provided a bedrock for us,

to Sean Roper, whose efforts to teach me to play
have been just as valuable as my attempts
to teach him to work,

to Matthew, Kenneth and Jeff McDougall who
represent God's gifts of love and joy in my life,

and

to the many children who have made us
keenly aware of the need for this work.

Acknowledgements

We appreciate so much the support and encouragement given to us by our counseling colleagues and especially by our Director of Guidance for North East ISD, Carol Churchill and by respective principals, Ruth Fowler and Jim Huston.

We are also grateful for the input and encouragement received by professionals in the medical community who provided valuable feedback. Dr. Steven Pliszka, Dr. John Burnside, Dr. Wayne Wilson Grant, Dr. James Wicoff, Dr. Melvin Cohen and Dr. Randall Sellers were all generous with their time and expertise.

This book could not have been as practical and applicable if it had not been for the enthusiastic work by the counselors who agreed to field test or review the materials and give us meaningful suggestions for improvement. Our dedicated field testers and contributors included:

- ☆ Mindi Acord and Janie de la Garza, The Winston School San Antonio (a private school for children with learning differences)
- ☆ Lois Bohl, Redland Oaks Elementary, NEISD
- ☆ Pam Brook, Thousand Oaks Elementary, NEISD
- ☆ Penny DeVoss, Encino Park Elementary, NEISD
- ☆ Sandy Foster , Kate Schenck Elementary, SAISD
- ☆ Shirley Gebhardt, Thousand Oaks Elementary, NEISD
- ☆ Carrie Hillman, Headmistress, St. Thomas Moore Episcopal Preschool
- ☆ Patti Johnston, Northwest Crossing , NISD
- ☆ Shawn Langford, Therapist in private practice
- ☆ Lynn Lavelle, Behavior Interventionist Children's Intervention Center, NEISD
- ☆ Margaret Matthews, Encino Park Elementary, NEISD
- ☆ Teri Myers, Robert McDermott Elementary, NISD
- ☆ Cathy Ortiz, Weiderstein Elementary, Schertz-Cibolo ISD
- ☆ Tonda Pratt, Northwood Elementary, NEISD
- ☆ Jill Rithmeyer
- ☆ Doug Roper - artist
- ☆ Guy Roper, Psychologist in private practice
- ☆ Melanie Vaughn, Oak Meadow Elementary, NEISD
- ☆ Mellonee Villalobos, Carroll Bell Elementary, Harlandale ISD
- ☆ Cindy Woodlee, Helotes Elementary, NISD
- ☆ Eli Zambrano, NISD

Foreword

For several years we had been involved with colleagues in helping to create dynamic classroom guidance lessons for our district's counselors to use. Several of us commented on the need for well organized materials to use with small groups. We were disappointed in our search for resources specifically for groups of children with ADHD. True to the old phrase about necessity being the mother of invention, we finally decided to get busy and create our own curriculum.

As we neared the completion of this project, we found ourselves in search of a meaningful metaphor to describe the process through which this curriculum was produced. Childbirth came to mind, a sporting theme was tempting, but horticulture seemed more fitting for we have sown seeds, cultivated them over time as our own counseling experience allowed, weeded out what seemed extraneous, and pruned back what appeared to be unwieldy until, at last, we arrived at a point where we were fairly content with the foliage or arrangement and variety of ideas that have grown out of our fertile imaginations and the needs we have encountered within the student populations we've served.

As the "almost final" draft was field tested and we began to step back and view the work from a bit of a distance, its versatility became more apparent. We realized, along with others who were working with the materials, that the activities included could be utilized in a variety of ways.

   ☆ The sports theme could be de-emphasized or different sections of the book could be combined in numerous ways for use with varying types of small groups.
   ☆ Students in friendship groups could use the communication and teamwork sections as a focus for a meaningful group experience.
   ☆ Students needing specific help with study or classroom coping skills could benefit from the listening, paying attention, organization and goal setting sections.
   ☆ The sections on feelings, self concept, goal setting and communication would help students deal with feelings arising from poor self concepts or difficulties in the home setting.

In short, this curriculum could be used to meet the needs of many children who are not necessarily identified as having Attention Deficit Hyperactive Disorder. In the section on educational accommodations for children with ADHD, we mentioned that classroom modifications often prove to be useful for any child at some point in time. In the same way, large or small group guidance lessons can be adapted from the ideas and activities in this curriculum to enhance a guidance program for all children.

Table of Contents

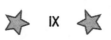

. . .why we wrote this

..from Janet

Shortly after Doug and I were married, the characteristics so typical of ADHD (inattentive type) that had initially attracted me to him - his spontaneity, incredible creativity, a wonderfully "laid back" personality, a free spirit - began to express themselves in less charming ways. He was so laid back that he couldn't seem to meet deadlines or stay on tract to complete jobs. His creative impulses were numerous, but follow-through and closure were rare. Spontaneity became tarnished as it lapsed into impulsive buying and his strong pleasure ethic clashed head on with my Germanic work ethic. Our marriage seemed to be on the road to ruin as frustration mounted and we experienced the painful shock of "real life" consequences that arose from our failure to impose some order on the chaotic life we shared.

Ten years later Sean was born. While he was one of the few important things in our life that we had carefully planned for, we weren't quite prepared for the gift we got. The old analogy about planning a trip to Hawaii, but winding up in Kansas instead, seemed to fit. It is not that Kansas is terrible; it's just not were we'd planned to go. As we learned to love our strong-willed bundle of energy we had to rethink things, gain familiarity with our little whirlwind, unpack the sun tan lotion and learn to weather some storms instead. Initially, as difficulties arose, I was neither creative nor supportive. I resembled a cross between a drill sergeant with PMS and an overbearing mother turned terrorist! Taking this stance was draining for me and unbearable for Doug and Sean.

As time went on, both my husband and son were diagnosed with ADHD, and we began to search for some "perfect plan" or technique to alleviate the symptoms and the stress associated with the disorder. While we haven't discovered any miraculous cure, we continue to believe in and apply meaningful insights gained with God's help and support from friends, family and mental health professionals:

- ☆ Time outs can be a **gift** for children and adults.
- ☆ Behavior management only goes so far.
- ☆ Valuing the "product" is not as important as recognizing the effort expended to produce it.
- ☆ Our family is not on this trek alone.
- ☆ You can catch more flies with honey than vinegar.
- ☆ Consistent tolerance and commitment are needed to build, repair and sustain relationships.
- ☆ Coping skills evolve **slowly**; expecting rapid, far-reaching change in behavior is about as reasonable and gratifying as trying to nail Jello® to a wall!
- ☆ There are inevitable ups & downs with ADHD; the depths of despair are extreme but so are the moments of joy!

Learning to be a "creative coach" doesn't happen in a vacuum or overnight. Prayer, private tutoring, therapy, medical intervention, rigorous behavioral contracting, special education support and meaningful contact with others on the same road have all been essential.

...from Nancy

When I compare the intense impact of ADHD on Janet's family life, I realize that this condition has affected my family differently. We hear of Attention Deficit as occurring on a continuum from mild to severe. My experience has been more at the mild to moderate end of the spectrum. My parents thought of me as a non-stop talker whose middle name by high school age had become "on the go." Even though I excelled as a student, I have suspected in retrospect that many of the study strategies and work habits I developed were actually ways to compensate for my distractibility and racing mind. I learned to take verbatim notes in classes to keep focused; to study for tests alone while using "white noise" to screen out distant auditory distractions; and to make constant "to do" lists. Expanding my interpersonal skills as I earned my counseling degree must have paid off, since friends at my ten-year high school reunion commented on my social "late bloomer" status.

Learning to organize a household with three boys (born within an eight-year span), a husband who is a concrete sequential engineer, and a professional career has been made more difficult with my random nature. Of our three sons, Jeff and Matt tend to be more like their father. Our middle son Kenneth seems to have inherited my tendencies to procrastinate, a comfort level with "piles," and creative energy that keeps him involved simultaneously in many different projects. He has experienced the flip sides of ADHD, from losing car keys, wallets, textbooks, and assignments to juggling a schedule of AP classes, award-winning drama productions, band competitions, and as he puts it, "my ever-expanding harem of women." Unlike Janet's family, ours used medication only briefly and accessed family therapy on a short-term basis.

Since both Janet and I have experienced this long trek personally, we are humble enough not to make unrealistic claims about incredible improvements arising from this curriculum. The journey IS worth taking as long as we don't expect to jog 20 miles a day along side these kids or expect them to achieve Olympic levels of performance overnight. Our faith in God has helped us to maintain a healthy perspective, to remember that all people are His unique and intentional creations and to enjoy the peace that passes understanding even in the midst of chaos.

Our decision to write the *Creative Coaching* curriculum arose out of our personal investment and out of the realization that an extensive, formalized program did not exist. Because we have experienced the benefits of having a well-prepared classroom guidance curriculum in our district, we believed that other programs could be enhanced by materials especially designed for use with specific groups.

Using various versions of this curriculum, we have conducted educational support groups for children with ADHD for the last six years at each of our elementary schools. We first got the courage to do these groups when our district secured the limited services of outside therapists to co-lead groups with school counselors. At that time, we requested support for starting groups for children with ADHD. It seemed like a simple request; but as it turned out, coordinating our school schedules with private therapists was tougher than anticipated. A psychologist came to work on campus, however was able to follow through with only one group meeting. Surprisingly, we discovered we could do fine on our own, especially with a structured plan in place.

We are confident that other professional educators and mental health practitioners will bring their own expertise and insights in the successful application of this curriculum. We appreciate any feedback from those of you who will be using these materials and encourage you to write us in care of YouthLight, Inc., P.O. Box 115, Chapin, SC 29036.

. . .getting started!

Prior
  Planning
    Prevents
      Poor
        Performance

TIP!!

Most Commonly Asked Questions About *CREATIVE COACHING*

1. What is this program and who is it for?

2. What is covered in each of the fourteen sessions?

3. Why is a small curriculum-based group approach needed?

4. How have children and adults responded to the program?

5. Who can lead a *Creative Coaching* group?

6. What kind of parent support would you need?

7. What other kinds of support are needed (teacher, administrative, etc.)?

8. What are the "nuts and bolts" of implementing the group?

    ☆ Responsibilities of a group leader
    ☆ Session format
    ☆ Rewards and reinforcements
    ☆ Handling problem behaviors in group

Questions & Answers About
CREATIVE COACHING

1. What is this program and who is it for?

This program is a practical resource for conducting educational groups for children. Short-term, educational, curriculum-based groups provide a supportive and nurturing environment within which children can learn and practice specific life skills. And, although applicable for almost all children, *Creative Coaching* can be specifically referenced when working with children who have Attention Deficit Hyperactivity Disorder. In addition to providing specific suggestions for learning objectives and activities, this program includes detailed instructions for implementing groups and resource materials which provide training for teachers and parents who wish to enhance student skills.

2. What is covered in each of the fourteen sessions?

The curriculum offers fourteen sessions from which a group leader can design the most effective sequence and content of concepts for any particular group of children. Following is a brief summary of relevance to the "real world" and description of learning objectives in each session.

SESSION 1 - INTRODUCTION

This is the session in which students become familiar with how the group will operate. The group leader uses a sports team metaphor to establish the relevance of rule making, skill development, improved performance, and teamwork. Students begin to establish group cohesiveness as they are involved in initial activities, learn about the token reinforcement system to be used, and are offered opportunities to become personally invested in this particular group.

SESSION 2 - LISTENING

Just as successful players learn to listen to their coaches even in the midst of distractions, group members learn the steps to listening effectively and have opportunities to demonstrate their skills in a variety of activities. Through these group experiences, students identify both positive consequences of listening effectively and the negative consequences that occur when they choose not to listen.

SESSION 3 - UNDERSTANDING ADHD - PART 1

This session is based on the assumption that the more children learn about ADHD the better they will know themselves and be able to capitalize on personal strengths while compensating for limitations. Students learn characteristics and the underlying physiological basis of ADHD. Students are encouraged to view ADHD as a condition that may be characterized more as a difference than as a disease or disorder. Group members have an opportunity to listen and respond to children's books about ADHD.

SESSION 4 - PAYING ATTENTION

Most students have experienced situations in which they must concentrate in order to perform well. Focused concentration is as essential in the classroom as it is in the athletic world. Students identify, practice and evaluate basic attending skills within group activities. Specific strategies for handling distractions are discussed and applied.

SESSION 5 - ORGANIZATION

The process of becoming and staying organized requires, like biking and hiking, a great deal of stamina and endurance resulting from time and energy invested on a daily basis. Because organization can be boring, emphasis is placed on the positive benefits and the need to accept coaching from a third party. Group members participate in practical, down-to-earth activities that result in orderly notebooks and desks.

SESSION 6 - SELF CONCEPT

Group members have opportunities to share their own strengths and weaknesses with one another. The emphasis is on self acceptance and personal effort as modeled by popular sports figures who accept wins and defeats gracefully, learn from mistakes and strive to improve their skills. Students are encouraged to acknowledge the variety of gifts and talents others possess and to make choices about which personal attributes they want to enhance through practice.

SESSION 7 - GOAL SETTING

Goal setting is the skill that bridges the gap between intention and action. Students participate in group and individual goal setting using the SMART criteria; that is, effective goals are Specific, Measurable, Accountable, Realistic and "Totally Mine." Students are encouraged to set a goal and periodically share with the group their progress toward attainment. This practical application helps to teach the concept that any goal worth achieving comes at a price. Parallels with the world of athletics are drawn from discussions of athletes, like swimmers, who have to do boring, repetitive and frequent workouts in order to achieve record performances.

SESSION 8 - FEELINGS

The emphasis in this session is on identification and appropriate expression of feelings. While all feelings are valid, some, like anger, are more difficult to express in ways that are not harmful to oneself or to others. Because of heavy media exposure, students are very familiar with the way famous athletes handle strong emotion. Group members learn consequences of lack of self control and strategies for maintaining positive attitudes in the face of frustration.

SESSION 9 - CONTROLLING IMPULSES

Knowing how far you have to go, when to back off, how far to push (an issue), when to stop (boundaries), how risk taking to be and how fast or slow to go are all skills that help us "go the distance" in the race of life. Students learn specific strategies to help them stop and think before overreacting and examine the consequences of not pacing themselves appropriately. Parallels are drawn from racing strategies where speed is usually not the only factor in winning.

 8

SESSION 10 - LEARNING TO RELAX

Great athletic or academic performance depends on knowing when and how to relax mentally and physically. For students to deal successfully with the stress of daily living, they must be able to clear out their mental clutter, relieve their anxieties, and focus on the task at hand. Students have an opportunity to experience relaxation exercises and are asked to identify times in their lives when relaxing is important.

SESSION 11 - COMMUNICATION

The world of sports provides a great variety of examples of both verbal and nonverbal communication. While children of almost any age can identify sportsmanlike versus unsportsmanlike behavior, mastering the subtleties of basic communication skills presents a real challenge. Students develop awareness of their personal responsibility to send and receive clear communication signals. Group members identify common blocks to effective communication and generate more positive approaches.

SESSION 12 - FRIENDSHIP

Students learn through experiential play that when it comes to having and keeping friends, it's how you play the game that counts! Emphasis is placed on respecting others' personal space and resolving conflicts while being part of a team. This session includes many fun, interactive opportunities for team building.

SESSION 13 - UNDERSTANDING ADHD - PART 2

This session reinforces many of the concepts introduced in Session 3, with the added opportunity of students being able to ask questions in a medical context. Group members explore the difference between understanding ADHD as an explanation for their actions and using ADHD as an excuse for their misbehaviors. Students learn that believing in themselves and being persistent may be among their most important abilities. As they gain insight into this life-long trek, they will know themselves better and be able to capitalize on strengths and compensate for attributes holding them back.

SESSION 14 - CLOSING CELEBRATION

Although planning a special event to bring closure for students requires extra effort, this type of celebration provides a unique opportunity for parents to be totally focused on their children and encourages them to continue "coaching" to ensure ongoing progress. The entire process of group work and participatory learning is validated as parents are engaged in some of the same activities their children completed in group. This session includes specific suggestions for various centers that could be prepared.

3. Why is a small, curriculum-based group approach needed?

Small groups can be an essential component in the overall treatment plan for students who have primary characteristics of ADHD without significant comorbid features of anxiety or depression. Groups, like the type proposed in this curriculum that are conducted within the school setting, have the distinct advantage of providing a "real world" arena in which students can develop and practice skills during the course of a "normal" day. Often, children have a more difficult time generalizing skills learned in the isolated and artificial environment of a therapist's office. The school is more likely to embody the concept of "taking a village to raise a child" as children are encircled and supported by peers within the group, by the group leader who serves as advocate and by concerned teachers and parents who reinforce and encourage them as they apply their skills at home and at school. When students need additional support from the medical or mental health community, this positive group experience often helps them to be more receptive to other therapeutic experiences.

In an interview with Dr. Steven Pliszka, a nationally recognized expert in the field of ADHD, he explained that existing research seems to indicate that no one isolated treatment produces lasting results. Several studies have tried to determine the effectiveness of varying combinations of treatment. In a recent review conducted by the National Institute of Mental Health (*J. Am. Acad. Child Adolesc. Psychiatry*, 1995, 34, 8:987-1000), researchers have been able to show that "the combination of clinically useful medication with appropriate psychosocial treatments directed to specific child and family functioning deficits yielded unexpectedly positive outcomes."

Dr. John E. Richters, at the National Institute of Mental Health, is heading a comprehensive, multimodal, scientific research study being conducted over a five-year period throughout six different research centers, each using common methodologies. After beginning with a year-long review of current literature, project directors discovered several questions that have not been successfully answered in previous research studies. Representatives from several sites using common procedures will generate comparative data to answer the questions of "under what circumstances and with what child characteristics . . . do which treatments or combinations of treatments (stimulants, behavior therapy, parent training, school-based interventions) . . . have what impacts . . . on what domains of child functioning . . . for how long . . . to what extent... and why" (*J. Am. Acad. Child Adolesc. Psychiatry*, 1995, 34, 8:987-1000).

4. How have children and adults responded to the program?

The response to *Creative Coaching* from parents and children has been overwhelmingly positive! This feedback has been invaluable and has resulted in the addition of several features which enhance communication between school and home and have provided additional opportunities for parents to interact with their children. We even received word from one administrator that parents were requesting that middle school staff continue such educational groups. In addition to children asking to be included in group, parents report receiving the following feedback from their children about their participation in group:

☆ "Very little detail, but always "I really loved it, Mom".
☆ "He gets excited about going."
☆ "He liked going; it's fun. Didn't want to be specific."
☆ "He seemed to have a positive experience."
☆ "He enjoyed the group sessions without relaying specific details; his mood was very positive. We saw an overall improvement in his day-to-day behavior - no anger."
☆ "He enjoyed being able to share his feelings and not feeling like he was all alone."

When asked what parts of the program they thought their children benefited from the most, parents responded:

- ☆ "He was affirmed as a special and neat person. It was good for his self-esteem."
- ☆ "Knowing he's not alone & just being part of the group."
- ☆ "Just being with his peers."
- ☆ "Knowing others in the group have had the same problems. He also liked the relaxation exercises."
- ☆ "Self-control - dealing with anger."
- ☆ "Learning how to temper his feelings and not get so disappointed."

When we asked for suggestions that would improve the program, most indicated they would like it to be extended. However, both children and parents commented that it was difficult to miss other activities in order to attend group.

- ☆ "Nothing was least helpful. To improve, have maintenance classes (one every four weeks) on application of skills."
- ☆ "Missing music or PE (once a week) was tough on him. To improve, maybe offer some techniques for the parents to use at home."
- ☆ "None was least helpful. To improve, I would like to see the group session continue as a form of behavior modification for the kids."
- ☆ "Expand it to be incorporated into the LD child's regular program."

Based on parent feedback, an initial orientation meeting is critical to the overall effectiveness of the program. Many parents commented that they would have been "clueless" without the group overview, and experience confirmed that the poorest parent response was from those who were not able to receive an explanation of how important their support was. Specific comments from those who attended the parent meeting included:

- ☆ "I wouldn't have known what it was about. Michael didn't elaborate too much."
- ☆ "Very helpful meeting other parents."
- ☆ "Gave insight to what was ahead."
- ☆ "Very appreciated."
- ☆ "Excellent time to share feelings with other families with similar experiences."
- ☆ "I appreciated being able to share our experiences with others who are experiencing the same or similar difficulties."

How beneficial was the final evening family celebration dinner and activity night?

- ☆ "Beside the good food, having Matthew guide us through what he was interested in and seeing other ADHD kids & parents."
- ☆ "Danny had us all to himself!"
- ☆ "Seeing the activities he's learned and most of all, just spending time alone with my son."
- ☆ "Role playing was great!"
- ☆ "Role playing (role reversals)."
- ☆ "Sharing with Michael in the activities and enjoying a good laugh."
- ☆ "Showing me the different techniques to help Brian at home. He enjoyed so much showing me how to do these things."

These comments about the final family celebration meeting seem to confirm the idea that spending one-on-one time with their children is of great value. The most telling comment we received was from a mother of a boy with "pure" ADHD, that is, with no comorbid features. She wrote:

"Mike started behavior modification with a psychologist three months ago. I discontinued when this group started. He had one session with the therapist. This eight-week program helped him cope with his frustration and inability to get his work done. His performance/behavior at home is 100% improved; he does better than his brother (who has ADHD) at organizing his after-school time. I no longer see the need to continue with the psychologist. Thanks for a terrific program."

Now, obviously, having only one session with a private therapist was not long enough time to see any beneficial effects of private therapy. Many children with ADHD, particularly those with accompanying features of anxiety, depression or oppositionality, can benefit greatly from private therapy. However, many do not have complicating features with the ADHD and seem to do well with support within the school atmosphere.

5. Who can lead a *Creative Coaching* group?

The *Creative Coaching* curriculum is designed to be detailed and comprehensive enough to enable various types of professionals in the fields of education or mental health to implement a successful program. Such group leaders might include school counselors, social workers, special education teachers, behavioral interventionists or psychologists. No matter what the professional credentials, an effective group leader would ideally have the ability to:

☆ Establish rapport with children of varying academic and behavioral abilities.
☆ Communicate effectively with children and adults.
☆ Interact comfortably within a group setting.
☆ Modify plans and approaches as needed to meet children's needs.
☆ Lead discussions.
☆ Facilitate interactive learning.
☆ Be flexible enough to capitalize on "teachable moments."
☆ Apply behavior management strategies.
☆ Coordinate supportive efforts of teachers and parents.
☆ **And Walk on Water** (optional).

After reading this list of characteristics, it would be easy to feel overwhelmed and underqualified! It is important to remember that there is no perfect group leadership style. Group facilitators learn to live with the fact that groups do not always operate smoothly. Perhaps caring about children, persistence and the ability to learn from experience are the most important assets a group leader can have.

6. What kind of parent support would you need?

It is often beneficial to hold an evening meeting for parents to familiarize them with the objectives, methods,and activities before the student group begins. For specific suggestions and handouts to prepare for an initial parent meeting, refer to the "nuts and bolts" section beginning on page 16 . Whether it is over the phone or during a parent meeting, it is crucial to clarify and emphasize your specific expectations about the various ways parents can offer support to ensure that their child obtains the most from this group experience. Although it is not realistic to expect every parent to follow through on all of your recommendations, it is important, nevertheless, to provide them with a standard to aim for. Parents should be encouraged to:

☆ Be receptive to professional educators' suggestions about their child participating in a group.
☆ Attend parent orientation and support meetings.
☆ Invite their child to share thoughts and feelings about group activities without "interrogating."
☆ Initiate Home Practice activities by setting aside a specific time and being willing to scribe for the child.
☆ Display or post the parent backing to the Home Practice sheet as a reminder of the weekly skills to be reinforced.
☆ Take multiple opportunities to coach children by commenting on social skill development at home.
☆ Record on the Parent High 5's form positive, realistic, evaluative comments about the child's behavior.
☆ Coach students with application of skills.
☆ Help with organization of group materials and timely return of sheets.
☆ Call the group leader if questions arise.
☆ Attend closing group celebration. (See pages 265 - 278 for program suggestions.)
☆ Continue expanding their knowledge of ADHD and related issues through materials and programs provided by the school and other community programs.

7. What other kinds of school support are needed (from administrators, teachers, etc.) ?

Those of you who enjoy wonderful administrative support will recognize the aspects of quality leadership listed below. Administrators can provide substantial support to group leaders if they:

☆ Are aware of what percentage of the population served by special education and counselors is ADHD. (They should be aware that ADHD is the most commonly diagnosed medical condition of childhood.)
☆ Are aware of the legal obligations to children with ADHD under 504 and IDEA legislation.
☆ Are willing to see the need for staff inservices about ADHD as a priority.
☆ Are generally familiar with research supporting the efficacy of groups as part of a multimodal treatment plan for children with ADHD.
☆ Encourage teachers to make educational and behavioral accommodations.
☆ Are sensitive to the impact of ADHD on the child's ability to follow the school's regular discipline plan.
☆ Are supportive of group leaders' needs for continuing education.
☆ Know enough about the group process to adequately respond to parent concerns.

 13

If you find that your administrators don't fit this description, it is important to determine what factors are making it difficult for them to assume a supportive stance. Stumbling blocks might include:

☆ Underexposure to basic information about ADHD or about educational group process.
☆ Worries relating to overstepping educational boundaries and violating medical boundaries.
☆ Believing that ADHD is more behaviorally than physiologically based.
☆ A very negative past experience in which ADHD was inappropriately used as an excuse.

Classroom teachers need not only the training and levels of awareness desired from administrators, but also a willingness to spend extra reserves of energy and time to meet the needs of children with ADHD on a daily basis. The persistent, frequent occurrences of seemingly minor, off task behaviors can be a constant drain on a teacher's spirit. It is critical to avoid overwhelming teachers when you ask them to consider additional interventions. Begin by expressing appreciation for the inordinate amounts of time they are already investing in these children, and ask them to consider focusing their efforts in three positive arenas: identifying the child's major areas of need; providing intentional, ongoing feedback about effort in these areas; and implementing an individual management plan where meaningful consequences take the place of continual verbal redirection.

When teachers complete a needs assessment, the data can be used to help group leaders prioritize which sessions and activities to emphasize with group members. While many such forms are available (see *Skill Streaming the Elementary Child* listed in the bibliography), usually the simpler and more concrete the scale, the more likely the teacher will be to complete and return it. See the following page for a sample Behavioral Needs Assessment.

Probably the most powerful and practical responses we need from teachers are their ongoing awareness of what skills need to be reinforced, the willingness to prize individual effort towards a goal as much as goal attainment, and following through with completion of the High 5's form on a weekly basis. There is very little that happens in the group that is as significant to the children as hearing the written comments of their teachers being read aloud in group. This written feedback, combined with consistent variable, intermittent verbal reinforcement within the classroom, will help the teacher and the student maintain a more positive relationship.

If teachers and administrators on your campus have little knowledge about Attention Deficit Hyperactivity Disorder, consider using the information in the "Involving Parents and Teachers" section (page 279) of this manual to provide inservice opportunities for your staff.

Behavioral Needs Assessment

Name _____   Date _____

Completed by _____

Please complete this rating scale to help prioritize this child's needs.

1 = Never   2 = Rarely   3 = Occasionally   4 = Frequently   5 = Consistently

Listening & Paying Attention					
Uses listening skills to make and keep friends	1	2	3	4	5
Uses listening and attending skills to follow directions	1	2	3	4	5
Appears to be listening with appropriate eye contact	1	2	3	4	5
Controls body movements (fidget-free; quiet)	1	2	3	4	5
Appears to be listening by making appropriate responses	1	2	3	4	5
Is able to listen without interrupting	1	2	3	4	5
Is able to ignore distractions appropriately	1	2	3	4	5
Seems focused in classroom (with little daydreaming)	1	2	3	4	5
Can sustain focus on most important issues in class	1	2	3	4	5
Organization					
Is aware of organizational strengths and weaknesses	1	2	3	4	5
Is willing to accept suggestions about improving organization	1	2	3	4	5
Attempts to apply suggestions about organization	1	2	3	4	5
Takes time routinely to organize materials	1	2	3	4	5
Displays age-appropriate organizational skills	1	2	3	4	5
Self-concept and Goal-setting					
Has realistic view of own strengths and weaknesses	1	2	3	4	5
Seems motivated to improve personal weaknesses	1	2	3	4	5
Likes him or herself despite areas needing improvement	1	2	3	4	5
Can set realistic goals for self	1	2	3	4	5
Can sustain effort toward goal attainmen	1	2	3	4	5
Feelings					
Expresses most feelings appropriately	1	2	3	4	5
Expresses anger and/or frustration appropriately	1	2	3	4	5
Recognizes and generally respects feelings of others	1	2	3	4	5
Understands consequences of releasing feelings inappropriately	1	2	3	4	5
Controlling Impulsivity & Relaxation					
Is able to stop and think before overreacting	1	2	3	4	5
Thinks ahead to anticipate consequences	1	2	3	4	5
Paces self appropriately with different activities	1	2	3	4	5
Knows & uses skills for relaxing and slowing down	1	2	3	4	5
Communication					
Is able to read body language of others	1	2	3	4	5
Uses body language appropriately	1	2	3	4	5
Asks for what is needed or wanted in an appropriate way	1	2	3	4	5
Accepts responsibility for own actions	1	2	3	4	5
Friends					
Respects other people's personal space	1	2	3	4	5
Resolves conflicts in respectful ways	1	2	3	4	5
Exhibits good sportsmanship	1	2	3	4	5
Plays and works cooperatively with peers	1	2	3	4	5

What are the "nuts and bolts" of implementing the group?

CHECKLIST FOR GROUP LEADER RESPONSIBILITIES

☐ 1. Inservice staff about Attention Deficit Hyperactivity Disorder.

☐ 2. Examine your master schedule to determine how many groups you will be able to conduct within the current semester and schedule a time for each.

☐ 3. Identify the children who would benefit from group participation.

☐ 4. Distribute tentative group list and schedule to staff. Update this with finalized version after receipt of all parent permission forms.

☐ 5. Have teachers complete a needs assessment for each potential member of a group to be held that semester.

☐ 6. Make the initial contact with the parents of the children involved.

☐ 7. Plan the overall scope and sequence of weekly activities.

☐ 8. Determine the final size and composition of each group.

☐ 9. Plan and conduct parent orientation meeting.

☐ 10. Prepare for the first session by assembling initial handouts and other paperwork. Decide how you will organize all of your group materials.

☐ 11. Speak with each parent by phone about midway through the group sessions.

☐ 12. Plan final group celebration event, send parent invitations, and secure parent evaluations from any who are not able to attend closing event.

RESPONSIBILITIES OF A GROUP LEADER

1. Inservice staff about Attention Deficit Hyperactivity Disorder.

Using resource materials provided in the back of this manual (beginning on page 279), develop an inservice for your staff. Coordinate with your administration to determine if a series of short, after-school sessions would be preferable to one lengthier workshop. Consider inviting a community expert in the field of ADHD to speak. A thorough seminar should include information from the following categories:

- ☆ Characteristics and diagnosis
- ☆ Differing perspectives and attitudes about ADHD
- ☆ Current research findings
- ☆ A typical treatment plan
- ☆ Educating the child and parent about ADHD
- ☆ Educational and behavioral accommodations in the school setting
- ☆ The role of behavioral contracting and sample contracts
- ☆ Understanding medications frequently used and their potential side effects
- ☆ Overview of the *Creative Coaching* program and specific teacher support for students involved in groups.

2. Examine your master schedule to determine how many groups you will be able to conduct within the current semester and schedule a time for each.

The chart entitled "*Coaching Strategies At A Glance: Scheduling Sessions*" on the next page summarizes several pertinent planning issues. It is important to be realistic about how many groups you can comfortably conduct within one semester. Variables such as amount of experience in leading groups and time limitations imposed by other job responsibilities must be considered. Balance the quality of your interactions with the great number of students needing to be served. Having as few schedule changes as possible will be the most beneficial to this group of children who need structure and generally don't handle change well! But, allow for some flexibility to accommodate makeup times because of field trips or other special events.

There is no ideal time to schedule a group within the school setting. Scheduling groups during academic time may prove difficult because you are likely to encounter significant teacher and parent oppositions since the burden of helping students make up missed work will fall on the adults involved.

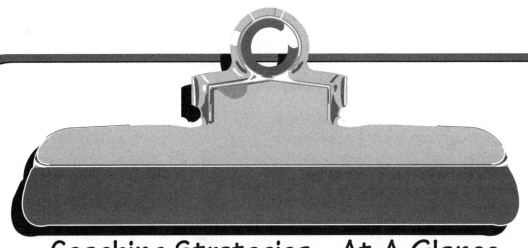

Coaching Strategies - At A Glance

Scheduling Sessions

How Many Sessions Should be Planned?

We recommend conducting 10-12 sessions. *Creative Coaching* features enough activities for children to participate in groups for 2-3 years with little repetition. Be creative & flexible. Consider meeting weekly all year long if a group is working well together.

When Are Groups Scheduled?

There are no perfect times with "pull out" programs. Check your schedule for optimal times. Preferably, avoid lunch, critical academic instruction times, & before or after school, if transportation is a complicated issue.

How Long is Each Session?

We recommend 45-50 minutes from sit down to exit. Practically, if school schedules severely limit available time, sessions can be adapted to work within 30 minute blocks with minimal changes.

How Often May Meetings Be Scheduled?

Most group leaders meet with children at least once a week, especially if the group members are "pulled out" of other classes. Some group leaders find that two meetings per week work better with younger children.

How Many Students May Be In A Group?

We recommend that no more than 5-6 children be included. Group leaders will want to take several factors into account: age of children, number of unmedicated children, & the number of extremely hyperactive or emotionally disturbed children.

Holding groups during the lunch hour can be tricky since many students will be at the end of their medication cycle. Also, they need to eat quickly and complete their meal before the actual activity begins. Generally, students will participate in group for about thirty-five minutes. Considering the time it takes to gather all the students from various homerooms, you will probably use a total of about forty-five minutes.

Conducting groups before or after school is complicated by bus schedules or individual transportation arrangements. However, in some instances, this may be the only way to have access to some students. Again, with after school meetings, the issue of medication wearing off has to be considered.

Scheduling groups during teacher conference times may be the most practical approach for group leaders. It helps to talk ahead of time with teachers of special classes (like PE, music, library or other electives) to secure their cooperation and provide them with a complete listing of students and the proposed dates and times of meetings. Even though students hate to give up these special classes, they can usually adapt to missing them only once a week.

3. Identify the children who would benefit from group participation.

If time has lapsed since teachers have received inservice training on ADHD, ask for time to review the scope of the *Creative Coaching* groups with teachers during their grade level meetings. Have teachers identify students whom they feel would benefit from participation in the program. If more students are suggested than you could possibly work with during the current semester, assist teachers in prioritizing needs. Ask each teacher to consider which of their children are least functional academically, socially and emotionally but seem open to improving their own behavior and are willing to attempt positive interaction with peers. This sort of educational "triage" attempts to identify "who needs group experience the most" and who is able and willing to benefit from it.

Note: It is extremely important to personally contact older children individually to be a part of the group. They need to feel like the decision to join a group is theirs. It is not necessary to go into great detail about the group, but to describe it as a club or team that meets for just a season of a few weeks. If the child seems uncertain, ask him or her to attend the first meting and then decide.

4. Distribute tentative group list and schedule to staff.

All of a child's teachers need to be aware of what plans you have for pulling students from their classes. By distributing a list of groups, you will inform all special teachers (PE, music, resource, speech) in addition to the teacher who completed the needs assessment on the child. Update this list with a finalized version after receipt of all parent permission forms.

5. Have teachers complete a needs assessment for each potential member of a group to be held that semester.

The sample Behavioral Needs Assessment (page 15) has already been referred to under the section discussing types of teacher support. Have teachers complete the needs assessment only for those students whom you intend to work with during the current semester. You may want to have special teachers complete an assessment in addition to the one collected from the classroom teacher.

6. Make the initial contact with the parents of the children involved.

Parental attitudes toward their children's involvement tend to be more positive if the group leader has had an opportunity to explain the purpose and nature of the group before they send the permission letter home (see sample letter on page 21). The group leader can do this by phone if a rapport already exists.

For students new to the school whose parents indicate that a diagnosis of ADHD already exists, the group leader could discuss how and when the diagnosis was made, what interventions have been undertaken so far, what the parents' level of understanding about ADHD currently is, and what additional support they might need. Make parents aware of campus and community resources available. Describe the *Creative Coaching* program as an option for them to consider. If they are interested, invite them to the introductory parent meeting. You may choose to send a parent permission letter at this time, or plan to distribute it at the orientation meeting.

Many parents of children who are experiencing "classroom difficulties" because of behaviors characteristic of ADHD, feel comfortable with their child participating in the group because they are learning skills that will be helpful to them whether they actually have ADHD or not. In groups where everyone fits the behavioral profile, but several group members are not formally diagnosed, the leader will need to decide how to address the material on Understanding ADHD. This may be done individually or with a subgroup of diagnosed individuals.

7. Plan the overall scope and sequence of weekly activities.

Using both the teacher's needs assessment data and information obtained from parent contacts, select the session topics you wish to address. See "*Coaching Strategies - At A Glance: Modified Group Formats*" (page 22) for groups with a particular focus. After an introductory session to introduce group format and components, this curriculum includes clusters of concepts that can be addressed in various sequence, depending on the needs of the children in the group.

☆ **Study Skills Groups** - Listening, Paying Attention and Organization can be thought of as a cluster of specific classroom coping or study skills that parents and teachers are most often concerned about addressing immediately.

☆ **Personal Growth Groups** -This cluster of sessions could allow students an opportunity to develop realistic self-concepts through recognition of individual strengths and weaknesses and practicing goal-setting. Learning to recognize and expressing feelings while practicing relaxation and other techniques to control impulsivity appropriately are especially important to children with ADHD.

☆ **Interpersonal Skills Groups** -A group of this type would give students opportunities for listening, communication and cooperation with friends.

Finally, for groups including only children diagnosed with ADHD, an understanding of ADHD is imperative to help them "get a handle" on their own learning and personality style. For all groups, it is important to find an appropriate closure, to help students celebrate their learning.

Dear Parents of _____,

As part of our school's developmental guidance program, students are invited to participate in small curriculum-based support group sessions once a week for _____weeks. Membership in the ALL-STARS! group is based on parent, teacher or counselor referral. If, after reading the following description, you think that your child might benefit from participation in this group, please complete the form below and return it to your child's teacher or to the counselor.

This group has a sports theme and involves creatively "coaching" your child to improve his or her skills in the following areas:

Effective Listening & Paying Attention   Organizational Skills
Positive Self Concept   Setting and Reaching Goals
Handling Feelings   Controlling Impulses
Learning to Relax   Teamwork
Successful Communication

Participation in this group will involve meeting _____ minutes a week (during their PE/Music/Assistant or lunch time). "Home Practice" activities will be sent home each week to allow you to do some "coaching" and to enjoy spending some quality time with your child! Since teachers are part of the "coaching staff" too, they will complete "High Five" forms which are designed to encourage your child to incorporate the skills they have learned in group into daily practice. Your child will earn points for "their team" when they return the "Home Practice" and "High Five" forms, so please help them use their special group folder to bring papers back and forth from home to school.

I would love to discuss specific details about the ALL-STARS! curriculum and am anxious to answer any questions that you may have at a special parent meeting in:

_____ on_____ from _____ to _____.

_____
Group Leader Signature

☆☆☆☆☆☆☆☆☆☆☆☆☆☆☆☆☆☆☆☆☆☆☆☆☆☆☆☆☆☆☆☆☆☆

_____Yes, I give my permission for my child,_____, to participate in the ALL-STARS! group.
_____Yes, I am planning to attend the special parent meeting.
_____I will need child care for children.
_____No, I do not wish for my child to participate in this group.

_____   _____
Parent Signature   Date

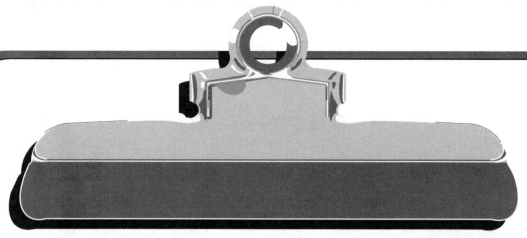

Coaching Strategies - At A Glance
Modified Group Formats

Don't limit yourself only to groups for ADHD children. Consider adjusting the curriculum for groups with a different focus! After an introductory session to begin the group bonding process, select 2-4 sessions from each concept.

Study Skills Group

- ☆ Listening
- ☆ Paying Attention
- ☆ Organization

Personal Growth Group

- ☆ Self Concept
- ☆ Feelings
- ☆ Goal Setting

Behavior Management Activities

- ☆ Feelings
- ☆ Controlling Impulsivity
- ☆ Relaxation
- ☆ Goal Setting

Interpersonal Skills Group

- ☆ Listening
- ☆ Communication
- ☆ Friendship

8. Determine the final size and composition of each group.

Although it might be tempting to involve more students, a group of about six children seems to be the optimal size. Consider talking individually with older students or any student that you anticipate may be reluctant to participate, before involving them in a group. When making final decisions about how many and which children should be in a group, take the following factors into consideration:

☆ How many are diagnosed ADHD (hyperactive, impulsive or combined type) versus ADHD (inattentive type). A group in which all six are very hyperactive would be ill advised!

☆ The severity of impairment of children diagnosed with or displaying characteristics of ADHD (mild, moderate or severe).

☆ The number of group members who are medicated.

☆ The grade level of the group. Generally, the younger the children, the smaller the group should be as greater individual attention and guidance are required.

☆ The gender of the students. Characteristically, there will be more boys than girls participating in groups, but it is prudent to avoid having only one boy or girl in a group.

☆ Any previous socialization patterns. If at all possible, separate individuals who have experienced ongoing conflicts into different groups.

Regardless of group composition, providing a set structure and sticking to it will enhance the functioning of any group.

9. Plan and conduct a parent orientation meeting.

You may choose to distribute parent permission letters at this time. On the next page is a sample "Outline for Introductory Parent Meeting."

Consider having parents participate in several of the activities you will be using with their children and explain what objectives these activities will be illustrating. Go easy using complex, diagnostic terms if parents are not already familiar with them. Be very concrete about when and where the group will meet, how many students will be involved, and what part of the day it will take place. During the introductory meeting, show them samples of specific folders, Home Practice sheets, High "5's," etc. Stress the importance of at-home tasks as discussion starters between parent and child. Stress that you want parents to "scribe" for their child on Home Practice sheets. We want group "homework" to enrich, not add stress to, an already busy evening.

SAMPLE OUTLINE FOR
PARENT INTRODUCTORY MEETING

A. Share the basic **scope** of the curriculum.

B. Explain the **rationale** of using a coaching analogy.

C. Explain the details of the **format** of the curriculum.
(45 minute session, once a week, time scheduled, for how many weeks)

D. Explain the format of each **session.**
(pregame warmups, connection to the real world and objectives, the activities, discussion questions, and closure wrap-ups including directions for the Home Practice & High 5's.)

E. Overview of **Objectives** for each session and brief description of some sample activities. (If time allows, let parents actually participate in an activity.)

F. Specifically address the sessions on Understanding ADHD - Trek 1 and Trek 2. At this time, consider giving Note to Parents : "Perceptions, Realities & Myths about ADHD." Discuss under what conditions you will present information from these sessions, particularly if you have children who have not been diagnosed ADHD participating in group.

G. Secure parent permission for students to participate in a group meeting with a physician if you have scheduled one.

H. Clarify your **expectations** of exactly how parents can be supportive of their child as he or she participates in this group.
1. Ask for folder weekly, on group day & help to see it returns.
2. Make Home Practice activities fun. Emphasize the importance of "scribing" for children to prevent from adding additional stress.
3. Be a positive coach who notices improvement in skills and verbally reinforces and writes initials on form!
4. Plan to attend the end-of-group celebration event to spend individual time with your child.

I. **Disclaimers** - Participation in this group will NOT CURE ADHD! ADHD in "pure form" is rare; so if parents suspect problems with anxiety, depression or other significant conditions, ask them to consider consulting their physician to discuss the need for additional private therapeutic support.

10. Prepare for the first session by assembling initial handouts and other paperwork. Decide how you will organize all of your group materials.

If you plan to follow this curriculum closely, it generates a lot of paperwork by the time you consider a possible activity page, a Home Practice sheet with parent backing, and High 5's teacher reinforcement sheet for each student each week. It is helpful if each student has an individual folder within which to keep items. Since buying folders for each student can be costly, you may consider one of two options. Have each student bring his or her own folder, or beg teachers for large sheets of construction paper from their art supply closet and fold, cut and staple them into folders. Label the front of each folder with the name of the group ("All Stars" or whatever unique name the group comes up with if you allow them to name themselves), the student's name and homeroom teacher, and the day, time, and possibly the place of meeting.

To keep student folders from "bulging" as time goes along, consider having a separate spot to "keep" completed home practice sheets which can be returned to students at the end of the group. Also, you might consider having a volunteer mother come in weekly to run new papers or possibly file completed ones. Using colored paper is one option for helping students locate these assignments in the snowstorm of white papers that go back and forth between school and home daily.

11. Speak with parents by phone about midway through the group sessions.

This contact is particularly important for those students who have not been following through on returning home practice sheets. Schools send home so many papers that parents often need additional reminders! Also, you may have communicated previously with one parent but the message was never passed on to the other parent, who may be the one who goes through the backpack nightly!

12. Plan final group celebration event.

There are a number of different types of group closings that you can plan. The *"End-of-Group Celebration"* section (page 265) describes an evening program involving parents. Because you have asked parents and teachers to give consistent feedback throughout a number of weeks, this is a golden opportunity to "cement" the experience in everybody's mind and to obtain some good evaluation input both verbally and in writing. The temptation after a few groups is to skip this event, but we have found that it diminishes the overall effect of the group experience. If an evening activity is not at all practical, sometimes a morning breakfast of sweet rolls and beverages can be arranged. Be sure to send parent invitations (and call to remind them) about the event. Also, remember to secure parent evaluations from any who are not able to attend the closing event.

PLAY BOOK

SESSION FORMAT

Children with ADHD function best within predictable, consistent environments. Having a set format for each session provides the boundaries they need to feel safe and encourages them to stay focused. We have provided a "Typical Session Format" on the following page which incorporates the specific sports analogies of this curriculum. Essential elements of the format include:

☑ A **beginning ritual** that awards earned points and reviews concepts, rules and token system (rituals in the form of group handshakes, symbols or nicknames also help establish group cohesiveness and bonding and takes about 5 minutes).

☑ An **introduction of new concepts** to help students focus on the main ideas to be learned (perhaps in the form of a group "huddle" and takes about 5 to 8 minutes).

☑ An **activity** through which concepts are concretely experienced and skills practiced (takes 15 to 20 minutes).

☑ **Debriefing** and processing of activity through discussion to emphasize main ideas and help students to generalize from the specific activity to areas of application in their lives (takes 5 to 8 minutes).

☑ Some type of **closure** activity which may include awarding points for appropriate behavior in group, a brief description of Home Practice activity that allows parents the opportunity to reinforce concepts their child has learned in group, and an opportunity for students to share positive comments with each other (takes 5 to 8 minutes).

TYPICAL SESSION FORMAT

PREGAME WARMUP

Review group rules & token system
Discuss any returned Home Practice sheets
Read High 5's comments
Acknowledge & reward on-task behaviors

CONNECTING TO THE REAL WORLD

Discuss how the concepts fit into the athletic arena
& into the students' everyday world.

OBJECTIVES

Explain the main ideas to be covered in this week's lesson.

ACTIVITIES

Select the best activity for your group. Each activity includes:
Equipment needed
Game Plan or procedure for activity
Discussion questions for debriefing & processing
Home Practice sheets to extend skills

POST GAME COMMENTARY

Tally points & reward behavior by evaluating both individual and group
Make necessary announcements
Allow students to share positive comments with one another

REWARDS & REINFORCEMENTS

Using rewards and reinforcements is a very individual matter depending on personal preference and working style. Some people tend to be very random and have a difficult time using one system for any length of time. Other people are very concrete and sequential and use the same reinforcers each week. Pick a system that fits your style. There are many possibilities.

Use a ticket punch system where the child is randomly awarded punches for appropriate behaviors in group. In addition, each child receives punches or points for returning Home Practice and High 5's reinforcement sheets from parents and teachers. Students can claim privileges or rewards when the predetermined number of punches have been earned.

Place small cups containing tokens or chips in front of each child. Throughout the entire group meeting

add or remove tokens as behavior dictates. This system has the advantage of being more immediate and tangible for younger students and can include the aspect of taking away tokens for significant off-task behavior.

Using any type of token system means that you can reward at specific point intervals (10, 20, 30) as well as designating rewards for higher point values. This allows you to accommodate children who like to delay gratification as well as those who prefer immediate gratification.

Group rewards may be used in addition to individual reinforcers to build a sense of cooperation. For example, you can tell the group that when all individual points are added together and total a given amount (i.e., 250 points), that the group can earn a special reward that all can enjoy.

Whatever system you decide to use, make it work for you. If Home Practice and reinforcement sheets are not coming in, reevaluate your reinforcement system to see if you are providing enough point values to make it "worth their while" to bring items in or if the reinforcers you are offering, are meaningful to the students.

HANDLING PROBLEM BEHAVIORS IN GROUPS

In spite of all the expertise and careful planning invested in implementing this program, group leaders would be wise to anticipate the inevitable behavioral issues that will arise from time to time. See "Coaching Strategies at a Glance - Handling Personal Fouls," on the following page   for a brief overview of specific intervention strategies. Some general rules of thumb to consider include:

☆ Ignore behavior that is not incredibly disruptive or distracting.

☆ Be very intentional and consistent about calling attention to appropriate behavior.

☆ Model positive comments and provide time for group members to compliment each other.

☆ Don't be afraid to "push the pause button" during an activity to help the group respond to inappropriate behavior.

☆ Routinely help students identify and anticipate consequences of behavior.

☆ Model and give group members permission to say how they feel about functional and dysfunctional behaviors.

☆ Create opportunities for students to redeem themselves by using such techniques as "pushing the rewind button - if you could go back and do that again, how would you do that differently?"

As much as possible, try to emphasize the use of positive reinforcers to control behavior within group as opposed to consequences such as time-out or removal from group for inappropriate behavior. However, do not allow a specific child to control or sabotage group interaction. Since not all children may be at a point where they are able to function within a group, you may have to give as many as two verbal warnings and one time-out in any one session before asking a student to return to class for the day. If this occurs, schedule an individual conference with the child to process what happened. Consider dropping a child from group who shows no improvement after having been given several time-outs or after having been returned to class more than once. If you permanently remove a child from group, it is advisable to contact the child's parents and teachers to discuss the rationale for your actions.

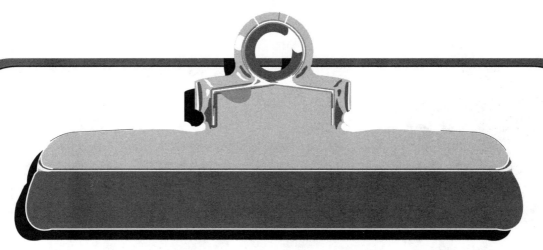

Coaching Strategies - At A Glance
Handling Personal Fouls!

☆ Ask: What are you doing? How does that help? What else could you do?
☆ Use "I" messages & short time-outs as needed.
☆ Use "instant replays" to practice correcting the behavior.
☆ Set up bonus tokens for specific behaviors if needed.

What if a Child...

Calls Names
Let students know that anyone who name calls will have to give 2 sincere compliments (in front of the group) or take a time-out to think about more appropriate behavior.

Fidgets
Briefly touch the student & provide nonverbal direction. Say, "When you fidget, I get distracted." Ask the group to take a deep breathing break if several fidget.

Gazes Off
Ask the child, "What is making if difficult for you to pay attention to what's most important right now?" Or invite the group to comment on the general quality of attention.

Interrupts
Give "proximity praise" to others who <u>are</u> listening. Ask the person who's been interrupted, "How does it feel when you aren't able to

Invades Space
Ask the person whose space is violated, "Does that bother you? What would you like to happen instead?" Suggest ways the "space invader" could get needs met.

Talks Too Much
To prevent a student from dominating the discussion, have an informal rule that no one talks a second time until all have had a chance to talk once.

Whines
Say to the whiner, "How could you say that in a different way?" Have him do so & appreciate the improvement out loud!

. . . .of what if's and, yes, but's?

COACHING TIP:

Do not look back in anger or forward in fear, but around in awareness.

TIP!!

How many of you remember learning about "yesssbuttts" in your professional training? Yes, we mean those people who responded to suggestions with "Yes, that might work, but I already tried that and.. . ." Our professors warned us about trying to give our wise advice to others because most people, if they were of normal intelligence, would have already considered what we were suggesting and would have ruled it out for some sane or insane reason. Well, after working as educators for several years now, we've discovered that we do as much "yes butting" as our clients do.

Whenever we come across a new idea for a program, group or lesson series, and especially one that is not of our own origination, we get excited about trying it, until we get down to practical application. It seems like there is always such a big gap between an idea and its actual implementation. Well, in case any of you are at the stage where you are seriously thinking of conducting a small group for children with ADHD, here are some answers to the "**What if's**" and "**Yes**, that's a great idea, **but** I don't think it would work for me" thoughts that you already have or may think of. We have provided the following two-page chart that summarizes the major doubts and then offer a more comprehensive discussion for each concern.

"WHAT IF'S..." - AT A GLANCE

Still have doubts about starting a group? Refer to page numbers listed for additional discussion about each issue.

WHAT IF...	OFFENSIVE STRATEGIES
No official diagnosis of ADHD is made, but child fits behavioral profile for group (page 35).	☆ Utilize any spontaneous comments made in group about medication or doctor's visits to discuss ADHD. ☆ Omit Trek 1 & 2 from the group's curriculum. ☆ Secure parent permission for children formally diagnosed with ADHD, to listen to an invited physician to speak at another scheduled time.
Child (or parent) asks why they were selected for group (page 35).	☆ Teacher thought child would enjoy participation. ☆ Child has potential for being a "good team player". ☆ To strengthen specific skills. ☆ To serve as a positive role model for others. ☆ To improve child's comfort level with peers.
Child doesn't want to be in group (page 36).	☆ Optimize positive nature of being included in group. ☆ Have a one-to-one dialogue to explore reasons. ☆ Consider other scheduling options. ☆ Negotiate trial attendance at 2-3 sessions.
Group has too many children who are hard to control (page 36).	☆ Establish structured routines for smooth flow. ☆ Modify activities to meet specific group needs. ☆ Consider dividing the group into two smaller units.
Limited parent support for child in group evidenced by few Home Practices returned (page 37).	☆ Emphasize parent responsibility at orientation meeting. ☆ Consider distribution of "packet" containing all Home Practices & High 5 sheets at orientation meeting.
Limited teacher support for child in group - evidenced by few High 5's returned (page 37).	☆ Prior to group, stress importance of positive input. ☆ Streamline process for dispersing & returning forms. ☆ Send weekly reminders & thank you's for completed High 5's.

WHAT IF...	OFFENSIVE STRATEGIES
Suggested activity or material seems inappropriate to use or unavailable (page 37).	☆ There is no perfect method or material. Be creative & substitute an alternative, concrete focus or method. ☆ Increase structure of activity or "rehearse" lesson with another group before using with children who are ADHD.
There are children whose improvement goes unnoticed by others (page 38).	☆ Remind others that children require repeated reinforcement to change behaviors & those with ADHD have great fluctuations in performance. ☆ Have teacher update needs assessment & note any differences. ☆ Suggest further interventions (i.e., private therapy, behavioral contracting, medical re-evaluation, etc.) ☆ Ask parents & children for feedback at end of group.
Educator has insufficient time in schedule to run small groups (page 38).	☆ Distribute planned guidance schedule to staff. ☆ Begin with a minimum 3 hours per week for groups. ☆ Include frequently-seen individuals within a group. ☆ Schedule individuals during recess or before school.
Leader feels inadequate facilitating groups (page 39).	☆ Develop a network of peer support to discuss or improve group functioning. ☆ Consider having a co-leader in the group. ☆ Hang in there - excuses are for losers!
Parental criticism or challenge to conducting groups in school (page 39).	☆ See page 40 for differences in educational support groups and therapy groups.

What if . . . "everybody" thinks a child really has ADHD but the official diagnosis hasn't been made yet? Should this student be in a group?

Almost everyone faces this situation. Participating in one of our first groups were two boys whose parents had indicated the need for full support from the school but who had not received a medical consultation yet. When the group began, Nancy delayed introducing the concept of ADHD. She called the group "Classroom Coping Skills" and went through eight weeks of introduction, self concept, feelings, paying attention, controlling impulses, relaxation, and social skills, planning to end with a book about ADHD and discussing medication as appropriate. As the actual week of discussing "it" approached, she grew more anxious about how to discuss these issues, especially since not everyone in the group was diagnosed and not all were on medication.

Fortunately, one of the boys, during "care and share" time, talked about how neat it was when he went to the doctor to have a "brain wave" test and had all these wires put on his head. He concluded by saying that he was going to be starting on some medicine for something called "ADD." Several of the other boys responded excitedly by saying, "Oh, yeah, I had that done too." "Yeah, I take Ritalin and it helps me to concentrate." They all seemed surprised that other people had actually experienced the same things and didn't realize that this common characteristic was the criteria for their selection in the group. So, Nancy whipped out several children's ADHD books and said, "Well, it looks like you guys have a lot of questions, and I 'just happen' to have a couple of books here that talk about that very thing! Let's take a look at them and see if they can answer any of your questions." Talk about a smooth transition; things worked out beautifully.

Yes, but . . . how do you handle it when a child or a parent asks why they were picked to be in a group?

Well, if you are talking about ANY generic type of small, educational support group that students are invited to participate in, you could give a general answer like, "Well, I asked teachers who they thought would enjoy the experience of being in a group and she thought you might enjoy participating." Students can be given the privilege of signing up for a group, sometimes even with a choice of type of group (friends, family, study skills, leadership, decision-making groups). It is extremely important to include "average" children as much as possible in small group programs, or the group leader soon gets the reputation of working only with the "trouble-makers". That is the kiss of death as far as the children themselves are involved and as concerns the parents' willingness to have their children participate in a group. Many "average" students will need a particular skill strengthened, and teachers will want them to be in a group. If the community thinks that you work with only "troubled" children, believe me, mom or dad will be on the phone the minute they receive the note about why their child needs to be in a group. And, who would blame them? The way news travels in some communities, every mom on the street has told everybody else when she comes home from volunteering for the teacher, how Suzanne and Joshua go to a social skills group EVERY Thursday! Word definitely gets around.

Beyond considering children's privacy and reputation issues, it is beneficial to include some positive role models in groups. Clustering all challenging children together and expecting them to learn social skills from one another is ludicrous. Even in groups intended for children with ADHD, it is important to achieve a balance of students. Including children who are inattentive but not impulsive creates stability for those who are hyperactive.

What if . . . a child says he or she doesn't want to be in a group?

Determine the reasons the child is hesitant to participate in group. If the group leader has handled the "invitation" smoothly, has talked with the child about the group and clarified what the group will be doing, has talked with the parents about the child's participation, and the child still does not want to join, then several factors may be at play. A supportive school program should provide numerous opportunities for all children to participate in small group activities, so students do not have to worry that they must have a "problem" to be involved. If these opportunities are not given, educators will see increasing numbers of children opting not to participate.

Sometimes children are hesitant to participate in a new or unknown arena, often approaching new situations with an initial negative outlook. If this seems to be the case, most children can be encouraged to try coming to group for two or three times to see if they like it with the option of dropping out at the end of their initial trial if they so choose. In almost all cases, if hesitancy is the reason, the child will be "hooked" and will remain with the group.

More frequently, children do not want to participate because of the timing of the group. If group meetings are held during PE, music or recess times, some students will really object to missing these other activities. After some discussion, most will admit that missing a favorite activity only once a week is not too much to ask, for all the fun they'll have in group. However, the bottom line is, forcing a student to remain in a group will not be beneficial for that child and will wind up being detrimental to the entire group. It's simply not worth it. Make sure, however, that if a child does choose not to participate, he or she assumes the responsibility of contacting his or her parents to secure their written approval of the decision. Parents can also be encouraged to consider engaging the child in activities or therapies outside of school which will provide additional support to their child's study and social skill development.

What if . . . I get too many students in group and their behavior is just too wild for me to control?

Actually, the children are usually better behaved than you'd expect them to be. The key is to be in charge with plenty of structure outlined and explained from the very beginning. Routine and repetition of group procedures help the students know exactly what to expect and to feel "safe". It doesn't take long to discover what type of activity a particular group can handle and what it can't. Remember, don't ever "meld" yourself to ANY lesson in a particular way. Be willing to adapt to the needs of your group. There was an experienced and talented primary teacher once who shared that she loved to do a special activity with students carving pumpkins, roasting the seeds and then writing about the experience. But one year she said, "You know, I just can't do that type of activity with this year's class because no matter what I try, they can't stay in control during these more interactive, fun activities." We have all had to do the same thing with various activities and adapt to a level of involvement that works for the group.

Another thing to remember is that just because an activity doesn't work with one group, doesn't mean it might not work for another. One year, Nancy had several fifth grade boys referred for help with social skills; and they wouldn't all fit in one group. She very carefully split them into two groups with the personalities that seemed to work best together. It turned out that for one group, ANYTHING she planned worked beautifully and the guys bonded so well that they made significant growth! She was tempted to believe it was all due to her amazing leadership skills. However, as you have probably discovered, failure is often a prelude to humility. For you see, with the second group, NOTHING she did, not even identical activities, seemed to work at all. The second group was beset with absentee problems, upset and surly boys who scorned any activity proposed, and a general disgust displayed toward one another by all group members. If this had been the only group of the two that she had done, Nancy would have taken the failure very personally and decided that she didn't know what she was doing or else blamed it on the "lousy" curriculum! As much as we hate to admit it, there are sometimes circumstances beyond our control that will affect the group - sometimes in positive ways, but also often in negative ways too. If your group begins to resemble your worst nightmare, don't hesitate to ask for help and support from a fellow professional to help you regain perspective and confidence.

What if . . . the reward system doesn't seem to be effective in motivating students to return Home Practices or High 5 sheets?

Honestly, reward systems can be a real pain! They require constant monitoring and readjusting, especially since children with ADHD can get bored easily with any particular system. It is a continual challenge to combine consistency with flexibility. The first thing to do is to double check to make sure the following steps in the process are in place:

☆ Have parents been notified to expect the weekly Home Practice and High 5's sheets? By phone, remind them about specific details and expectations: day of week the group meets, their involvement with paper completion, their assistance in filing papers in folder or backpack, etc. If parents are aware that their child is one of the few in the group with no points, they usually respond with heightened interest.

☆ Is the teacher clear on expectations, procedures and importance of High 5's? Consider sharing medical professionals' comments about the importance of positive reinforcement within the child's daily environment. Check to see if minor procedural changes could create a more effective time to complete the charts (note on child's desk, thank you note from group leader in teacher's box when a High 5 has been received, etc.).

☆ Are you as group leader spending sufficient time and giving plentiful verbal praise along with the token reinforcements on a consistent basis? Are reinforcers given frequently enough to be motivating? Do students need to be more involved in the selection of reinforcers?

☆ Finally, are there any procedural changes or environmental adaptations that could help? For example, students could return forms any day during the week instead of waiting till the next group meeting. Bonus points could even be given for early returns. Think of creative ways to "up the ante!"

What if...I just can't find a particular book or material suggested in this curriculum or think a certain activity seems awkward, uncomfortable to me, or not practical for my population?

No material in ANY curriculum book is sacred! If you can't access a particular resource, design your own or find another focus to get the same point across. Often when people first start to teach a concept or skill, whether it's social skills, reading or science, they are tempted to teach in an activity-driven way. "Oh this looks like a good activity" instead of "What idea am I trying to convey and where is there a parallel in everyday life that would bring this point home?" If Jaime Escalante of *Stand and Deliver* fame can put on a chef's hat and carve up food to teach fractions to high schoolers, we should be no less daring in devising exciting ways to help our students learn important concepts. Remember that you tend to remember 10% of what you hear, 20% of what you see and hear, and 60% of what you do.

You are the prime ingredient here! Modify, combine, cut lessons, recreate to make them your own. (Write and share your ideas with us too, by the way!) That's why we've called this *Creative Coaching*! What works for one group leader won't work for another, just like what works for one group doesn't always work for the next. And if you are like most educators, just having a plan to follow helps when you don't have time to develop lessons during the course of the hectic week. Often, each week as a group leaves, leaders glance at their notes for the following week, and think, "I can do this better; I'm going to ...before next week." But, there are only so many hours in the day, and another group or student or teacher or class is waiting, and there is no time to develop new ideas. So, for those "in the trenches," here is a plan that hopefully will be workable until summer comes along and you have time to revise it the way you really want to!

Yes . . . I know it's important to have small group support, but . . . it just doesn't fit into my schedule and I have so many individual children to work with that I just can't do it.

If not careful, professional educators tend to be crisis-driven in their jobs, and therefore not as effective. For example, our recommended guidance plan in Texas calls for elementary counselors to spend about 40% of their time in guidance and small groups. Some people consider this an impossibility. We find it helpful to distribute guidance and small group calendars at the beginning of the month to the staff, so that when it comes time for parent-teacher conferences or seeing kids on an "emergency" basis, we can usually work around existing time slots. Give a distraught child a few minutes to calm down, discover the nature of the presenting problem, and give them a time to return if you are about to leave for a class or start a group. Usually, processing with the individual child goes more smoothly at a later time when they are not as agitated. Generally, children who have been dropping in frequently tend to need significantly less individual time if they are being seen in a group during the week.

Special educators often spend specific time at the beginning or end of the day reviewing behavioral expectations and may spend significant amounts of time redirecting inappropriate behaviors. We believe that this time is better spent teaching appropriate interactive skills through small group activities. Special education teachers are in a unique position to do this because of the smaller group setting, their specialized training, the availability of an assistant, and their cooperation with general education staff.

Yes, but . . . what if teachers say that they see no improvement in the students who are participating in the group?

Remind teachers that children with ADHD require repeated exposure with reinforcement over time to internalize and generalize behavior. Asking the teacher to update the needs assessment completed at the beginning of the program can be helpful as it may enable the teacher to see improvement in some specific, but perhaps isolated, behaviors. It can also be helpful to remind the teacher that INCONSISTENCY is the irritating hallmark of people with this type of "output" disorder. Give assurance that regardless of how fantastic the intervention, whether yours or theirs, ups and downs will occur. However, if you find yourself consistently redirecting the student during sessions, consider the possibility that he or she may not yet be ready or able to benefit from the group experience. You may want to suggest that parents pursue individual "coaching" regarding social skills with a private therapist, or you may want to work with the teacher and parents to develop a behavioral contract to address the most disruptive or distressing behaviors.

Yes . . . I know these students need group, but . . . I'm not a therapist! I might wind up doing them more harm than good. I don't feel like I have enough training to lead groups for them.

Once, a friend of ours, who had more experience in leading groups than we had, shared the same feeling with us about a group of troubled boys she was starting to work with. (It really helps to have a support system so you can realize you aren't the Lone Ranger! We all feel inadequate at times, and we need to talk with others to help us put things into perspective.) It seemed like she was really excited because her school had made arrangements with a local psychologist (Ph.D. trained) to come in and co-lead a group. She said it was the best learning experience in the world for her, but not for the reason you'd think. She had been hoping to learn some really special techniques from an expert for working with these tough children. As it turned out, he had no "tricks up his sleeve" and had just as much difficulty controlling the group as she did. He used the same techniques of clarifications, time outs, redirections, processing of what was happening in group, and modifying of the lesson. She was flabbergasted that she had as many practical skills about group dynamics and management as the psychologist did! The main benefit was having another trained person in the room and having someone to debrief with after the sessions.

Another time, Janet co-led a group with her principal and discovered that sometimes it just takes two - one to keep the group on task with the lesson and one to troubleshoot specific problems as they come up. Once an educator happened to be having a group session for children with ADHD in her room while the district's behavioral specialist was there writing a specific plan. The group leader was embarrassed because the students had needed so much redirection. She felt she had to control the group's behavior, in front of the behavioral specialist no less! She was surprised when this recognized authority commented, "That was a fantastic session!" and noted how wonderfully she had redirected and handled all the problems that had arisen.

The point is, it's not so much your specific skills and techniques that count. Beyond basic group management skills, stamina and an awareness of group dynamics and characteristics of ADHD, it's you and your genuine care and concern for kids that will come across and make the difference in the lives of children.

What if . . . somebody gets upset because I'm doing "therapy" with students in the public school? Can I get in trouble with parents, like those who are really conservative and think I'm trying to act like a shrink and "meddle with their kids' minds?"

There is a significant difference between conducting "curriculum-based" or educational support groups and holding "therapy" sessions. Few professional educators have expertise in the field of doing "therapy" and can feel somewhat inadequate in this area. We were thankful to be able to attend a presentation in Dallas for Rainbow Days, Inc., by Jerry Moe, a gifted leader of educational groups for children of alcoholics. He shared with participants the difference between "therapy" and "education support" groups and how to explain the distinction to staff, parents and community. To illustrate the major characteristics, a coworker of ours, Carrie Hilman, summarized his ideas in the included chart (see page 40). After recognizing the difference ourselves, we now experience a comfort level beyond any we had previously felt in working with children in groups at school. What we do is not "therapy" per se, but surely is therapeutic for children and can produce life-changing results!

A Comparison of Curriculum-Based Educational Support Groups and Therapy Groups

Curriculum-Based Educational Support Group	Therapy Group
1. Group focuses on building protective factors by presenting information on life skills (i.e., "All feelings are ok, People have special qualities," etc.).	1. Group resolves individual problems by focusing primarily on risk factors.
2. The support group becomes a safety net to try out newly learned skills in this "microcosm" of the world.	2. Each person has an Individual Treatment Plan.
3. Guided activities in group are based on a set curriculum that is clearly age-appropriate with objectives and measurable outcomes. Since group is content driven, you validate & affirm individuals & move on!	3. Group sessions are a "process" -we talk and talk," probe and confront!
4. Group provides a nurturing and supportive environment. It is ok just to sit & listen. Participants may choose to pass.	4. Group is nurturing and supportive, with confrontation for individuals as needed.
5. Group is led by trained facilitators with a blend of skills - loving & nurturing & listening to children. Facilitators access ongoing training and supervision as needed.	5. Group is led by a licensed therapist with at least 3000 hours of clinical supervision.
6. Group is limited to a set number of weeks, a set time & a "closed" membership (new members can't join once the group has begun.)	6. Group sessions are ongoing & open (children can come & go as they finish their issues.).
7. The cornerstone of the group is confidentiality by facilitator & kids. (Kids rarely breach!)	7. The cornerstone of the group is confidentiality.
8. Not every child is able to handle group interaction appropriately. When necessary, refer the child for outside assessment.	8. Assessment takes place within the group rather than outside!

Yes . . . I know these students need longer than six weeks in group, but . . . I'm afraid I'll never know if I've made an impact on any of them regardless of the number of sessions we meet.

You may never know. Face it. Teachers and counselors seldom do. After all, it's a very rare occurrence that an elementary teacher receives the honor of being selected as the most influential teacher a student ever had! That happened on our campus last year. When our district's National Merit Finalists were able to invite to a banquet the teacher that had the greatest impact on their lives, and one of our finest second grade teachers was selected to attend, it brought a sense of awe and wonder to all of us in the building. Just think what would happen if every student were given the opportunity to show their appreciation in this way!

Every once in a while, something will happen to let you know you've made a difference. One day, an occupational therapist came up to a school counselor and said, "You'll never know what an impact you made on Johnny the other day!" When the counselor didn't remember the incident, the therapist reminded her that she had passed Johnny in the hall on the way back to class earlier in the week and had said hello. Johnny had complained about hurting his arm over the weekend, and the counselor had given some typically "Eriksonian" response, like, "Gee, that must really have hurt when you threw that ball. I really hope you feel better soon." The therapist said that Johnny had told the same story to at least three other adults in the building who had nodded or responded minimally to him. After receiving an affirming response, however, Johnny had visibly brightened, straightened up and marched into the classroom, feeling validated at last. "You were the only one to respond to his hurt." Our school buildings are filled with people who genuinely care about children. They just don't all have the time to give that personal response that a child so often desperately needs.

One thing all group leaders need to do is provide opportunities for feedback. Include a parent as well as a student evaluation form at the end of small groups (possibly one like those included under the end-of-group celebration unit at the end of this book). As indicated earlier, parents have told us that their children excitedly looked forward to the day of their group meeting, recalled activities afterwards and loved knowing they weren't the only ones in the world who had these problems. Sometimes the child they were describing was the very child who came in each week with a mellow attitude, rarely opened his mouth in group and left as quietly as he came. You can't always tell who is being impacted the most by their group experience. And sometimes, the children and parents themselves won't know until farther into the future.

SESSION 1
GO FOR THE GOLD!

Connecting to the Real World

The group leader explains that the group will be conducted along a coaching theme. If students want, each "team player" will be allowed to bring their favorite team jersey or cap to wear each week. Just as teams have rules to live within, our group will develop rules to help us function. Even pro athletes stay in condition and sharpen their skills through practice in order to turn out excellent performances. Likewise, we will practice our skills and earn token points. And, just as winning teams have members who work well together and encourage one another, our team will gain points for positive interactions and encouragement among team players.

Students will take turns doing various jobs in the group. For example:

☆ The "assistant coach" will review group rules each week and collect and file Home Practices.
☆ The "time keeper" will keep the group on task and time activities as need.
☆ The "equipment manager" will hand out any needed equipment or handouts each week & remind people to take their folders and belongings when they leave.
☆ The "High 5's leader" will provide encouragement to team members throughout the session or keep track of when others are encouraging (for intermediate student groups). For younger groups, you may substitute "line leader" whose main responsibility will be to lead students to and from the group meeting place.

These group roles are certainly optional, depending on the group's maturity to handle them with direction and the comfort zone of the group leader. Assuming responsibility within the group will encourage more active participation and sense of belonging to the group.

OBJECTIVES

Students will participate in activities that emphasize the following concepts and skills:
I understand how our group will run.
I understand why the group leader has chosen a "coaching theme."
I will have opportunities to interact with others in the group.
I will begin to feel a part of the group.

PROCEDURE

Pregame Warmup

☆ As students enter the room, welcome them and explain that they have been selected to be part of a group which will help them learn more about themselves, identify personal strengths, improve study, friendship, & goal-setting skills, and have fun!

☆ Review "Connecting to the Real World" before beginning the first activity.

Activities
(choose one or more of the following)

Activity 1.1	Introduction
Activity 1.2	Everybody Up
Activity 1.3	Learning About My Teammates!
Activity 1.4	The Name Game
Activity 1.5	A What?
Activity 1.6	Well, I Never. . .
Activity 1.7	Tug of Friendship

Post Game Commentary

☆ Tally and record individual points gained during group.

☆ Explain "Compliment Corner" activity (used as part of each group's ending). In this activity, each stu dent will have an opportunity to give a compliment to anyone else in the group regarding any specific behavior that helped the group that day.

☆ Announce any housekeeping details (i.e. any change in meeting date and time).

☆ Give students folders in which to keep their Home Practice sheets and "High 5's" notes.
(Group leader may want to consider writing student's name, homeroom teacher's name and meeting time and date on the front of the folder.)

EXTENSIONS
Coaching Tips
High 5's for Teachers
Home Practice Backing for Parents

44

Activity 1.1 - Introduction

EQUIPMENT

"A Coach is Someone Who" sheet
"Team Rules and Roster" sheet
Job cards & "All-Star Tickets To Success"
Individual folder for each student to personalize, keep and return weekly
"Like Me! Not Like Me!" Home Practice Sheet

GAME PLAN

1. After welcoming students to group, discuss the structure of the sessions & post the "Typical Session Format" sheet. Refer to the team and coach concepts. Post and read "A Coach is Someone Who" sheet and

   review this week's Objectives.

2. Explain group job assignments; post laminated cards and write student names beside each. Jobs will rotate weekly. Devise a system to keep track of who has had each job.

3. Develop group rules. You may cover your own suggested list, but it is preferable to have group members give input or develop their own rules. Make sure that basic issues of confidentiality, taking turns speaking, listening and mutual respect are covered. Record group names and rules on the "Team Rules and Roster" sheet.

4. Explain how your token system works. Generally, team members who follow rules during sessions will earn 2 to 3 tokens. (Tokens can be paper clips, pennies, chips, points on a chart, punches on a "game ticket," etc.) You may decide to give each member tokens at the beginning of each session and take tokens away for excessively inappropriate behavior in group. The goal is to keep (or earn) as many tokens as possible. Team members who bring in completed Home Practice sheets or "High 5's" comment sheets from parents or teachers can earn additional points. This emphasis on "out of group" activities is to help students transfer knowledge from group into their everyday interactions.

5. Explain how students may redeem tokens weekly for small treats or save tokens for a larger reward at the end of the group. Another option is to have students earn rewards at predetermined point values (15, 20, 25, 50, 100 etc.). A token system should allow for flexibility.

6. Have students decide on a name for their "ALL-STARS" Team. If students have a hard time coming to consensus, consider using Sid Simon's concept of "values voting:" each student votes for his or her top three favorites, assigning 3 points to top choice, 2 points for the next, and 1 point for their last choice. If time allows, conclude the group with an additional activity as an ice breaker.

HOME PRACTICE

Have students take "Like Me! Not Like Me!" Home Practice sheets to complete with their parents. Return for points. (May be used at the end of any of this section's activities.)

A COACH IS SOMEONE WHO:

☆Has a sense of humor!
☆Helps you get in shape & keeps you on track!
☆Points out areas that need improvement!
☆Capitalizes on your strengths!

☆☆☆☆☆

☆Sets goals with you & drives you toward them!
☆Motivates, encourages & reminds you with a minimum of nagging!
☆Lifts you up & doesn't put you down!
☆Seizes the teachable moment!

☆☆☆☆☆

☆Expects your best!
☆Doesn't dwell on your worst!
☆Knows all players have good days & bad days!
☆Helps you create a vision of what you <u>can be</u>!

☆☆☆☆☆

☆Instills a positive "I CAN" attitude!
☆Doesn't give up & won't let you give up either!
☆Stresses the importance of practice!
☆Helps you know that you are a winner, not a loser!

> Within even the most resistant student, there is the desire to learn. That desire is inflamed in direct proportion to our belief in him or her.

GROUP JOB CARDS

ASSISTANT COACH

Reviews rules & assists Coach.
Collects & files completed Home Practice sheets.

TIME KEEPER

Helps group members be aware of time
& gives 10 minute warning.

EQUIPMENT MANAGER

Passes out & collects all materials in an orderly manner.
Reminds everyone to take folders home!

HIGH 5's LEADER

Encourages team members & leads group compliment time.

 # ALL-STARS

Team Rules & Roster

 Check it out!

Team Rules

_____

_____

_____

_____

_____

Team Members

1. _____

2. _____

3. _____

4. _____

5. _____

6. _____

_____

_____

_____

_____

_____

_____

_____

_____

_____

_____

_____

Name _____

This home practice is designed for you to show what you like to do in your spare time! Circle the things you like to do, and do nothing to the things that you don't enjoy. Be ready to share with group members next week!

Like Me! Not Like Me!

Swim

Play cards	Sing a song	Draw
Wash dishes	See a movie	Ride my bike
Jump rope	Skateboard	Build a fort
Go golfing	Mow the lawn	Play chase
Jump up & down	Paint a picture	Work a puzzle
Build with Legos®	Race remote control cars	Play catch
Play videos	Be on a team	Write a letter
Go to the mall	Camp with Scouts	Clean my room
Sleep	March in a parade	Read a book
Eat	Go to a park	Wash the car

ALL-STAR
Ticket to Success

ADMIT ONE

When you have ____ punches, you may redeem this ticket for _____

ADMIT ONE

When you have ____ punches, you may redeem this ticket for _____

© 2001, McDougall & Roper

Activity 1.2 - Everybody Up

EQUIPMENT

None

GAME PLAN

1. This activity is taken from the book *Silver Bullets* (see bibliography) and is only one example of many great interactive games. Explain that in this activity you are going to see how well the group works together as partners and perhaps as a whole group. Have students pair up with someone who is approximately their same size and sit on the floor facing each other. They should sit with their knees bent up and the bottoms of their feet touching each other's feet. The partners should lean in and hold hands tightly and try to pull one another up at the same time.

2. If pairs are successful, see if a group of three or four (up to the size of the whole group) can sit in a circle with feet touching and arms grasped and pull up as a unit.

3. Another way to have students work in pairs is to have them sit back-to-back, push evenly against one another and try to stand up as a pair. (Arms should not be locked because this could lead to possible dislocation of shoulders.)

HOME PRACTICE
(See Home Practice listed under Activity 1.1)

Remember to print the parent note entitled "Home Practice" on the back of each student worksheet. If you want specific objectives listed, use page 62 . There will be a backing with specific objectives given at the end of each session. If you want to write in your own objective, use the more generic form on page 64.

Activity 1.3 - Learning About My Teammates!

EQUIPMENT

Pencils or markers
"Getting to Know My Teammates" activity sheet

GAME PLAN

1. Distribute activity sheet and make sure each student puts his or her name by "This sheet belongs to..." since swapping gets confusing after a while.

2. Explain that this activity will be one way everyone can learn more about one another.

3. Have students walk around collecting at least two signatures from each group member. (This activity will give the group leader a good idea of which students will need extra attention with the skill of asking for what they want and feeling comfortable joining a group activity.)

DISCUSSION

☆ What was the toughest part about asking someone to sign your sheet?
☆ What was the easiest?
☆ What makes it difficult to meet new people in the classroom, at recess or on your street?
☆ Did you have anything in common with any of the other group members?
☆ How did it feel to be asked about yourself?

HOME PRACTICE
(See Home Practice listed under Activity 1.1)

GETTING TO KNOW MY TEAMMATES!

This sheet belongs to: _____

Make sure that everyone in the group signs at least twice. Find people in your group who:

Plays one of the same sports that you do _____

Has the same favorite color as you _____

Likes the same sports team _____

Has either a brother or sister _____

Enjoys watching cartoons _____

Loves to eat pizza _____

Has ridden a roller coaster _____

Plays video games every day _____

Hates to clean his or her room _____

Likes Math _____

Has a library card _____

Activity 1.4 - The Name Game

EQUIPMENT

"I'm An All-Star" Home Practice Sheet

GAME PLAN

1. If group members do not already know one another fairly well, play a name game to encourage everyone to learn one another's names.

2. Sitting in a circle, have a person in the group start by saying his or her name and a descriptive adjective that starts with the same letter as their name (or favorite food, sport, etc.).

3. As each person around the circle gets their turn, they have to repeat each other's names and descriptive adjective before they add their own to the list. The group leader will be the last to participate.

4. This may seem like a very basic activity and waste of time. But actually, while some children with ADHD become engrossed in incredibly small details, many often have difficulty remembering names! This lack of memory makes it more difficult for them when they try to interact with classmates, especially during those unstructured times. Also, Jerry Moe in *Conducting Support Groups for Elementary Children K-6* (see bibliography) says that bonding and group cohesiveness are increased by such rituals as having special nicknames that are used only in group. He has each student find a word that begins with the same letter of his or her first name and that describes them or something they like. He has been "Jelly Bean" for years to countless children!

DISCUSSION

☆ How did it feel when someone remembered your name and your special interest?
☆ How did it feel if someone forgot your name but was able to remember others?
☆ When at school, on the playing field or at home, is it especially important to remember other people's names?
☆ What are some important memory tricks you can use to remember names more easily?

HOME PRACTICE

Have students take *"I'm An All-Star"* Home Practice sheet to complete with parent.

I'm An All-Star!!

Dear Parents of _____,

Please put one letter of your child's name in each of the stars. (You may use a nick name or abbreviated form of the name if it is longer than 8 letters.) Working together, write as many words as you can that describe your child's positive qualities that begin with each letter! When you've finished, your child will truly feel like an "All-Star" son or daughter!

_____
Parent's Signature

☆ _____

☆ _____

☆ _____

☆ _____

☆ _____

☆ _____

☆ _____

☆ _____

Activity 1.5 - A What?
(best for intermediate age students)

EQUIPMENT
Two small objects that can be passed around a circle

GAME PLAN

1. The group leader holds up one of the objects and says, "This is a _____," and gives the object an imaginary name (i.e, a fizzle, a hitzel, etc.)

2. The group leader instructs the student on his or her right to respond, "A WHAT?" The group leader again repeats "a fizzle." Upon which the student is prompted to respond, "Ahhhh...a fizzle." The group leader passes object to student.

3. This student accepts the object and turns to the student on his or her other side and says, "This is a fizzle." Upon which the second student says, "A WHAT?"

4. The first student then turns back around to the group leader and asks again, "A WHAT?"

5. The group leader repeats, "a fizzle."

6. Then the first student turns to second student and says, "a fizzle," and then hands the object to the second student.

7. Play proceeds around the circle so that by the time the object has reached, the last student, each student in line is turning around asking, "A WHAT?" all the way back to the group leader and repeating "a fizzle" all the way back to the object.

8. Students get really tickled but can usually handle getting one object around to the starting point. If they can handle it, the group leader can start another round, but increase the difficulty by starting the "fizzle" in one direction, and starting "a hitzel" in the opposite direction. When both objects reach the same crossing point, things get really interesting!

9. This game is one of several that we will be using in upcoming lessons that come from a type of "adventure based" counseling. In the bibliography, there are several books listed that have numerous activities. We have found, however, that if you have the funds and can invest in the Adventure Based Resource Index System, hundreds of games and activities are catalogued by type and objective. This activity is taken from ABRIS card number 486.

DISCUSSION

☆ What did you have to do to be successful at this game?
☆ How did people respond when someone messed up?
☆ Is there anything that you would have liked to have happened differently?
☆ What made this a challenging game?

HOME PRACTICE
(See Home Practice listed under Activity 1.1 or 1.4)

Activity 1.6 - Well, I Never ...

GAME PLAN

1. In this game, you explain that everyone will have a chance to get acquainted. (It is also an effective way for the group leader to gauge life experiences of group members.) Each child is given three playing chips.

2. The first child completes the sentence: "Well, I never _____" by naming a place they've never visited, something they've never owned or something they've never done.

3. Any child in the group who HAS had that experience gives up a chip by putting it in the center of the table.

4. Play continues as the next child completes the prompt and others who have had the experience each forfeit a chip.

5. This game is over when only one player has chips left. The child with the fewest "things to brag about" actually wins - a nice turn of events!

NOTE: We borrowed this game idea from Lynn Lavelle, the behavior interventionist in our district.

DISCUSSION

☆ Can you think of one or two other people who have done some of the same things you have done?
☆ Is there any one in here you think you would like to get to know better? Why?
☆ How did if feel when someone remembered something specific about you?

HOME PRACTICE
(See Home Practice listed under Activity 1.1 or 1.4)

Activity 1.7 - Tug of Friendship

EQUIPMENT

A length of rope, about 10 feet long,
tied into a loop with a strong knot.

GAME PLAN

1. The purpose of this activity is to show how the group wins when everyone in the group does their part. Have students sit in a circle with knees up and bent and feet on the floor.

2. Lay the rope on the floor in the middle of the circle.

3. Ask students to take hold of the rope directly in front of them.

4. Explain that each person is to pull evenly on the rope at the same time (without jerking). If the group does this cooperatively, each person will be able to use the resistance on the rope to be pulled into a standing position. This process may take more than one trial. Encourage children to discuss problem solving techniques between tries.

NOTE: This activity is taken from ABRIS card number 160 (see bibliography).

DISCUSSION

☆ What did it take for the entire group to be successful?
☆ What were obstacles to success? (Encourage students to describe behaviors that hindered success, not to name the people who did the behaviors.)
☆ How did it feel when everyone was trying and the group still wasn't successful?
☆ How did the group eventually solve the problem?
☆ How did it feel when the whole group was successful?
☆ Explain that there will be many opportunities for challenges and learning in future group meetings. It will help if everyone "does their part" cooperatively within the group in order for our whole "team" to succeed. (If the group was successful on the first attempt, consider modeling what a disaster uncooperative behavior would have resulted in, with the group leader demonstrating the effect on others by not doing his or her part.)

HOME PRACTICE
(See Home Practice listed under Activity 1.1 or 1.4)

COACHING TIP:

From time to time, we'll include a few "asides" to suggest ways you may want to take a look at what is going on. At the end of your opening session, take a few minutes to evaluate how well the logistics of the group meeting went. Ask yourself:

How well did the space for the group work?
Were there "snags" in the seating arrangement?
What went well this week?
Did I stick to time limits needed to cover everything?
Do I need to take a more or less structured approach?
Is there anything that could be organized more effectively (tokens, job cards, material, etc.)?

If you have doubts about how things went or need specific suggestions, consider calling another educator or mental health professional you trust (or even e-mailing one) to describe any specific situation you were unsure of and ask for feedback from them!

TIP!!

Many professionals believe that children with ADHD have difficulty transferring skills learned in isolated therapy sessions to their everyday settings. Participating in their school's curriculum-based support groups allows children with ADHD to learn new skills in a less threatening and more natural environment. The more opportunities we provide in their daily lives to apply these skills, the more quickly they will see the benefits of using their new skills. With that in mind, we have included weekly reinforcement sheets for each child's teacher ("High 5's") and parent ("Home Practice and High 5's"). Each group session will have a specific form with objectives already written in. We have also provided a generic version in this introductory session in case a group leader wishes to use a simplified form or write his or her own objectives.

The "Home Practice" parent signature form should be duplicated as the backing of each Home Practice assignment sheet that the student takes home. Group leaders might want to consider duplicating the teacher's forms on colored half sheets that would be readily identifiable. Taking the time to let the teachers know how much you appreciate their efforts and energy to complete the "High 5's" would be reinforcing to professionals with an already overloaded schedule!

COACHING TIP:

If your group is one that needs to be up and active, another good introductory activity is to play *Group Juggle* (see Activity 9.1 under Controlling Impulsivity) during the first session. It's a great ice breaker and a good way for the group members to learn one another's names and a simple way to see how the group begins to function as a problem-solving unit. Then, since children tend to beg to play it again, you can redo it later as a quick ending or introduction and focus discussion questions on the controlling impulses aspect of the game.

TIP!!

Sporting Speech!

Running out of ideas for sports analogies? Here are a few:

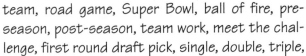

Making waves, pro, amateur, score card, team player, Olympic medalist (gold, silver, bronze), Dream Team, "3 strikes & you're out," home run, grand slam, RBI's, grandstanding, benched, cheering, good or bad sport, All Stars,

Hall of Fame, hurdles, World Series, MVP, striking out, penalties, stats, commentators, umps, referees, fielding, slam dunk, get a grip, stance, focus, defense, offense, photo finish, first down, 4-minute mile, conditioning, training, practice, quitter, home team, road game, Super Bowl, ball of fire, preseason, post-season, team work, meet the challenge, first round draft pick, single, double, triple, season, don't drop the ball, touch down, huddle, ball four - take a walk, take your pulse, free agent, marathon, home court advantage, fumble, on your mark, get set, & go!

Objectives:

Each week our **"Objectives"** will include essential information that we discuss & practice during our group time. It is very helpful for you, as a "Classroom Coach," to be on the lookout for times when this student has used these skills at school. Each week, you will be asked to record any compliments about his or her performance and effort.

Go For The Gold!

High 5's

Each week you will be asked to notice when _____ is practicing the skills and ideas in the "Objectives" on the left. Please "catch the student being good!" And, while it's great to know if he or she is practicing the specific skills we've covered for the week, we are also hopeful that students will continue to demonstrate skills from previous sessions as well. So, any positive behavior or effort that you observe may be recognized by complimenting and signing below.

_____

Teacher's Signature   Date

Objectives:

Each week our **"Objectives"** will include essential information that we discuss & practice during our group time. It is very helpful for you, as a "Classroom Coach," to be on the lookout for times when this student has used these skills at school. Each week, you will be asked to record any compliments about his or her performance and effort.

Go For The Gold!

High 5's

Each week you will be asked to notice when _____ is practicing the skills and ideas in the "Objectives" on the left. Please "catch the student being good!" And, while it's great to know if he or she is practicing the specific skills we've covered for the week, we are also hopeful that students will continue to demonstrate skills from previous sessions as well. So, any positive behavior or effort that you observe may be recognized by complimenting and signing below.

_____

Teacher's Signature   Date

HOME PRACTICE

Each week the Objectiveslisted in this section will include essential information that we have discussed & practiced during group. Since your child will probably remember the activity more than the "message" discussed, we will print the learning objectives each week so that you can reinforce them as much as possible during the week. During our initial meeting, we did not practice specific skills, but instead got to know one another & became familiar with the general sports theme and meeting format.

Pregame Warm up	reviewing group rules, token system & Home Practices
Objectives	concepts as they apply to sports & to everyday life
Activity	skills practiced within the context of an interactive learning experience
Discussion	questions designed to help students see the connection between the group activity & skills they need for everyday life
Post Game Commentary	rewarding of appropriate behavior and time for team members to recognize and reinforce one another

High 5's

Each week, you will be asked to notice when your child is practicing the skills & ideas in the **"Objectives."** And, while it's great to know if your child is practicing the specific skills we've covered, we are also hoping that he or she will continue to demonstrate skills from previous sessions as well. So, ANY positive behavior or effort that you observe may be recognized and commented on below! Your child will receive points in group for returning this completed & signed sheet.

Compliments & Comments:

_____

_____

_____   _____
Parent's Signature   Date Due Back

From Your Number ONE FAN

Objectives

<u>This week we focused on the topic circled below:</u>

Listening

Paying Attention

Relaxing

Positive Self Concept

Teamwork

Handling Feelings

Working on Goals

Communication

Being Organized

Controlling Impulses

High 5's

This week, I noticed _____ practicing the type of skill covered in group.

"Coach," please comment on times when this student successfully used these OR ANY OTHER skills this week.

_____

_____

_____

_____   _____
Teacher's Signature   Date

Objectives

<u>This week we focused on the topic circled below:</u>

Listening

Paying Attention

Relaxing

Positive Self Concept

Teamwork

Handling Feelings

Working on Goals

Communication

Being Organized

Controlling Impulses

High 5's

This week, I noticed _____ practicing the type of skill covered in group.

"Coach," please comment on times when this student successfully used these OR ANY OTHER skills this week.

_____

_____

_____

_____   _____
Teacher's Signature   Date

HOME PRACTICE

This week's **"Objectives"** for

The home practice on the other side is to help your child apply these skills in "real-life" situations. Please help record your child's ideas. **Your child will receive points in group for returning this completed & signed sheet.**

High 5's

I noticed my child applying ideas from **"Objectives"** learned this week **or in previous weeks.**

Compliments & Comments:

_____

_____

_____

_____

_____   _____
Parent's Signature   Date Due Back

From Your Number ONE FAN

I'M ALL EARS, COACH!

CONNECTING TO THE REAL WORLD

Many people in our lives act as "coaches." Parents and teachers coach us just as much as the "real" coach on our playing teams. A coach is someone who oversees proper nutrition and conditioning for developing the stamina and endurance required for the game, who teaches new skills and techniques, who supervises practice of those new skills, and who serves as an encourager and motivator. Doesn't this sound a lot like parents and teachers? When a player doesn't follow the coach's directions for a play, or only hears a part of the directions, usually the play goes wrong and the team suffers. Plus, the player may be benched! If we think of the game of football, we realize that many things can happen to distract a player from listening - the roar of the crowd, the antics of the cheerleaders, the cameramen and reporters, and challenges from the opposite team. Learning to listen in the presence of distracters is imperative if the team is going to win!

OBJECTIVES

Students will participate in activities that emphasize the following concepts and skills:

Listening makes it easier to follow directions.
Listening is a way to show respect.
Listening is important in making and keeping friends.
People can tell when I am listening.
(Discuss eye contact, staying still, asking questions or making appropriate comments.)
Listening is hard when I am confused, distracted or daydreaming.

PROCEDURE

Pregame Warmup

☆ As students enter the room, accept "High 5" forms and completed Home Practice sheets.
☆ Tally points using your selected method.
☆ Wearing your coach's hat and whistle, review group rules and point system.
☆ Briefly discuss completed Home Practices from previous week.
☆ Review "Connecting to the Real World" and Objectives.
☆ Introduce the selected activity for the week.

Activities

(choose one or more of the following)

Activity 2.1   I'm Going on a Road Trip
Activity 2.2   Emmitt Goes to Training Camp
Activity 2.3   Catching a Glimpse!
Activity 2.4   Score With Listening

Post Game Commentary

☆ Tally and record individual points gained during group.
☆ Encourage students to give one another "High 5's" by verbalizing ways in which they have seen each other be especially positive or helpful in group that day.
☆ Announce housekeeping details (any change in meeting date and time).
☆ Give students "High 5" reinforcement sheets to give to their teachers.

EXTENSIONS

High 5's for Teachers
Home Practice Backing for Parents

 66

Activity 2.1 - I'm Going on a Road Trip

EQUIPMENT

Tape recording of various noises and sounds
or a bag of things to make noises with
"Going on a Road Trip" Home Practice sheet
(Optional) toy microphone

GAME PLAN

1. Ahead of time, prepare a cassette tape of common noises or have a bag with various noise makers in it and make noises during the meeting as group members keep eyes closed. (Our friend, Margaret Matthews, made a tape that included: a whistle, phone ringing, faucet running, vacuum cleaner, door bell, snapping fingers, clapping, etc.) Have the group listen and guess what is making the sounds.

2. Consider playing the game, "I'm Going on a Road Trip." This is another activity adapted from one taught to us by Lynn Lavelle. In this game, the group leader explains that you are all members of a favorite local sports team going on a weekend road trip. Then the leader says he or she is going to take a toothbrush.

3. Ask each group member to add an object he or she would take. BUT, they must first recall each object previously named by other players. See how many times you can go around the circle before someone leaves an object out. Counselor Cathy Ortiz has adopted a fuzzy sports mascot that students hold as each speaks. She has found that it not only helps the children to focus better, it has also become an important part of their group ritual.

4. An alternate activity is the "Human Tape Recorder" game. Make a short statement and have a student repeat exactly what you say. Gradually increase the complexity of the statement. You may do this by lengthening the statement, or by making a statement that is nonsensical. Using a play or real microphone heightens the fun!

DISCUSSION

☆ In the first game, what did you have to do in order to be able to make good guesses?
☆ In the second game, how did you remember what others said in the correct order?
☆ Name some times during a regular day when it's important to listen.
☆ What makes it difficult for you to listen?
☆ How do you help remind yourself to listen well?
☆ Was it easier to remember things you understood or the phrases that made no sense?
☆ What happens when you do not listen carefully at home? . . .at school? . . .at practice?

HOME PRACTICE

Have students take "Going on a Road Trip" Home Practice sheets to complete with their parents. Return for points.

IS GOING ON A ROAD TRIP!

Dear Parents,

In group, we've been practicing listening & paying attention. When you listen to others, putting things in your "memory bank" & keeping them there is a challenge! Please take a few minutes this week to play this game while you wait in line, at supper, or another time when you have a few minutes to listen & concentrate.

Going on a Road Trip Game

1. The first player states that he or she is going on a road trip & selects one item that will be taken.
2. The second player says, "I'm going on a road trip, I'm taking an extra pair of shoes & a swim suit."
3. The next player repeats this & adds an item; on it goes until someone can't remember all the items!
4. Take a minute & discuss what everyone did to remember things so well! (some people try remembering only the first letter of the item, some visualize it in their minds, some repeat it silently, etc.)
5. You can also discuss other situations at home or school in which it's important to remember things in a certain order.

Activity 2.2 - Emmitt Goes to Training Camp
(A good introductory activity)

EQUIPMENT
Story of "Emmitt Goes to Training Camp"
"Key Words" Home Practice sheet

GAME PLAN

1. Tell the group that today they will be playing a fun listening game to sharpen their skills of listening for and responding to key words.

2. Divide students into groups of 2 or 3. Assign each group a key word to listen for ("EMMITT," "COACH" and "FIRST DOWN.") Younger children may be more successful if they respond in unison.

3. Tell the students that as you read the story, each of the groups will say their response in unison immediately upon hearing their own key word. (Responses include shouting "BIG BUCKS" when they hear EMMITT, "HUT! HUT! HUT!" when they hear COACH, and "GO TEAM!" when they hear FIRST DOWN.)

4. Tell the story and discuss how effectively and quickly they responded.

5. If time allows, do it twice, switching assigned key words.

DISCUSSION

☆ What did you have to do to listen effectively? (ignore distractions, focus on own task)

☆ What are some times at school or at home when you have to listen to key words?

☆ What are some important key words to listen for? (now, only once, quickly, after you're through, underline, use complete sentences, follow directions)

☆ In this game, we used responsive listening. In real life, what are some words or responses that adults expect you to use so they can know you've listened to and understood them? (yes sir, yes ma'am, I'll do it now, I will)

HOME PRACTICE

Take the story of "Emmitt Goes to Training Camp" and play with your parents. Complete the "Key Words" Home Practice sheet with your parents. Return for points.

Emmitt Goes to Training Camp

It was the first day of training camp for the Dallas Cowboys & most of the players had arrived. EMMITT Smith drove in just as the COACH said: "Boys, it's time to put on the pads & huddle up! Let's get to work! I expect to see lots of FIRST DOWN plays in practice today!"

Aikman was in good shape after having elbow surgery last season. None of his passes were under 30 yards long. EMMITT was in fine form, catching pretty nearly all those passes. Why, he even caught a sixty yarder! COACH said, "Way to go!" After the sixteenth FIRST DOWN, COACH said, "Let's take a break, boys!" It was so hot that the players drank buckets & buckets of their favorite sports drink.

During the break the COACH said, "Guys, I've got some bad news for you! I've had a talk with EMMITT & catching balls & scrambling for FIRST DOWNS is startin' to lose appeal. EMMITT's thinkin' of switching to baseball for a new career. I tried to tell him that it didn't work for Michael Jordan & it wouldn't work for him, but it seems like his mind's made up...."

EMMITT spoke up: "Aw, COACH, you know me. I was just a-foolin' you. I won't ever get tired of making downs – FIRST DOWNS or touchdowns! Why, the name, EMMITT, is synonymous with football!

Well, the Cowboys got a big laugh out of EMMITT's joking around, but they weren't gonna let him get away with it. Every time he made a FIRST DOWN during the rest of the week, they'd all yell: "It's a home run, EMMITT!" They about drove the COACH crazy, but he didn't mind too much as long as they kept making those FIRST DOWN plays!

KEY WORDS

Dear Parents,

When we read the story, *Emmitt Goes to Training Camp*, in our group meeting, we practiced responding (in silly ways) to certain <u>key words</u>. You'll see some key words listed below that "coaches" (teachers & parents) use in real life. Next to each key word, please help your child record a response that an adult would like to hear or see! Talk about situations in which they can expect to hear those key words most often (home, school, other). Discuss & add some of your family's favorite key words for fun!

Key Words	Best way to respond
"Pay attention"	_____
"Put away your…"	_____
"Do it quietly"	_____
"Read carefully"	_____
"Do it now"	_____
"Answer completely"	_____
"Go to time out"	_____
"Try it one more time"	_____
"Listen carefully"	_____

_____
Parent Signature

Activity 2.3 - Catching a Glimpse!

(A good introductory activity)

EQUIPMENT

(None)

GAME PLAN

1. Have students stand up in a circle. Explain that they are to subtly make eye contact with another person in the circle. As soon as eye contact has been established on both sides, students quietly switch places in the circle. Let this activity continue for a couple of minutes. Some students may move several times.

2. Then explain that on the next round, as soon as eye contact is established, give a "high 5" to each other as you exchange places. Continue for a minute or two.

3. In this round, students should whisper "You're cool!" to one another as they switch places after establishing eye contact.

4. Have students sit down to discuss questions below.

DISCUSSION

☆ How did it feel to be "contacted" several times in the circle?
☆ Why is it difficult to look people in the eye?
☆ What does this activity have to do with listening?
☆ How important do you think eye contact is in real life when you are just talking with friends?

HOME PRACTICE

(None)

Activity 2.4 - Score With Listening

EQUIPMENT

Mini poster of "*Listen Up*"
Score cards (optional - cut out,
pasted onto tag board and laminated for durability)
"*I'm All Ears*" Home Practice sheet

GAME PLAN

1. Describe steps for effective listening using the "*Listen Up*" sheet. Each step of the skill may be printed on a sheet of paper or index card. After explaining the steps, the group leader models them while a student speaks and other group members observe.

2. The group acts as a "panel of judges." For fun, give each child three "score cards" marked "Touchdown," "Field Goal" and "First Down." They can hold cards up to evaluate your listening and the role plays to follow. Each student must be able to give a reason for his or her scoring.

3. After the steps have been reviewed and briefly discussed, then students take turns being the talker and listener in a communication "dyad" format. Possible dialogue starters include: what I did this weekend, stuff I hate to do and why, my favorite vacation, a time I made the big play, what I like best about my teacher or my school.

4. At the end of each two to three minute dialogue, the speaker gives a "score" to his or her paired listener. Encourage students to practice listening during the week.

5. Discuss techniques students could use to help themselves refocus when they felt themselves losing attention. Examples could include: getting up to get a tissue, sitting up straighter, writing down key words, removing distracters, fidgeting "constructively" and unobtrusively by twiddling thumbs or rubbing something quietly in their hands while they continue to maintain eye contact with the speaker.

DISCUSSION

☆   What did the listener do well? Was there any way the listening could have been improved?
☆   How did it feel to have someone really listen to you?
☆   Tell about a time when it's most difficult for you to listen.
☆   What is your favorite refocusing technique?

HOME PRACTICE

Encourage students to use the "*I'm All Ears*" Home Practice sheet and ask a parent to "judge" them on their listening skills. Return for points.

Listen Up to Follow Directions

A wonderful way to help your child learn to follow directions is to verbally remind him or her to do these 4 things each time a direction is given.

LOOK AT THE SPEAKER

Maintain eye contact the entire time the direction is being given.

SAY "OK," "YES MA'AM," or "YES SIR"

Use a respectful tone of voice.

DO IT RIGHT AWAY

No excuses, arguing or stalling
(just a minute, in a little while, I'll do it later...)

CHECK IN WITH THE PERSON

Show them that you have followed the direction.

☆☆☆☆☆☆☆☆☆☆☆☆☆☆☆☆☆☆☆☆☆☆☆☆☆☆☆☆☆☆☆☆☆☆☆☆☆

Parents, you are being an <u>excellent coach</u> when you:

☆Say these steps aloud for your child

☆Ask him or her to repeat them aloud

☆Prompt your child to do the next step

☆Label unacceptable behavior aloud without emotion:
("What you are doing right now is arguing, making excuses, stalling...")

☆Compliment your child immediately when a direction is followed

Listening Score Cards

Dear Parents of _____, Listening & paying attention take SO much practice! This week, "signal" your child as to how well he or she is doing. Please complete the "Listening situation" information on all the Listening Score Cards that apply! Return form to ALL-STARS' folder.

Listening situation:

_____

Touchdown!

You are the referee! If the person you are observing did a great job & did <u>all</u> of the listening steps.

Listening situation:

_____

Field Goal!

You are the referee! If the person you are observing did a good job of using <u>most</u> of the listening steps, use this card

Listening situation:

_____

First Down!

You are the referee! If the person you are observing did a great job but did not seem to be listening <u>some</u> of the time, use this card.

I'm All Ears!

Dear Parents of _____,

Please take a moment & evaluate your child's listening skills. Start a conversation, give some directions or select some other situation in which you expect your child to listen. After a few minutes, please give him or her feedback using the checklist below. For fun, you can take turns role-playing effective & ineffective listening.

I wanted my child to listen to me when I was talking about:

_____

He or she was able to do everything checked off below!

_____ Looked at me while I was talking.

_____ Ignored distractions.

_____ Listened without interrupting.

_____ Used body language to indicate attentiveness.
(leaning in, looking interested, etc.)

_____ Asked a question or made a comment that showed understanding of what was said.

Please add compliments or comments:

_____
_____

_____
Parent's Signature

This week our Objectives included:

☆ Listening is important in making & keeping friends.
☆ Listening makes it easier to follow directions at home, school & at play.
☆ Listening is a way to show respect.
☆ If you wait to speak until others are finished, make eye contact, stay still, ask questions & make comments, others will know that you are listening.

"Coach", please be on the lookout for times when I have used these skills at school.

I'm All Ears, Coach!
Listening

High 5's

This week I noticed _____ practicing the skills & ideas in the "Objectives." I've circled on the left the areas I've seen improvement in this week. Below are compliments that "celebrate" his or her good behavior.

_____   _____
Teacher's Signature   Date

- -

This week our Objectives included:

☆ Listening is important in making & keeping friends.
☆ Listening makes it easier to follow directions at home, school & at play.
☆ Listening is a way to show respect.
☆ If you wait to speak until others are finished, make eye contact, stay still, ask questions & make comments, others will know that you are listening.

"Coach", please be on the lookout for times when I have used these skills at school.

I'm All Ears, Coach!
Listening

High 5's

This week I noticed _____ practicing the skills & ideas in the "Objectives." I've circled on the left the areas I've seen improvement in this week. Below are compliments that "celebrate" his or her good behavior.

_____   _____
Teacher's Signature   Date

HOME PRACTICE

This week's **"Objectives"** for _I'm All Ears, Coach!_ are:

☆ Listening is important in making & keeping friends.

☆ Listening makes it easier to follow directions at home, school & at play.

☆ Listening is a way to show respect.

☆ People can tell when someone is listening (when they have eye contact, stay still, ask questions or make comments, and don't interrupt).

☆ When your mind wanders, you're distracted or confused, it's hard to listen.

The home practice on the other side is to help your child apply these skills in "real-life" situations. Please help record your child's ideas. **Your child will receive points in group for returning this completed & signed sheet.**

High 5's

I noticed my child applying ideas from **"Objectives"** learned this week **or in previous weeks**.

Compliments & Comments:

_____

_____

_____

_____

_____   _____
Parent's Signature   Date Due Back

From Your Number ONE FAN

SESSION 3
(Paying Attention)

HANGING IN THERE

CONNECTING TO THE REAL WORLD

The group leader ask students if they have ever seen or been in a gymnastics, karate, skating or skiing competition. Each of these are often solo performances where the participant is "in the spotlight." Ask students how they think the soloist feels being in the spotlight. Ask if students are aware of how athletes prepare themselves for the big performance. Make sure they touch on the issues of mental as well as physical conditioning, skills and practice. Ask how soloists keep from being distracted by the crowd, the judges and any other events going on around them. Discuss focusing and how important it is to star athletes. Discuss what could happen to them in the athletic arena or at school. Explain that in these next few activities, the group will be sharpening their focusing skills.

OBJECTIVES

Students will participate in activities that emphasize the following concepts and skills:

Paying attention helps me follow directions.
I must concentrate (stay focused) to pay attention and ignore distractions.
When I pay attention, others enjoy being around me.
To pay attention, I notice what's going on, decide what's most important and stick to it.
I pay better attention to details when I take my time.

PROCEDURE

Pregame Warmup

☆ As students enter the room, accept "High 5" forms and completed Home Practice sheets.
☆ Tally points using your selected method.
☆ Wearing your coach's hat and whistle, review group rules and point system.
☆ Briefly discuss completed Home Practices from previous week. Review "Connecting to the Real World" and Objectives.
☆ Then introduce the selected activity for the week.

Activities

(choose one or more of the following)

Activity 3.1   Spotlight
Activity 3.2   The Dream Team Goes to the Olympics
Activity 3.3   Mirrors & Webs
Activity 3.4   Focused Memory

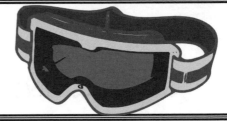

Post Game Commentary

☆ Tally and record individual points gained during group.
☆ Encourage students to give one another "High 5's" by verbalizing ways in which they have seen each other be especially positive or helpful in group that day.
☆ Announce housekeeping details (any change in meeting date and time).
☆ Give students "High 5" reinforcement sheets to give to their teachers.

EXTENSIONS

High 5's for Teachers
Home Practice Backing for Parents

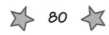

Activity 3.1 - Spotlight
(A good introductory activity)

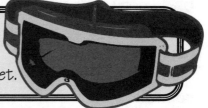

EQUIPMENT
Flashlight
"In The Spotlight" Home Practice sheet.

GAME PLAN

1. Ask students to imagine that when someone talks, there is a "spotlight" on them, much the same as if they were speaking in a play. In a play, the most important thing to pay attention to is in the spotlight and the spotlight moves from person to person to remind us of whom to look at and listen to.

2. Darken the room somewhat and ask one person to begin to talk. Provide a discussion starter if necessary, or have students share their Home Practice sheet from the previous group session. Focus the flashlight on the chest of the selected person and keep it there until someone in the group looks away, interrupts or otherwise sends a "signal" that they are not listening. At this point, either turn the flashlight off or aim it down toward the table top or floor. Then ask the group to tell you why the spotlight had to go off the origi nal speaker. It is useful to refer to this activity intermittently during other sessions. You can also ask "Who's in the spotlight?" to cue children to listen.

NOTE: This activity was adapted from the book, *Games People Should Play* (see bibliography).

DISCUSSION

☆ How did it feel when the spotlight shifted to another person?
☆ How did it feel to be the spotlight "stealer?"
☆ What can you do to stay focused when the spotlight is on someone else?
☆ What made it tough to keep the spotlight on a particular person?
☆ When are there times in the classroom when the focus is on a "soloist?"

HOME PRACTICE

Have each student take "In The Spotlight" Home Practice sheets to complete with their parents. Return for points.

Name_____

Draw a picture of a time when you really need to "spotlight" someone else.

IN THE SPOTLIGHT

List some things you would like your listeners to do when <u>you</u> are in the spotlight:

_____   _____

_____   _____

_____   _____

Activity 3.2 - The Dream Team Goes to the Olympics

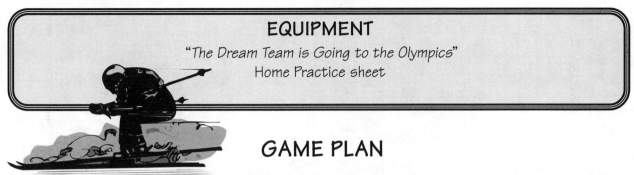

EQUIPMENT

"The Dream Team is Going to the Olympics"
Home Practice sheet

GAME PLAN

1. Play the game "*The Dream Team is Going to the Olympics.*" Begin by thinking of a CATEGORY of things, but do not share this with the group. For example, equipment, food, compact disc titles, red things, summer clothes, things that have zippers, words starting with a specific letter, etc. Then say: "The Dream Team is Going to the Olympics and they are taking a _____" and name an item that fits your preselected category.

2. Invite each child to make a guess about something the Dream Team might also bring along. If their guess fits the category, you say, "Yes, the Dream Team would like to take that."   If the item does not belong in your category, you say, "No, I don't think the Dream Team would take that." Go around the group and allow each child to take turns guessing. You will take a turn each time around the circle, giving another "clue" as to what would be taken.

3. Tell students that once they figure out how the game works, they ARE NOT to explain to others, but may go on giving good clues to those students who have not "caught on."

4. The group "wins" when every child is able to correctly select an item that the Dream Team would take. Then it can be revealed that you had to figure out the category and name an item from that category. This requires close and sustained listening and may take the group several tries to master!

DISCUSSION

☆   What was most challenging about playing "*The Dream Team is Going to the Olympics?*"
☆   How did it feel to have the category figured out quickly and have to wait for others?
☆   How did it feel to be one of the last to figure out the category?
☆   Are there ever times in class when it is difficult to figure out what is going on?
☆   How does it feel when you are in this situation? What can you do about it?
☆   Do you suppose you are the only person who is confused?

HOME PRACTICE

Give each student a Home Practice sheet to take home to play "*The Dream Team is Going to the Olympics*" so that students may play the activity with their family. Return for points.

The Dream Team is Going to the Olympics!

"The Dream Team is Going to the Olympics" is a new twist on an old game that involves paying attention & some "strategizing." Your child played this game in group this week & would like for you to play it with him or her at home. To be successful, you'll need to listen carefully as your child provides "clues" about what items would be taken to the Olympics by Dream Team members...

After you get the hang of it, you can rotate leadership & challenge your child!

Hang in there!

(Don't forget to model persistence & positive ways to handle frustration!)

Please sign below after you've played the game!

_____
Parent's Name

_____
Child's Name

Activity 3.3 - Mirrors & Webs
(A good introductory or closing activity)

EQUIPMENT
Ball of string or yarn

GAME PLAN

1. Making and maintaining eye contact is such an important issue with younger children that you may want to spend extra time practicing this skill by playing the "Human Mirror" game. Have two students at a time stand facing each other and ask one to be the "mirror." This student must copy everything the other student does for one minute. There is no talking until the time is up. (For added difficulty, let observers attempt to distract the "mirror" during the last 30 seconds.) Have students sit in a circle on the floor.

2. Discuss specific behaviors necessary to pay close visual attention. A transition into the web activity could be made by saying that paying attention in "real life" usually involves more than just using your eyes!

3. Have students sit in a circle on the floor. Pass a ball of string or yarn to the student across from you. Have each student continue to pass to someone across from them.

4. As a "web" begins to develop, students will either do what it takes to maintain the web pattern and sustain attention, or will do things that are inappropriate and irritate other members in the group as their attention wanders.

5. One way to increase the difficulty level of this activity is to try to tell a cohesive story as the yarn is passed from person to person. Each member tries to pick up the story where the last member left off. If they've been paying attention, the story should "flow."

NOTE: This activity is adapted from *Learning through Laughter* by Charlene Wenc (see bibliography). It has also been used in training sessions by the Johnson Institute.

DISCUSSION

☆ What happened when people paid attention?

☆ How did you feel about those people? What did you think about them?

☆ What happened that was NOT helpful?

☆ Make the point that any discussion or game really has its own "invisible web." Since this is so, how you handle your part of the web affects others.

☆ In what situations do others depend on you to pay attention and do your part?

☆ If you get "off track," what could you say to yourself to get refocused?

HOME PRACTICE
(None)

COACHING TIP:

Consider sharing this imaginary tip that students can use in the classroom with their teacher's permission. "Pretend you are an alien stranded in a classroom on a different planet. Your teacher is the source of communication with your home base. Inside the corner of your desk is a small, smooth object (like a stone or block) that allows you to communicate with your home planet. Whenever the teacher says she is going to give directions and to listen very carefully, that is your cue to pick up the object and hold it still in your hand. Imagine that this device forces your eyes to stay glued to the teacher and your hand to be "frozen" still. Concentrate  carefully on the meaning of the coded message your teacher is relaying. When the teacher says that it is time to "get to work," that is your signal that the transmission is broken. Then return your signaling device to its safe place in your desk and complete your assignment. DO NOT pick up the signaling device except during transmission times, as this will weaken it and bring undue notice of this device to the alien creatures seated near you who might be tempted to take it or ask too many questions about it. Good luck with your 'secret mission' of receiving coded messages from the teacher!"

Activity 3.4 - Focused Memory

EQUIPMENT

TV tray, cookie sheet, or box lid & cloth to cover the tray
Variety of home, school, or office objects small enough to fit on the tray or lid
Paper and pencil for each child
"Object Search - Part A" and "Object Search - Part B" activity sheets
"Staying Alert on the Slopes" or "The Thrill of Victory & The Agony of Defeat"
Home Practice sheets.

GAME PLAN

1. This activity involves using a "now you see it, now you don't" type of activity to improve visual memory and focusing of attention. Place a variety of items on a tray (about 15-20 for third through fifth graders; less for younger students).

2. Explain to students that they will have two minutes of total silence in which to study the items on the tray. After the two minutes are up, cover or remove the tray and distribute pencil and paper to each student.

3. Ask students to list by name or draw all the items they can remember having seen on the tray. Encourage individual work at this point; sharing will come later. After about five minutes, allow students to share what they have remembered.

4. Discuss. Consider teaching students a system of classifying to help them remember all the items by color, by materials, by shape or by first letter in the name of the object.

5. Allow students to try again after having discussed classification systems.

6. If time permits, remove some items to see if students can name which have been removed.

7. A variation is to show a picture of items on "Object Search - Part A." Ask students to remember everything on the page. Remove "Part A." Give "Object Search - Part B" to all students and ask them to circle every item that was NOT on "Part A." Share results.

8. Ask if any students divided the page up into sections and focused on one part at a time. Discuss how this could be a help.

9. Be inventive. Depending on the nature of the group, you can encourage them to let you know when they are finished and make a point of writing down their time for completion. Also, at any time, you can be very "distracting" and see how it affects students' studying.

DISCUSSION

☆ What helped you to remember? How did practicing help?

☆ Did anything (external or internal) interfere with paying attention and remembering (especially identify feeling confused, overwhelmed or "bored" as blocks)?

☆ What happened, or would happen, if someone divided the picture into smaller parts?

☆ When at home, school or playing sports, is it important for you to pay attention and remember more than one thing at at time? (examples could include: where things go if you are asked to pick up or clean up, multiple step directions in the class or at home)

☆ Does it help to rush through tasks? Why or why not? (stress accuracy versus speed)

☆ What can you do to remind yourself to slow down and examine things carefully?

☆ In which school subjects is this skill needed? Which chores are best done slowly ?

☆ Is there a difference between just "listening" and really concentrating to pay attention?

HOME PRACTICE

Have students take either "Staying Alert on the Slopes" or "The Thrill of Victory & The Agony of Defeat" Home Practice sheet to complete with their parents. Return for points.

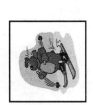

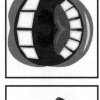

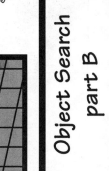

Object Search
part B

Staying Alert on the Slopes

_____
Name

Dear Parents & Teacher,
Please put a check beside any behavior you observe this week.
Please emphasize paying attention in as many different situations as possible.

☐ Paid attention when directions were given.

☐ Ignored distractions and finished work.

☐ Followed two to three-step directions.

☐ Finished work by following a written list of directions.

☐ Could repeat oral directions when asked.

This All-Star also paid attention by:

_____

_____

_____

Parent's and/or Teacher's signature

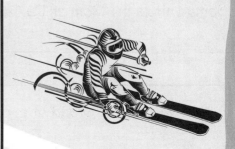

PAYING ATTENTION

Dear Parent of _____,

One of the toughest parts of paying attention involves <u>ignoring distractions.</u> Please help your child to circle the things below that are especially difficult for him or her to ignore. Share some of the things you do to stay focused! Finish by completing the statements at the bottom of the page together.

Some tips for successfully gaining your child's attention are:
Be in the same room when you want them to hear you or stay focused on a specific task, touch them to gain attention, insist that they respond when spoken to, turn off the TV, ask them to repeat what you have said, <u>enthusiastically appreciate eye contact</u>, compliment them for ignoring or minimizing distractions, be intentional about acknowledging when things are distracting & problem solve about ways to stay focused!

NOISES

THE PETS

THE URGE TO DRAW & DOODLE

TV & NINTENDO

WHAT ELSE?

day dreaming

EVEN THE THOUGHT OF PLAYING!

WHAT ELSE?

FUNNY PEOPLE OR THINGS

COMPUTER

It's really tough to pay attention when _____

Some things my Mom or Dad do to stay focused are:

_____   _____

_____   _____

A time when I was proud of my child for ignoring distractions was:

_____

This week our Objectives included:

☆ Paying attention makes it easier to follow directions.
☆ Paying attention requires concentrating & ignoring distractions.
☆ When you notice what's going on & select the most important thing to stay focused on, you are paying attention.
☆ Taking your time allows more careful attention to detail.

"Coach", please be on the lookout for times when I have used these skills at school.

Hanging In There!
Paying Attention

High 5's

This week I noticed _____ practicing the skills & ideas in the "Objectives." I've circled on the left the areas I've seen improvement in this week. Below are compliments that "celebrate" his or her good behavior.

_____   _____
Teacher's Signature   Date

- -

This week our Objectives included:

☆ Paying attention makes it easier to follow directions.
☆ Paying attention requires concentrating & ignoring distractions.
☆ When you notice what's going on & select the most important thing to stay focused on, you are paying attention.
☆ Taking your time allows more careful attention to detail.

"Coach", please be on the lookout for times when I have used these skills at school.

Hanging In There!
Paying Attention

High 5's

This week I noticed _____ practicing the skills & ideas in the "Objectives." I've circled on the left the areas I've seen improvement in this week. Below are compliments that "celebrate" his or her good behavior.

_____   _____
Teacher's Signature   Date

HOME PRACTICE

This week's **"Objectives"** for _Hanging in There!_ are:

☆ Paying attention makes it easier to follow directions.

☆ Paying attention requires ignoring distractions & concentrating.

☆ Paying attention means noticing what's going on, selecting what's most important & sticking to it.

☆ Taking your time allows more careful attention to detail.

The home practice on the other side is to help your child apply these skills in "real-life" situations. Please help record your child's ideas. **Your child will receive points in group for returning this completed & signed sheet.**

High 5's

I noticed my child applying ideas from **"Objectives"** learned this week **or in previous weeks**.

Compliments & Comments:

_____

_____

_____

_____

_____   _____

Parent's Signature   Date Due Back

From Your Number ONE FAN

NO PAIN, NO GAIN!

CONNECTING TO THE REAL WORLD

Biking and hiking, two activities that require a great deal of stamina and endurance, need daily conditioning to build up to a marathon-level workout. It takes daily investment in time and energy or all benefit of building muscles and increasing stamina is lost and has to be regained. It helps to have an encouraging coach who will be with you during your daily exercise. Daily workouts are often boring, require personal discipline and can be "a pain," but are essential to success. The same can be said of taking the time to do boring organizational tasks like filing papers, straightening your desk, emptying your backpack and cleaning up your room. But, going a day or two without taking the time to get organized leads to piles, clutter and confusion. Remember, as the old saying goes, "No pain, no gain!"

OBJECTIVES

Students will participate in activities that emphasize the following concepts and skills:

I need to be aware of when I'm organized and when I'm not.
I can learn to be more organized and orderly.
When I put things in order, my life is easier!
It takes a little time each day to stay organized.
As I get older, others expect me to be more organized.
Sometimes I need help from "coaches" to be organized.

PROCEDURE

Pregame Warmup

☆ As students enter the room, accept "High 5" forms and completed Home Practice sheets.
☆ Tally points using your selected method.
☆ Wearing your coach's hat and whistle, review group rules and point system.
☆ Briefly discuss completed Home Practices from previous week.
☆ Do introductory Card Relay Race game before explaining the topic of the week.
☆ Review "Connecting to the Real World" and Objectives.
☆ Then introduce the selected activity for the week.

Activities
(choose one or more of the following)

Activity 4.1   Card Relay Race
Activity 4.2   Shaping Up
Activity 4.3   Putting Things Together
Activity 4.4   Keeping My Desk in Order
Activity 4.5   Keeping My Notebook in Order

Post Game Commentary

☆ Tally and record individual points gained during group.
☆ Encourage students to give one another "High 5's" by verbalizing ways in which they have seen each other be especially positive or helpful in group that day.
☆ Announce housekeeping details (i.e., any change in meeting date and time).
☆ Give students "High 5" reinforcement sheets to give to their teachers.

EXTENSIONS
High 5's for Teachers
Home Practice Backing for Parents

Activity 4.1 - Card Relay Race

(A good introductory activity)

EQUIPMENT

Deck of cards - one suit placed in order in one box
and the other suits scattered randomly and placed in another box.
Two boxes (about the size of a duplicating paper box)

GAME PLAN

1. Explain that today in group, before discussing what the topic will be, we are going to do a relay race to demonstrate a study "principle."

2. Divide into two groups and let the groups pick which side they will line up on. (Have your boxes already in place at one end of the room or hallway; that way, the teams cannot accuse you of favoritism at the end of the race! Depending on room arrangement and size, you may need to scoot some desks around or move to the hall to allow for two "running lanes.")

3. Explain the rules: Each team will send one runner to the end of the room to pick up a card and lay it on the desk (outside of box). Then they will return to the end of their line and the next runner will advance. Cards are to be picked up in order of value (i.e., Ace, K,Q,J, 10,9,8,7,6,5,4,3,2). The teams are unaware that one card pile is already in order and the other pile is disorganized!

4. After one team has won, return to seats without comments.

DISCUSSION

☆ How did it feel to be on the winning team? . . . on the losing team?
☆ Was it a fair race? Were the winners smarter or did they cheat?
☆ Why did one team find the task so much easier that they easily won?
☆ What skill does this game teach us about keeping track of our things that could help us at school?
☆ How could this skill help us at home too?
☆ How could organization help save study time in class? . . . with homework? . . .with finding belongings?
☆ Does being organized give a person an advantage?
☆ Who are you being unfair to if you stay cluttered?

HOME PRACTICE

(None)

Activity 4.2 - Shaping Up
(Best for intermediate students)

EQUIPMENT

NOTE: Several days before group, have each child's teacher complete
a copy of "How Organized Am I?" Checklist for each group participant.
One taped headband for each person (headband can be cut out of manila folder
or construction paper strips about 2 inches by 15 inches)
Copies of checklists of "How Organized Am I?" for each student and for each teacher
"Something to Cheer About" Home Practice sheet - intermediate level

GAME PLAN

1. The group leader explains that the activity today will involve group members playing roles of students in Mrs. McGillicutty's class. Each of these students is well known in class for a particular behavior and other students tend to react to them in certain ways.

2. The group leader puts a labeled headband on one student without letting him or her see what is on the label. Other students are asked to give clues without using any words that are on the label to see if the student can guess what behavior he or she is known for. Clues may be a description of, reaction to or statement that someone might say about that behavior.

3. After having guessed the label being worn, the student selects another group member to wear the second label. This process continues until all have had a turn.

4. Using questions, Part 1 from below, debrief this activity before continuing.

5. The group leader explains that it is important to know what our own individual organizational styles are. Distribute & ask students to complete the "How Organized Am I?" activity sheet.

6. After students have completed the checklist, ask if they would like to hear how their teacher views their organizational style. (Since most children with ADHD do not self evaluate accurately, you might want to prepare them for the fact that often others do not see us as we see ourselves. Since some teachers are very frank in their evaluations, it is best to have summarized their comments pointing out areas of agreement and areas where the teacher has rated the child differently.) Discuss questions in Part 1 & Part 2 following.

DISCUSSION

Part 1
☆ How did it feel to have the label you wore?
☆ What kinds of behavior lead to disorganization? . . . or to organization?
☆ How did people treat others differently when they wore a negative label as compared to when they wore a more positive label?
☆ Is it fair that people are treated differently? (Point out that life is not always fair and certain behaviors usually get certain responses.)
☆ Without using specific names, can you think of people in your class who are well known for being disorganized or organized?

Part 2

☆ Did anything about the teacher's comments surprise you? (Point out that each person tends to have a preferred style of organizing things and if the student's and teacher's styles don't match, it can cause problems.)

☆ What are the advantages and disadvantages of being organized at school? . . .at home?

☆ Who are the people at school and at home that help you to be more organized?

☆ What is so hard about being organized?

HOME PRACTICE

Have students take "Something to Cheer About" Home Practice sheets to complete with their parents. Return for points.

Something to Cheer About!

Intermediate

_____
Name

Check any of the following things your child has done this week. Take this opportunity to discuss your favorite organizational strategies with your child. Organization can include time management, initiating tasks, & neat arrangement of belongings.

School Stuff

_____ Organized notebook or folders

_____ Put name and date on papers this week

_____ Has filed homework papers

_____ Brought home parent notes about PTA, etc.

_____ Responded positively to a reminder about organizing school materials

_____ Brought home an accurate list of homework

_____ Brought home all materials needed to do work

_____ Received teacher reports of classwork completed in a reasonable length of time

Compliments or comments:

_____

_____
Parent's signature

Home Stuff

_____ O.H.I.O. (Only Handle It Once) trashed it, acted on it, filed it or put it away

_____ Sorted toys or games

_____ Got up on time*

_____ Was ready to leave for school or another appointment on time*

_____ Made a chore list*

_____ Checked items off chore list as they were completed*

_____ Started homework or chores without being told.

_____ Completed homework in a reasonable length of time*

_____ Picked up after self without being told

*(without excessive reminders)

Keeps things in place

Finishes work on time

Forgets homework

Has a messy desk

Loses papers

Studies hard

Makes good grades

Doesn't finish & gets low grades

 102

How Organized Am I?

Student Copy

Dear _____,

As we begin the part of our group work that deals with organization & study skills, it would help if you could take a few minutes to complete this checklist by placing an (S or N) in each blank.

S = Satisfactory   N = Needs Improvement

Your teacher will also complete it. Write some specific things you would like to do to improve your study or organization skills during the next few weeks.

____ I file papers.

____ I put my name and the date on my papers.

____ I keep my notebook organized
       (my best time to do this is _____).

____ I keep my desk clean
       (my best time to do this is _____).

____ I clean up my work area without reminders.

____ I finish my work neatly.

____ I finish work within a time limit.

____ I finish work accurately.

____ I turn in homework on time.

____ I work independently with few reminders.

Some things I do really well are:

_____

I could improve _____ by:

_____

How Organized Is This Child?

Teacher Copy

Dear Teacher of _____,

As we begin the part of our group work that deals with organization & study skills, it would help if you could take a few minutes to complete this checklist (**use S or N**) for this student.

S = Satisfactory   N = Needs Improvement

<u>This information will be shared with the student after he or she has completed the same checklist.</u> You will be asked to remark on any improvement you see during the next few weeks. **Please return to** _____ NO LATER THAN _____.

____ Files papers.
____ Puts name and the date on papers.
____ Keeps notebook organized
     (best time to do this is _____).
____ Keeps desk clean
     (best time to do this is _____).
____ Cleans up work area without reminders.
____ Finishes work neatly.
____ Finishes work within a time limit.
____ Finishes work accurately.
____ Turns in homework on time.
____ Works independently with few reminders.

Some things this student does really well are:

_____

_____

_____

_____
Teacher's signature

Activity 4.3 - Putting Things Together

(best for primary students)

EQUIPMENT

Three or four sets of items to be sorted
(old keys, socks, pencils, buttons, building blocks)
A plain sheet of paper for each group
A set of Item Cards & "Where Do I Put It?" activity sheet for each student
"Something to Cheer About!" Home Practice sheet - for primary level

GAME PLAN

1. The group leader explains that today we are going to do an activity where we group things together. Putting things together is one way of starting to be organized.

2. Divide the group into pairs or triads and give each group a different set of objects to be sorted. Tell them they will all have to agree on how they are going to sort them (by color, size, shape, etc.) and will have about five minutes to finish. (Counselor Sandy Foster suggests a more active alternative by taking students to the teachers' parking lot, dividing them into pairs of "parking attendants" and having them make a plan for parking the cars in a way that would make it easy for them to locate later.)

3. Discuss Part 1 questions.

4. In order to make the transition from sorting things in general to organizing and putting them away in order, hand each pair a sheet of paper and ask them to pretend this is a drawer and to put their set of items away as neatly as possible "in the drawer."

5. After putting all previous sorting items "away," the group leader explains that now we are going to use the idea of sorting things and putting them in their right places to help us see what to do with our school materials. Distribute "Where Do I Put It?" activity sheet and a set of Item Cards to each student. (Group leader can decide whether to tri-fold the paper and have cards already cut out and paper clipped to each sheet, or to have students fold paper and cut their own cards out during group, depending on time allowed.)

6. Tell students to spread their cards out and then sort them into the appropriate folder or box on the sheet using the OHIO method - "Only Handle It Once." Let them do it several times for fun (actually for help in increasing the neural pathways!)

7. Discuss Part 2 questions.

DISCUSSION

Part 1

☆ Did anything interrupt the organizing process? (kids playing with material, kids disagreeing on how to do it, watching others, etc.)

☆ What helped your group to organize or sort the materials?

☆ What are some things you really have to sort at home? . . .at school?

Part 2

☆ Why was putting things on the smaller area of the sheet of paper a challenge?

☆ What things do you most often lose or misplace at school?

☆ Do you ever get in trouble (as in, miss recess) because you can't find something?

☆ Did you have a tough time in the card sort game figuring out where the cards should go?

☆ Do you ever have a hard time with your real papers in figuring out where they should go?

☆ Who could help you figure out where certain papers go?

HOME PRACTICE

Have students fold their "Where Do I put It?" sheets into thirds and paper clip their game cards to the sheet. The students can take it home to play with their parents. Have them discuss with their parents what the advantages are of keeping their things in order. Return for points.

Item Cards for use with "Where Do I Put It?" Game

THINGS IN _____'S DESK

Spelling Test
1. Cat
2. Dog
3. Hat

Spelling test from last month

Art work

Other school supplies

Come to PTA on Oct. 30 for a great program!

PTA Notice

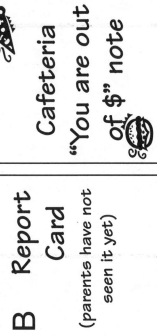

Cafeteria "You are out of $" note

A paper airplane

Half-finished math sheet

A+
B   Report Card

(parents have not seen it yet)

B+
Now is the time for all good men to come to the aid of their country.

Graded handwriting paper

Pens and Pencils

Note from teacher on a job well done!

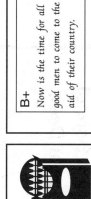

Crayons or scissors

I love

Paper you scribbled on

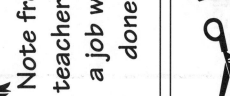

Scraps of paper

⭐ 107 ⭐

WHERE DO I PUT IT?

Name _____

School Box in Desk	Stay at School Folder in Desk	The Trash Can	Take Home Folder

Pretend that your teacher has asked you to clean out your desk. Sort the items from your desk into either your school box, "stay at school" folder, "take home" folder or the trash. Discuss the reasons for your choices with the group. Keep your game cards & playing sheet. Take the game home to play it with a parent.

Something to Cheer About!

Primary

_____
Name

Check any of the following things your child has done this week. Take this opportunity to discuss your favorite organizational strategies with your child. Organization can include time management, initiating tasks, & neat arrangement of belongings.

School Stuff

_____ Put name on papers

_____ Organized papers - none loose in desk

_____ Brought home parent notes about PTA, etc.

_____ Has taken completed work papers home

_____ Responded positively to a <u>reminder</u> about putting away school materials

_____ Brought home take home folders & necessary materials

_____ Received teacher reports of wise use of time in class

Compliments or comments:

_____
_____
_____
_____
_____
  Parent's signature

Home Stuff

_____ O.H.I.O. (Only Handle It Once) trashed it, acted on it, filed it or put it away

_____ Sorted toys or games

_____ Got up on time*

_____ Was ready to leave for school on time*

_____ Checked items off chore list as they were completed*

_____ Started homework or chores without being told.

_____ Completed homework in a reasonable length of time*

_____ Picked up after self without being told

*(without excessive reminders)

Activity 4.4 - Keeping My Desk In Order

(best for intermediate students)

EQUIPMENT

Tub or box for holding contents of one group member's desk
An empty student desk
Trash can
Marker for labeling
"House Rules" Home Practice sheet

GAME PLAN

1. As you pick up children for the group session, spot check each student's desk & make positive comments when merited. Select the most disastrous desk. Make sure the student feels comfortable with the group helping to organize the materials. Empty the contents into a plastic tub or box and carry back to the group room.

2. Complete routine opening activities. Tell the group that they will play a game where they have to think like a professional equipment manager, specifically, Mr. "Can Find-it." Discuss why it would be important to have an equipment manager for a pro sports team, and then link this idea with the importance of managing one's own possessions appropriately.

3. Using the contents from the tub, have students take turns thinking like the organized Mr. "Can Find-it" as they place materials one at a time into the empty desk. Have them explain their reason for placing items in a particular spot in the desk.

4. Ask if anyone would do it differently and emphasize that there are many ways of organizing materials. However, students should also be aware of and follow their teachers' organizational preferences. To follow up and encourage continuing practice of organizational skills, consider reinforcing clean desks by periodic desk checks. You might leave a tangible reinforcer such as a note, treat or other recognition. (Some group leaders who can not fit regular checks into their schedules can often find an instructional assistant, teacher or parent volunteer to follow-up.)

DISCUSSION

☆ How does it help a student to have an organized desk?
☆ What are some unpleasant consequences of having a messy desk?
☆ How does it feel when your things are in order? When they are out of place?
☆ How do others (students, teachers, parents) feel being around you when your things are scattered or missing? Give examples.
☆ What are some ways that you can make organizing easier for yourself? (for example, straightening up a little bit each day, choosing what is the best time each day to clean, cleaning out backpacks weekly, taking unneeded items to store at home).
☆ How important is keeping your things in order at home?

HOME PRACTICE

Have students take "House Rules" Home Practice sheet to complete with their parents. Return for points.

House Rules!

Name _____

If you sleep on it... **make it up**.

If your wear it... **hang it up**.

If you drop it... **pick it up**.

If you eat out of it...**wash it**.

If you open it... **close it**.

If you turn it on... **turn it off**.

If you empty it... **fill it up**.

If it rings... **answer it**.

If it howls... **feed it**.

If it cries... **love it**!

Anonymous

Dear _____

Have your parents initial the line beside each thing you've done this week. (Then you can cut the House Rules out & keep them at home if you'd like to!)

_____

_____

_____

_____

_____

_____

_____

_____

_____

_____

If your child used the **O.H.I.O.** (**Only Handle It Once**) principle & put an item where it went the first time he or she touched it, sign here:

_____
Parent's Signature

Dear Suzy,

You should have seen all the teachers gathered around today talking about My...yes...my desk!!!

They were so amazed at how clean it really was! My teacher said she hadn't seen it so clear of loose papers all year long! She even looked at my notebook – and you know what a mess it can be – and declared that all the papers were filed correctly and the dates were even on all the papers (well, most of the papers).

I love to know that I am being "Fair to myself" and getting a head start in class!!

Love,

THREE CHEERS
FOR GREAT EFFORT
IN KEEPING
YOUR "STUFF" IN
ORDER!!!

Name

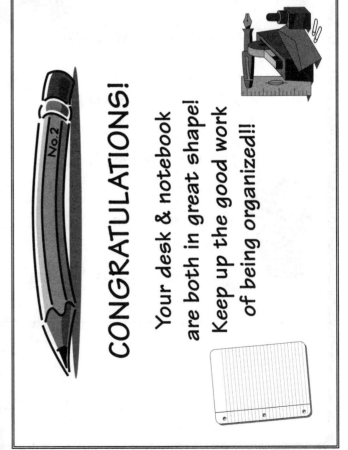

CONGRATULATIONS!

Your desk & notebook
are both in great shape!
Keep up the good work
of being organized!!

You are winning the race...

...of keeping up with your stuff!
Keep up the hard work

_____

_____
Date

THUMBS UP!
CLEAN DESK AWARD

Awarded to:

_____

for a job well done! Keep up the great
job of organizing your desk!

NO BETTER NOTEBOOK

AWARDED TO

_____

FOR TAKING EXTRA TIME TO
FILE PAPERS NEATLY!

_____
DATE

IN ALL THE WORLD!!

HIP! HIP! HOORAY!

THE NO LOOSE PAPERS AWARD!

Hereby given to _____

this _____ day of _____,

20__.

None in desk!

THUMBS UP!
CLEAN DESK AWARD

Awarded to:

_____

for a job well done! Keep up the great
job of organizing your desk!

THREE CHEERS
FOR GREAT EFFORT
IN KEEPING
YOUR "STUFF" IN
ORDER!!!

Name

Activity 4.5 - Keeping My Notebook In Order
(for intermediate students)

EQUIPMENT

Student notebooks
Extra organizational items like subject dividers, sticky notes,
transparent plastic sheets for inserting important papers,
agendas or homework charts, hole punch, reinforcers, etc.
"*Tour de Notebook*" Home Practice sheets

GAME PLAN

1. Check desks if you pick up students and reward for neatness. (Also notice cubbies, backpacks.) Ask students to bring their notebooks and <u>all loose papers</u> from their desks and backpacks.

2. Play link-up. The first person says: "Something I'm proud of that I organized this week is _____." Any other player may link arms with the first one if they have ever done the same sort of thing and say, "I've also done a good job of _____ and names another example of how they've been organized. Game continues until all have linked up in a circle. Celebrate being organized by doing a group High 5.

3. Define and list characteristics of a "PERFECT" notebook. Include best tips for keeping it organized. The group leader records the group ideas so that students can refer to it during the notebook exchange.

4. Sitting in a circle, students are directed to hand their own notebook to the person on their right. Allow three or four minutes to evaluate the notebook (on a scale from one to ten), using the list generated earlier as a guide for scoring. Then, ask each student to share two positive things about the notebook, one thing that could be improved upon, and the score they gave.

5. Return notebooks to owners, divide into pairs, and ask them to help one another get their notebooks into shape according to suggestions discussed above. Have available and offer extra materials to aid in organization.

DISCUSSION

☆   Where is the best place to put pages that need to be completed for homework?
☆   Where do you put schedules, your agenda, or other important notices to take home?
☆   Discuss the "out of sight, out of mind" principle.
☆   Discuss this statement: "If you're in charge of yourself and your stuff, no one has to NAG!!!"
☆   How can you tell if a paper is "too old" to keep in your notebook? Where do you put these papers ?
☆   Ask students if they have a "landing and launching" pad (a specific spot) at home in which to put their backpack, completed homework, etc.

HOME PRACTICE

Have students take "*Tour de Notebook*" Home Practice sheets to complete with parents. Return for points.

_____

Name

WORKING WITH YOUR PARENT -
put a check in each box that describes
your notebook & the organizational
habits that you have used this week.
_____

O.H.I.O Gazette

Tour de Notebook
U.S. Team Wins First Place!

U.S. Team Shares Winning Strategies!

The Perfect Notebook has:

❑ Big enough rings to hold all paper

❑ NO loose pages (flies like an eagle)

❑ All papers filed by subject

❑ One special place for ALL homework

❑ A place for reminder notes to yourself

❑ NO old or useless papers

❑ NO duplicates of pages

❑ A completed homework list (everyday!)

Note from the Editor to parents:

Please sit down with your child & look carefully at his or her notebook. It would be great if you could give generous praise for any & all signs of organization that you see!

Tremendous Tour Tips

Winners Learn To:

❑ **O.H.I.O.** (Only handle things once) Don't stuff or stack them; put them where they go the first time you pick them up!

❑ Put DUE DATES on all homework or unfinished work.

❑ WRITE YOURSELF NOTES about work to be done. Remember: If **YOU** take charge of your business, others won't need to!

❑ HIGHLIGHT HOMEWORK on the agenda.

❑ Keep IMPORTANT PAPERS in the front of the notebook. (Out of sight is out of mind!)

❑ TAKE TIME DAILY to sort things out.

❑ CLEAN OUT YOUR DESK & BACKPACK at least once a week!

Note: <u>If there are not very many papers in your child's notebook, there's a pile somewhere else! (Feel free to do a desk check next time you're at school!)</u>

 116

This week our Objectives included:

☆ It's important to know your own organizational strengths & weaknesses.

☆ It is possible to be more organized & orderly.

☆ Putting things in order makes life easier.

☆ It takes time each day to keep things in order. No Pain, No Gain!

☆ As we get older, others expect us to do more of our own organizing.

☆ Kids sometimes need support & encouragement from parents in order to become responsible for their own things.

"Coach", please be on the lookout for times when I have used these skills at school.

**No Pain, No Gain!
Organization**

High 5's

This week I noticed _____ practicing the skills & ideas in the "Objectives." I've circled on the left the areas I've seen improvement in this week. Below are compliments that "celebrate" his or her good behavior.

_____   _____
Teacher's Signature   Date

- -

This week our Objectives included:

☆ It's important to know your own organizational strengths & weaknesses.

☆ It is possible to be more organized & orderly.

☆ Putting things in order makes life easier.

☆ It takes time each day to keep things in order. No Pain, No Gain!

☆ As we get older, others expect us to do more of our own organizing.

☆ Kids sometimes need support & encouragement from parents in order to become responsible for their own things.

"Coach", please be on the lookout for times when I have used these skills at school.

**No Pain, No Gain!
Organization**

High 5's

This week I noticed _____ practicing the skills & ideas in the "Objectives." I've circled on the left the areas I've seen improvement in this week. Below are compliments that "celebrate" his or her good behavior.

_____   _____
Teacher's Signature   Date

HOME PRACTICE

This week's **"Objectives"** for <u>No Pain, No Gain!</u> are:

☆ It's important to know your own organizational strengths & weaknesses.

☆ It is possible to be more organized & orderly.

☆ Putting things in order makes life easier.

☆ It takes time each day to keep things in order. No Pain, No Gain!

☆ As we get older, others expect us to do more of our own organizing.

☆ Kids sometimes need support & encouragement from parents in order to become responsible for their own things.

The home practice on the other side is to help your child apply these skills in "real-life" situations. Please help record your child's ideas. <u>**Your child will receive points in group for returning this completed & signed sheet.**</u>

High 5's

I noticed my child applying ideas from "**Objectives**" learned this week **or in previous weeks.**

Compliments & Comments:

_____

_____

_____

_____

_____   _____
Parent's Signature   Date Due Back

From Your Number ONE FAN

SESSION 5
(Self-Concept)

I'M AN ALL-STAR!

CONNECTING TO THE REAL WORLD

Ask students what it would be like if all players on a team had exactly the same qualities (like everyone on a baseball team had high "RBI's" but couldn't catch, throw, or run very well). Emphasize that even pros have to practice. Explain that even super stars like Michael Jordan have areas of strengths and weaknesses (and remind them how "average" a baseball player he was, even though he was great at basketball). Discuss how mature pro players keep a positive attitude about their performances, accept wins and defeats gracefully, learn from their mistakes, strive to improve their skills, and focus positively on the next game.

⭐ 119 ⭐

OBJECTIVES

Students will participate in activities that emphasize the following concepts and skills:

Everybody has strengths and weaknesses and that's ok!
As I get older, I can improve upon my strengths by caring enough to practice skills.
I might not be the best at something, but I can always get better!

PROCEDURE

Pregame Warmup

☆ As students enter the room, accept "High 5" forms and completed Home Practice sheets.

☆ Tally points using your selected method.

☆ Wearing your coach's hat and whistle, review group rules and point system).

☆ Briefly discuss completed Home Practices from previous week.

☆ Review "Connecting to the Real World" and Objectives.

☆ Then introduce the selected activity for the week.

Activities

(choose one or more of the following)

Activity 5.1   I'm OK
Activity 5.2   The Spring Training Catastrophe

Post Game Commentary

☆ Tally and record individual points gained during group.

☆ Encourage students to give one another "High 5's" by verbalizing ways in which they have seen each other be especially positive or helpful in group that day.

☆ Announce housekeeping details (any change in meeting date and time).

☆ Give students "High 5" reinforcement sheets to give to their teachers.

EXTENSIONS

High 5's for Teachers
Home Practice Backing for Parents

Activity 5.1 - I'm OK

(Best for primary students)

EQUIPMENT

A wrapped gift box with a removable lid onto the bottom
of which a mirror has been taped
A book highlighting some aspect of self-esteem,
like *Quick as a Cricket* or *Stellaluna* (see bibliography)
Soft modeling clay (small amount for each student)
"*My Playing Field*" Home Practice sheets

GAME PLAN

1. Write the word "unique" and show it to the students. Ask if anyone knows the meaning of the word (Make sure the definition includes at least one of the following: something special, one-of-a-kind, the only one in the whole wide world, so valuable that it could never be exactly replaced, and must be handled with great care!)

2. Ask students if they can keep a surprise for a short time. Then have each child come to peek in the box to get a look at something "really unique!"

3. After all have had a turn, ask what it was they saw in the box that was unique. Some will say, "a mirror." Others will realize, "Each one of us is really unique."

4. Reinforce the concept of being unique by selecting a favorite children's book like *Quick as a Cricket* or *Stellaluna* (see bibliography). The first book emphasizes that it is okay to act a lot of different ways, depending on where you are. *Stellaluna* tells the story of how a young bat had to adapt himself to "bird" life and eliminate his "bad" bat characteristics before coming to an understanding that there are lots of ways of being!

5. As students discuss the story, have each one create an animal in clay that reminds them of themselves. Be sure to emphasize the session objectives during the discussion.

6. If time allows, student can make their favorite sports cap out of clay and put it on their animal.

DISCUSSION

☆ Discuss how character(s) in the book were unique.
☆ Have each child share one way in which they believe they are unique.
☆ Talk about the way circumstances and settings (home, classroom, etc.) can dictate which traits are useful or appropriate and which are not. (for example: If you were playing baseball, would it be better to be quick as a cricket or slow as a snail?.... loud as a lion or quiet as a mouse?)
☆ Ask students to select a picture or idea from the story that reminds them of themselves.
☆ Go back through the book and have students pick a picture that shows one way each one would like to be more often. When would that be and how come?
☆ Then, have students pick a picture that shows a way they don't like to be. Process the effect of behavioral consequences on their choices. How could they avoid being this way?

HOME PRACTICE

Have students take "*My Playing Field*" Home Practice sheets to complete with their parents. Return for points.

Name _____

Draw a picture
or use words to
complete all parts

I'm not good at

I don't like

I'm good at

I like

My Playing Field

© 2001, McDougall & Roper

Activity 5.2 - The Spring Training Catastrophe

EQUIPMENT
Story of "Spring Training Catastrophe"
"I'm A Pro and Even Pros Practice" Home Practice sheets

GAME PLAN

1. Read the story "The Spring Training Catastrophe."

2. Discuss using questions below.

DISCUSSION

☆ What were the unique qualities (strengths and limitations) of each of the players in the story?

☆ What message or moral does this fable teach us?

☆ How did each player feel when they were attempting to do what was most difficult for each of them?

☆ What could the players have said to themselves that might have made them feel differently?

☆ Do you ever feel like the players in this story?

☆ What are your personal strengths?

☆ What things are difficult for you to do?

☆ Are there ever times when it is a good idea to practice things that are not in your area of strength?

HOME PRACTICE

Have students take home and complete "I'm a Pro and Even Pros Practice" Home Practice sheet. Return for points.

TIP!!

COACHING TIP:

Think of a time when you felt like you were being asked to perform "out of your element." If appropriate, share with students. Ask students to talk with their parents about their most embarrassing moment or the toughest battle they ever had with self doubts or in dealing with others' unrealistic expectations. In working with parents and teachers of students with ADHD, encourage them to believe that most of these students will, as adults, be involved in vocations that allow them to be imaginative, creative, sensitive, flexible, and rapidly moving! Very few will stay put in jobs that require sitting still while giving close and continuous attention to detail. And, as stressed above with the students, even though it is important to broaden one's skills and practice areas that are not personal strengths, we don't have to cement our feet in positions that make us miserable! Remember to have patience with the child who may be tomorrow's Robin Williams or Steven Spielberg.

"THE SPRING TRAINING CATASTROPHE"

Joey was really excited because it was the first day of spring training for his "Eagles" baseball team. Last year they had won several contests in their city, and he and the other guys on the team couldn't wait to get started again. When he showed up for practice, he was surprised to find that they were going to have a new coach.

"I sure hope this coach has had experience in working with Little League teams," said Henry, Joey's friend and the team's fantastic first baseman. "Well, we don't have a lot of choice, do we?" replied Albert. "I only hope my RBI's wind up being as high this season as last year's. I've been putting in lots of hours at the batting cage this summer and I think I'm really ready!"

"Well, just as long as you can still catch all those pop flies at home, catcher!" responded Joey. Just then, their new leader, Coach Russo called the team to order and explained his philosophy of coaching. "Boys, I believe in having really well-rounded players! I think it's important for all of us to be able to play all positions just in case somebody gets sick and has to fill in. So, we are all going to practice all of the positions on the team! We are going to be prepared for anything!"

The boys didn't think it would work, but followed the coach's orders as he ran them through a practice game with players switching positions every inning. At the end of play, Coach gave out practice assignments and expected them to be followed strictly. Since Joey, last season's star pitcher, was having difficulty with his running speed and couldn't ever get to the ball in time to catch flies out in right field, Coach Russo had him practice running laps for a whole month before their first game. Even though he put his heart into it and was building up great endurance, Joey's short little legs just couldn't carry him fast enough.

Albert, who usually did a great job as catcher snagging fouls at home plate, did a horrible job with his long distance throws to home when he was out in left field. Since he wasn't in the middle of the action, his attention tended to wander whenever he played that position. So, the coach had him practice throwing long pitches every night. Albert was determined to get better, because he wanted the Eagles to win all their games this season. But the night before their first game, his arm was so sore that he wasn't sure he could play the next day.

Henry usually did a bang-up job at first base. He had a quick reaction time and could pay close attention to signals from home and from the pitcher. Hardly anyone ever got past him! Coach told Henry to practice squats for the catching position! But Henry was a little full around the middle and had a hard time squatting. Even the catcher's breastplate didn't fit him around the middle. So, coach had him doing aerobic exercises during practice for a month to improve his flexibility and help him to lose weight. The day before the big game, Henry's knees were so sore and inflamed that he went to his doctor!

Well, as you can imagine, the Eagle's didn't win their first game. Coach Russo just didn't understand it. How could things have gone so wrong? He wondered if more practice would help the team, or if they needed to take another approach. What do you think?

I'm a Pro...

Name _____

Ask your parents, teachers, & friends to write what's great about you & one area that they see you needing to improve.

_____
Parent

_____
Teacher

_____
Friend

_____
Friend

_____
Teacher

_____
Parent

... & Even Pros Practice

Activity 5.3 - All About Me

EQUIPMENT

Activity sheet entitled "All About Me"
Soft ball or some object to toss
Four bean bags for "bases"
"Four Bases" questions
"My Ump's Breastplate" or "My ALL-STARS Card" Home Practice sheet

GAME PLAN

1. Have students complete "All About Me" and share results.

2. Using a soft ball or object, select 4 to 5 sentence starters (depending on the attention span) from the handout and ask the speaker to hold the ball while speaking. Holding the object is used to heighten interest and focus attention; it also provides some movement and acceptable fidgeting. Students may pass or gently toss to the next child when it is their turn to respond. If you decide you would like for students to respond to sentences other than those they have already written on their handouts, other suggestions could include: tell about the nicest thing they ever did for someone or that someone did for them; if they could break any world record, what would it be and why; what is one area in which they excel and could teach others about.

3. If time allows, consider asking students to do a more active form of sharing. Arrange four bean bags to simulate first, second, third, and home bases. These can be in a tiny field pattern inside, or actually taken outside while keeping the field small enough for all participants to hear responses. Ask students individually to try for a home run by answering the question on each base (see "Four Bases").

NOTE: This activity is adapted from "Three Perspectives" found in ABRIS card number 69 and "Quickies II" card number 114.

DISCUSSION

☆ What did you learn about others in the group?
☆ What are some ways you are like others in the group?
☆ What are some ways you are different from them?
☆ Emphasize that differences are GOOD and that it is important to accept and respect individual differences.
☆ Have students look back over items and put a "plus" next to comments that they feel positive about.

HOME PRACTICE

Have students take "My Ump's Breastplate" or "My ALL-STARS Card" Home Practice sheet to complete with parents. Return for points.

ALL ABOUT ME!

_____

In the thought bubble, draw a picture of how you feel about school. Then, complete the following sentences:

I think I am _____

One change I'd make in school is _____

The best part about me is _____

Other kids say_____

My parents think I am _____

Kids in my class _____

The hardest thing about school is _____

At recess, I feel_____

When the teacher is talking, I _____

If I get in trouble at school, it's because _____

I wish I could do better at _____

I hope that in this group we will_____

FOUR BASES

FIRST BASE

Pretend this base stands for when you were in preschool or younger. Tell what you remember about yourself when you were this age.

SECOND BASE

Pretend this base stands for the age you are now. Tell something about yourself that describes you now.

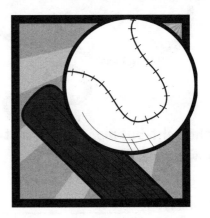

THIRD BASE

Pretend this base stands for when you are old enough to be in middle school. Tell something about what you think your life will be like then!

HOME PLATE

Pretend this base stands for when you are old enough to have a job. Tell something about yourself then!

MY UMP'S BREASTPLATE

_____
Name

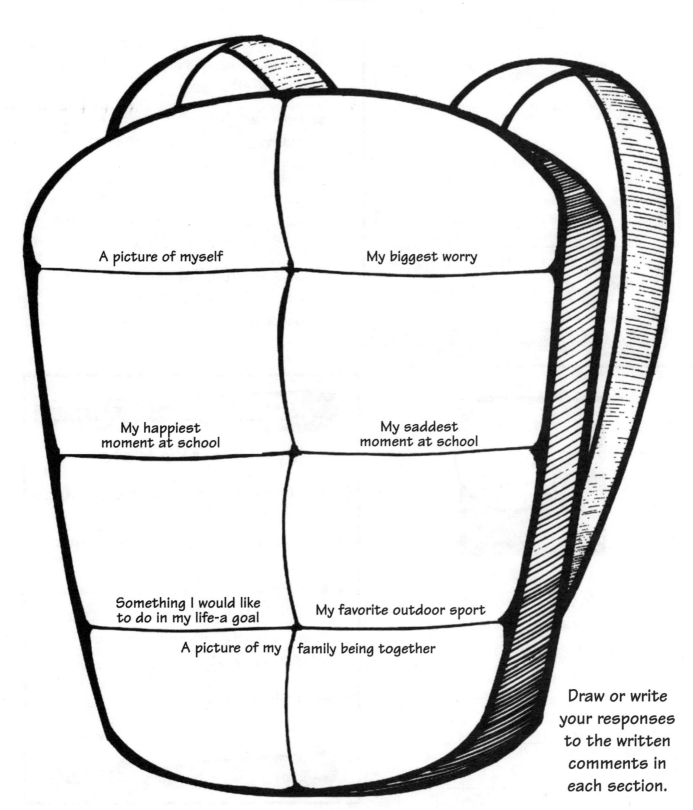

A picture of myself

My biggest worry

My happiest
moment at school

My saddest
moment at school

Something I would like
to do in my life-a goal

My favorite outdoor sport

A picture of my / family being together

Draw or write
your responses
to the written
comments in
each section.

My All-Stars Card

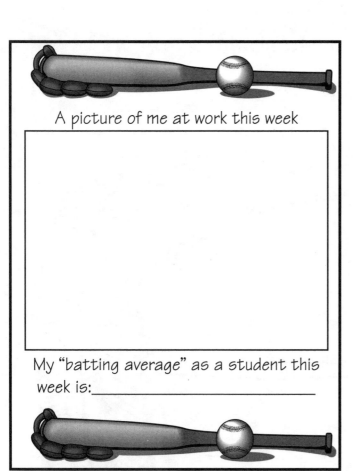

A picture of me at work this week

My "batting average" as a student this week is: _____

☆ Think about your "batting average" in class this week.

☆ Do you think that your work in class would have qualified you for the ALL-STARS team?

☆ How badly do you want to be considered an ALL-STAR student?

☆ Practice your skills to improve your performance and fill in the statustics you earned this week on the "back" of your ALL-STAR card below.

☆ On the "front" of the card on the left, draw a picture of yourself being successful in class this week!

What are some things you can do to increase your student "batting average" for the next week?

_____
_____
_____
_____
_____

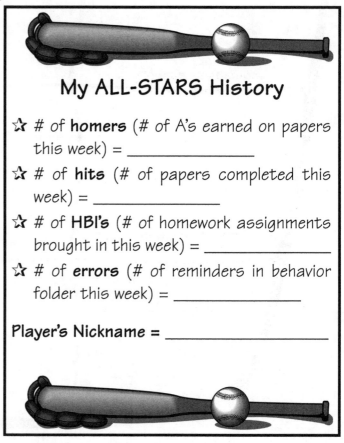

My ALL-STARS History

☆ # of **homers** (# of A's earned on papers this week) = _____

☆ # of **hits** (# of papers completed this week) = _____

☆ # of **HBI's** (# of homework assignments brought in this week) = _____

☆ # of **errors** (# of reminders in behavior folder this week) = _____

Player's Nickname = _____

I'm An All-Star
Self-Concept

High 5's

This week our Objectives included:

☆ Everyone's unique qualities include strengths & weaknesses.
☆ It's important to be realistic about one's qualities.
☆ Personal limitations may be due to lack of development, lack of practice, or low motivation.
☆ No one can be the best at everything, but everyone can get better at something.

"Coach", please be on the lookout for times when I have used these skills at school.

This week I noticed _____ practicing the skills & ideas in the "Objectives." I've circled on the left the areas I've seen improvement in this week. Below are compliments that "celebrate" his or her good behavior.

_____   _____
Teacher's Signature   Date

- -

I'm An All-Star
Self-Concept

High 5's

This week our Objectives included:

☆ Everyone's unique qualities include strengths & weaknesses.
☆ It's important to be realistic about one's qualities.
☆ Personal limitations may be due to lack of development, lack of practice, or low motivation.
☆ No one can be the best at everything, but everyone can get better at something.

"Coach", please be on the lookout for times when I have used these skills at school.

This week I noticed _____ practicing the skills & ideas in the "Objectives." I've circled on the left the areas I've seen improvement in this week. Below are compliments that "celebrate" his or her good behavior.

_____   _____
Teacher's Signature   Date

HOME PRACTICE

This week's **"Objectives"** for _I'm An All-Star!_ are:

☆ Everyone has unique qualities which include strengths & weaknesses.
☆ It's important to be realistic about these qualities.
☆ Personal limitations may be due to lack of development, practice, or motivation.
☆ Even though a person may not be the best at something, he or she can always get better!
☆ It's important to accept yourself, even while striving for improvement.

The home practice on the other side is to help your child apply these skills in "real-life" situations. Please help record your child's ideas. **Your child will receive points in group for returning this completed & signed sheet.**

High 5's

I noticed my child applying ideas from **"Objectives"** learned this week **or in previous weeks**.

Compliments & Comments:

_____

_____

_____

_____

_____   _____
Parent's Signature   Date Due Back

From Your Number ONE FAN

SESSION 6
(Understanding ADHD - Part I)
THE LIFELONG TREK - BEGINNING THE JOURNEY

CONNECTING TO THE REAL WORLD

Every time we meet, we have a connection that compares athletes in the world of sports with things that happen in our everyday lives. So, who are the important players we are really talking about here? Us, of course; and we are all playing one long, exciting game called "Life." Everyday we are in training for upcoming challenges. And each day we experience winning plays and painful defeats. Sometimes we work alone to improve our personal best. Other times we work as a valuable part of the teams we call our class, friends, family, or church. Whether working alone or with others, we are all on a life-long trek.

Just like every other player on these teams, we each have strengths and limitations. Sometimes, we may not be happy with our performances. So, we have a choice. We can either make excuses and limit our dreams for success, or try to understand what is happening and change what we can. It's a great challenge to learn to accept ourselves and each other. Just like athletes, we are all born with certain abilities and learn to develop other skills. We all have a unique perspective on the world. Having ADHD is only one part of who some of us are. The more we learn about ADHD, the better we'll know ourselves and be able to capitalize on strengths and compensate for things that hold us back. No matter where we are ability-wise, though, winning in life means never giving up.

OBJECTIVES

Students will participate in activities designed to emphasize the following concepts and skills:

☆ Kids and adults who have ADHD can learn more about how they tend
to think, feel and act and can be very successful in life.

☆ Many kids and adults have a condition called ADHD that may make it harder for them
to pay attention, to think before acting and to sit still. But they also tend to be
people who are very energetic, creative, sensitive, and inventive.

☆ Scientists think ADHD is caused by physical differences in the chemicals in a
person's brain, but they haven't yet figured out exactly how the differences work.

☆ Some doctors think that "attention deficit disorder" is not
named correctly and should be called an "attention difference."

PROCEDURE

Pre Game Warmup

☆ As students enter the room, accept "High 5" forms and completed Home Practice sheets.

☆ Tally points using your selected method.

☆ Wearing your coach's hat and whistle, review group rules and point system.

☆ Briefly discuss completed Home Practices from previous week.

☆ Review "Connecting to the Real World" and Objectives.

☆ Then introduce the selected activity for the week.

Activities

(choose one or more of the following)

Activity 6.1   Books and Bags
Activity 6.2   It's In the Bag

Post Game Commentary

☆ Tally and record individual points gained during group.

☆ Encourage students to give one another "High 5's" by verbalizing ways in which they have seen each other be especially positive or helpful in group that day.

☆ Announce housekeeping details (any change in meeting date and time).

☆ Give students "High 5" reinforcement sheets to give to their teachers.

EXTENSIONS

High 5's for Teachers
Home Practice Backing for Parents

  134

Activity 6.1 Books & Bags

EQUIPMENT

"Coach Wants to Know About" activity sheets
Children's book about ADHD (can be selected from the bibliography)
"Perceptions, Realities & Myths" summary sheet and *"Note to Parents"*
"Agree, Disagree, Not Sure" cards
Optional: *"It's In The Bag"* activity and *"Going on a Trek"* direction sheet, bags for each student

GAME PLAN

1. Give students five minutes to begin *"Coach Wants to Know About"* sheet. Explain that they will complete it at home, but you want them to think about how they would describe themselves before you read a book to them.

2. Select a book that addresses ADHD at an appropriate level for your age group. See bibliography, but consider one of the following: *Sometimes I Drive My Mom Crazy, But I Know She's Crazy About Me, Learning to Slow Down & Pay Attention, Eagle Eyes, I Would if I Could, Shelley-The Hyperactive Turtle,* or *Otto Learns About His Medicine.*

3. Explain to students that different experts have described ADHD in different ways and that you are interested in knowing what the students believe. Together discuss the most appropriate statements from the *"Perceptions, Realities & Myths"*. As you read each theory or statement, have students use their voting cards (Agree, Disagree, Not Sure) to indicate what they think. Briefly discuss students' reasons. Stress that not even the experts agree on all the right answers.

DISCUSSION

☆ What was the main point of this book? (Review story content to ensure for understanding.)
☆ Can you think of ways you are like (or different from) the character in the book?
☆ What are some facts about ADHD mentioned in the book?
☆ What are some advantages and disadvantages of having ADHD?
☆ What are some things about ADHD that you wonder about?
☆ Was there anything mentioned in the book that upset or worried you?

HOME PRACTICE

Have students take home *"Coach Wants to Know About"* sheet and a copy of *"Perceptions, Realities, & Myths"* with *"Notes to Parents"* section. This will encourage parents to discuss facts about ADHD with their children. If you have chosen to do *"It's In The Bag"* activity as a Home Practice instead of an activity in group, have students take bags and directions. They are to bring their creations to the next meeting.

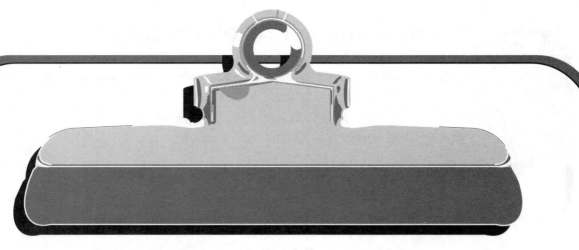

Coach Wants to Know About

Put a check next to each item below that describes _____

My opinion about me: My Parent's opinion about me:

____ I don't like waiting for my turn (in class, during games.)   ____

____ I lose my temper easily.   ____

____ Lots of times I call out answers without raising my hand.   ____

____ It's hard for me to stop once I get going!   ____

____ The longer I write, the sloppier my handwriting gets.   ____

____ I hear noises from kids in the classroom next door.   ____

____ I take a lot of time to "cool off" when I get upset.   ____

____ I like to draw & plan ideas & projects in my head.   ____

____ I usually jiggle my feet.   ____

____ I think of things in a creative, unique way!   ____

____ I still have energy left when others are tired.   ____

____ I like to work with my knees up in the seat or standing up.   ____

____ I tap my pencil & hardly realize it till someone tells me.   ____

____ My brain can shift from one idea to another very quickly.   ____

____ I often forget things.   ____

____ Sometimes it looks like I'm not listening, even when I am!   ____

____ Sometimes I don't finish work because my mind wanders.   ____

____ I get bored easily. I like to try new things.   ____

____ Sometimes my teacher says I rush through my work.   ____

____ I get out of my chair in class a lot.   ____

____ My desk is usually messy.   ____

____ My room at home is usually messy.   ____

____ Classmates sometimes tell me I bother them by talking.   ____

____ I argue with people a lot.   ____

____ I have a hard time getting started on my work.   ____

____ Sometimes I feel really different from most kids I know.   ____

Circle the item you would most like to change.

Perceptions, Realities & Myths about ADHD

PERCEPTIONS

Hunter-Farmer Theory (from Thom Hartmann)

☆ People with ADHD are like hunters who scan the scenery, notice small details, are alert, like to explore, and are quick to act.

☆ People without ADHD are like farmers who keep focused on one task at a time and patiently complete it.

Gene Pool Theory (from Dr. Edward Hallowell)

☆ People who discovered and settled America (like Columbus, the pilgrims, and later immigrants) were "hunter, adventurer" types. Since many of us in America today are descended from them, this may explain why more people in the United States have ADHD than in Europe.

Impulse Inhibition Theory (from Dr. Russell Barkley's explanation of language development theories)

☆ It's hard for people with ADHD to stop, think and talk silently to themselves before they act.

☆ People with ADHD find it hard to learn from past mistakes (because they have not taken the time to "verbalize" in their heads and neurologically store what they have learned.

☆ It's easier for people without ADHD to think and plan ahead.

☆ People with ADHD tend to experience feelings more strongly (because they haven't separated feelings from what is happening in the situation).

REALITIES (statements believed to be true)

Having ADHD is sort of like being nearsighted and having to squint to focus and see clearly. Having a doctor look at your eyes to see if glasses would help is kind of like having a doctor diagnose ADHD and prescribe something to help.

Many people with ADHD find it hard to begin a task or to finish a task.

Often people with ADHD like "piles" better than "files."

There are advantages and disadvantages to having ADHD.

People with ADHD can get bored faster doing ordinary things than people without ADHD.

People with ADHD can be "hyperfocused" on things they really enjoy!

Many people with ADHD may need more reminders because they forget a lot.

People with ADHD tend to be intelligent, creative, and sensitive.

Medication is to ADHD what glasses are to a nearsighted person.

ADHD is a condition - not a disease or pathology.

Some people who take medication like Ritalin for ADHD act differently but may not feel physically any different.

Not everyone who has ADHD needs medicine.

Having food allergies or eating too much sugar rarely, if ever, contributes to ADHD.

Regular exercise and spending time learning to relax can be helpful for all people, especially for those who have ADHD.

ADHD tends to run in families like hair color, height and weight, or other physical characteristics.

MYTHS (statements that are not true)

Most people with ADHD are just too lazy to pay attention, listen, stay on task, use self control, be organized, and remember things. *(These activities are really difficult for many people with ADHD because of a difference in their brain chemistry.)*

Medication can make a kid with ADHD behave. *(Medication can help a person's brain work correctly, but that person still makes choices about how to behave.)*

Taking pills for ADHD means that you are "sick." *(Many medications, like Ritalin, vitamins, minerals, insulin, or enzymes are given to healthy people to supply missing chemicals to the body.)*

Very few kids, about one in a hundred, have ADHD. *(Many doctors estimate that as many as seven boys out of one hundred have ADHD; the number of girls per hundred is at least three and possibly higher.)*

If you are not "hyper," you don't have ADHD *(Many people can have an "inattentive type" of ADHD and have no problem with being impulsive or hyper but have difficulty paying attention. In fact, doctors used to call this type of condition, "ADD" instead of ADHD. Now they use the term "ADHD, inattentive type" and "ADHD, hyperactive/impulsive type" or "ADHD, combined type" to describe the variations of this medical condition. Some people still say just "ADD" when they talk about attention deficit.)*

If you get the right doctor, ADHD can be cured! *(ADHD is not a disease to be "cured" but a medical condition that can be managed with help.)*

You always grow out of ADHD when you are a teenager. *(About 60% of people may outgrow ADHD or learn so well how to compensate for it that few people realize that they have it.)*

NOTE TO PARENTS

"Perceptions, Realities & Myths about ADHD"

The attached sheets include statements that were discussed in our group session this week. Your child had an opportunity to respond to many of these comments read orally by voting "Agree," "Disagree," or "Not Sure" depending on what they thought to be accurate. We are sending home a copy of "Perceptions, Realities & Myths about ADHD" so that you will be aware of what was discussed. Often, as time passes, children may get confused or forget which ideas represent truth and which do not. And, although every attempt was made to determine the accuracy of these assertions as based upon current research and review by qualified physicians, there are always more studies being completed and varying interpretations of data which could lead to further discussion. But most of all, a child learns and remembers critical information best from discussions with a loving and concerned parent who shares insights in line with their own personal family values. For these reasons, we encourage you to review the questions below.

☆ If your child is medicated, how have you addressed this issue with your child? What is your child's perception of how this medication works to help them function more effectively? If your child is not medicated, how have you addressed important adaptations that will be necessary for your child to experience success in meeting the demands of everyday life?

☆ In which of these two ways have you presented the condition of ADHD: the "disability" model or the "difference" model?

☆ Consider making a list with your child that includes the personality traits that tend to complicate each of your lives (like being a starter and not a finisher). Then make a list of personality traits that each of you have that enriches your lives (having a great imagination or being flexible, creative, sensitive or whatever).

- -

Detach and return the section below for your child to earn points and for giving feedback about this exercise.

Parent Comments: _____

_____

_____

_____

Parent's Signature:_____   Date: _____

AGREE!
You bet!

NOT SURE!!
???

DISAGREE!
No way!

Activity 6.2 - It's In the Bag
(Use for Home Practice or an in-group activity)

EQUIPMENT
(for intermediate ages)
6 each of rubber bands, index cards, paper clips, and popsicle sticks
1 dozen each of plastic straws and cotton balls
1 balloon and one "blob" of clay, about one inch in diameter, in a small baggie
Plan to have students provide their own scissors, markers & glue
"Going on a Trek" directions sheet
Equipment per student (for primary ages)
One small bag of gumdrops & one box of toothpicks

GAME PLAN

1. Explain to students that today they are going to get a chance to be really creative and use their imaginations. Read the directions from "Going on a Trek." Distribute bags that have several different types of supplies inside.

2. Let students talk their ideas out for the first few minutes. Then divide students up to allow for privacy during building time. Play soft music as students build quietly without talking. (Use folders as appropriate to ensure "privacy".) Allow as much time as possible for building (perhaps 15 minutes or so) while remembering to save time for sharing and debriefing.

3. Consider taking pictures of the students' creations to post in the room (especially if primary students want to eat their creations instead of taking them home)!

DISCUSSION

☆ Did your creation turn out like you had originally planned for it to?

☆ How did you work? Did you plan completely and then carry out your plan? Did you change your ideas as you built? Did you get angry or frustrated at running out of time?

☆ Is it easier for you to create something alone or when you work with others?

☆ Which is easier for you: thinking up an idea or actually making it a reality?

☆ Do you ever find it difficult to pay attention in class because you are using your imagination to think up creative ideas for projects?

☆ Can paying attention to a speaker (like your teacher) and using your imagination to dream up a plan or a project both happen at the same time?

☆ So, then, is imagination a bad thing to use at school? (Stress the importance of timing.) At school, when are the best times to use your imagination? To stay focused and attentive?

HOME PRACTICE

Have students take home their "It's In The Bag" creations (or instant snapshots of them) and discuss with their parents how they used their imaginations. Return with parent comments for points.

Name ─────────────────────

"Going on a Trek"

Pretend that you are going on a trek through strange and exciting territory and happen to see something unusual! This object could be a person, an animal, a plant, a piece of equipment, or a part of the scenery. Create what you have imagined by using only the items in your bag along with scissors, markers, and glue or tape. Give your creation a name or title and be able to describe what it does, what it's like, or how it's used. You may talk to others (like your parents) for ideas, but you should be the only person to actually touch your materials. Have fun using your imagination and creativity!!! Bring your completed creation to the group room on or before our next meeting!

Parents: Any comments on this activity?

_____

_____

_____

_____

_____

Parent's Signature

This week our Objectives included:

☆ Many kids & adults have a condition called ADHD that may make it harder for them to pay attention, to think before acting & to sit still. But, they also tend to be people who are very energetic, creative, sensitive & inventive.

☆ Scientists think ADD & ADHD are caused by differences in the chemicals in a person's brain, but they haven't figured out exactly how the differences work.

☆ Some doctors think that "Attention Deficit Disorder" is not named correctly & believe that it should be called an "Attention Difference".

☆ Kids & adults who have ADHD can learn more about how they tend to think, feel & act. They can be very successful in life.

"Coach," please be on the lookout for times when I have used these skills at school.

The Lifelong Trek - Beginning the Journey Understanding ADHD - Part 1

High 5's

This week I noticed _____ practicing the skills & ideas in the "Objectives." I've circled on the left the areas I've seen improvement in this week. Below are compliments that "celebrate" his or her good behavior.

_____   _____
Teacher's Signature   Date

- -

This week our Objectives included:

☆ Many kids & adults have a condition called ADHD that may make it harder for them to pay attention, to think before acting & to sit still. But, they also tend to be people who are very energetic, creative, sensitive & inventive.

☆ Scientists think ADD & ADHD are caused by differences in the chemicals in a person's brain, but they haven't figured out exactly how the differences work.

☆ Some doctors think that "Attention Deficit Disorder" is not named correctly & believe that it should be called an "Attention Difference".

☆ Kids & adults who have ADHD can learn more about how they tend to think, feel & act. They can be very successful in life.

"Coach," please be on the lookout for times when I have used these skills at school.

The Lifelong Trek - Beginning the Journey Understanding ADHD - Part 1

High 5's

This week I noticed _____ practicing the skills & ideas in the "Objectives." I've circled on the left the areas I've seen improvement in this week. Below are compliments that "celebrate" his or her good behavior.

_____   _____
Teacher's Signature   Date

HOME PRACTICE

This week's **"Objectives"** for _The Lifelong Trek - Beginning the Journey!_ are:

☆ Many kids & adults have a condition called ADHD that may make it harder for them to pay attention, to think before acting & to sit still. But, they also tend to be people who are very energetic, creative, sensitive & inventive.

☆ Scientists think ADD & ADHD are caused by differences in the chemicals in a person's brain, but they haven't figured out exactly how the differences work.

☆ Some doctors think that "Attention Deficit Disorder" is not named correctly & believe that it should be called an "Attention Difference."

☆ Kids & adults who have ADHD can learn more about how they tend to think, feel & act. They can be very successful in life.

The home practice on the other side is to help your child apply these skills in "real-life" situations. Please help record your child's ideas. **Your child will receive points in group for returning this completed & signed sheet.**

High 5's

I noticed my child applying ideas from **"Objectives"** learned this week **or in previous weeks.**

Compliments & Comments:

_____

_____

_____

_____

_____   _____
Parent's Signature   Date Due Back

From Your Number ONE FAN

☆ 144 ☆

SESSION 7
(GOAL SETTING)

AIMING HIGH

CONNECTING TO THE REAL WORLD

Athletes who grow and improve learn how to set high but attainable goals and to work persistently to achieve those goals. Often working toward a goal involves practicing the skills that may be the hardest and least interesting to do. For example, an archer who has great eye-hand coordination may not enjoy doing weight training to build up arm strength. A swimmer may hate running daily laps required to build stamina and muscles essential for setting swimming records. Successful athletes depend on their coaches to help them decide what reasonable goals to set. Coaches also help them to keep track of progress made. Although some goals can be accomplished quickly, others will require mastery of smaller steps over a long period of time in order to reach the desired level of performance. Experienced athletes know to expect temporary setbacks when they work toward their goals. But they refuse to be discouraged by these setbacks. Any goal worth achieving will require a lot of work. Thomas Edison's quote "Genius is one percent inspiration and ninety-nine percent perspiration" reminds us that in sports or in the classroom, it may well be that "Genius is one percent ability and ninety-nine percent sweat - or hard work!"

OBJECTIVES

Students will participate in activities designed to emphasize the following concepts and skills:

I can choose to improve things about myself.
I can change by setting and reaching my own goals.
SMART goals are the best. (Specific, Measurable, Accountable, Realistic and "Totally Mine."

PROCEDURE

Pregame Warmup

☆ As students enter the room, accept "High 5" forms and completed Home Practice sheets.
☆ Tally points using your selected method.
☆ Wearing your coach's hat and whistle, review group rules and point system.
☆ Briefly discuss completed Home Practices from previous week.
☆ Review "Connecting to the Real World" and Objectives.
☆ Introduce the selected activity for the week.

Activities

(choose one or more of the following)

Activity 7.1   Balancing and Believing
                (Dowels and Potatoes)
Activity 7.2   Clearing the Hurdles
Activity 7.3   A Tale of Two Boys

Post Game Commentary

☆ Tally and record individual points gained during group.
☆ Encourage students to give one another "High 5's" by verbalizing ways in which they have seen each other be especially positive or helpful in group that day.
☆ Announce housekeeping details (any change in meeting date and time).
☆ Give students "High 5" reinforcement sheets to give to their teachers.

EXTENSIONS

Coaching Tips
High 5's for Teachers
Home Practice Backing for Parents

 146

© 2001, McDougall & Roper

Activity 7.1- Balancing & Believing (Dowels and Potatoes)

EQUIPMENT

1 dowel (2-3 feet long) for each student
1 potato (raw) for each student
1 sturdy straw (NOT with flexible neck) for each student
"*I Believe In Me*" and "*Take Aim*" Home Practice sheet

GAME PLAN

1. Ask students to define what a goal is and briefly discuss types of goals (personal, group, short-term, long term). Suggest that reaching most goals requires effort. Explain that it is usually best for each individual to set his or her own goals, but you're going to make an exception and set one for them. The goal is that each group member will be able to balance a dowel in the (open) palm of their hand for at least 8-10 seconds.

2. Demonstrate by balancing a dowel in your hand. (You'll need to practice ahead of time. Even though the key is to keep your eyes on the very top of the dowel, don't share this with the students initially.)

3. Distribute the dowels and allow all group members to attempt the balancing act! Without giving away the "trick," call attention to anyone who has any degree of success. If others don't catch on, you may need to remark, "Where is Sean keeping his eyes?" Stop and discuss the first two questions below. Then, invite each member to try balancing again with encouragement from peers.

4. Explain that there are many things to consider when setting a reasonable goal for yourself, such as believing that you can actually achieve the goal. As a demonstration, ask how many of them believe that you can make a straw go all the way through a raw potato. Grasp the straw in your fist. Little of the straw should protrude from the top of your fist. Hold the potato in your other hand. Take a couple of "practice jabs" in the air, remind yourself silently that it IS possible, then push the straw through the potato in one smooth, firm movement.

5. Invite group members to try it one at a time! Most should be able to do it, but might require more than one try. It is amazing how encouragement helps! Complete the rest of the discussion questions.

DISCUSSION

☆ Acknowledge effort on everyone's part. Then ask why they think certain members of the group were able to balance the dowel longer than others. Stress how you had to keep your eyes at the top of the dowel. Invite students to brainstorm other reasons for success. (practice, perseverance, self confidence).

☆ How is balancing the dowel like working toward a goal? (takes sustained effort & focus, isn't always easy, takes people different amounts of time to get the hang of it).

☆ Name a goal you have set for yourself lately. Name a goal that others have set for you.

☆ What makes it difficult for you to believe that you can achieve a goal? Is believing in yourself important?

HOME PRACTICE

Have students take "*I Believe in Me*" or "*Take Aim*" Home Practice sheets to complete with their parents. Return for points.

I Believe In Me!

_____
Name

Complete these sentences:

I wish I could...

A. _____

B. _____

C. _____

Something I can't do is...

D. _____

E. _____

F. _____

Now look at these ideas differently

Select either A, B or C & complete these thoughts: I will...

_____

_____

_____

I will tell _____

that I am going to do it.

I think it will take _____

(how long) to be able to do it well.

I want to do it because _____

_____

Select either D, E or F & complete one of the statements below that is most true for you:

I don't want to _____.

I won't _____

_____.

I can, if I try.

Activity 7.2 - Clearing the Hurdles

EQUIPMENT
Soft ball
Watch with second hand or stopwatch
Outside playing area or large indoor space
Two 8-foot lengths of rope
Tape measure
"Personal Best" activity sheet and pencil for each student
"Quotable Quotes" Home Practice sheets

GAME PLAN

1. The group leader explains that participants will experience setting group and individual goals in the activities for today. If weather and space allow, take the group outside and have members stand in a circle.

2. Explain that the goal for the entire group is to pass a ball as quickly as possible to each member. Do the trial run and record the time.

3. Ask the group to discuss strategies for improving their performance time and make a plan. Anything that seems feasible and safe is acceptable. For example, the group doesn't really have to stand in a circle.

4. Do several trials and document times. Challenge the group to beat "the record" of two seconds!

5. Discuss questions in Part 1 before proceeding to the next part of the activity.

6. The group leader explains that in this next activity students will pretend that they are competing in the state long jump competition. Explain that their jumps will be successful if their feet clear (but don't touch) the two ropes which have been placed on the ground approximately one foot apart and parallel to each other.

7. Before the first round of trials, distribute the *"Personal Best"* activity sheets and pencils and ask each stu dent to complete these without discussing their responses. Students will estimate the longest distance they will be able to jump.

8. After the group leader collects all the pencils and forms, complete the first round of jumping trials. Emphasize individual effort and improvement from trial to trial, not competition between group members.

9. For each consecutive trial, the group leader moves the ropes one to two feet farther apart. Continue until each student can no longer clear the two ropes. Students should remember their best distance, but the group leader may wish to record distances as well.

10. Return group to inside setting, complete *"Personal Best"* activity sheet and complete discussion question in Part 2.

(NOTE: If you are unable to take the group outside, or if you have any concerns about the group handling this more strenuous activity, we recommend doing the alternative standing high jump. Using a measuring tape, mark with masking tape the heights on your door jam or wall. Starting at about five feet, mark at two to three inch intervals up to about seven feet. Students will stand and jump vertically, one at a time. The highest point their fingertips touch will be their standing height.)

DISCUSSION

Part 1

☆ Were members of the group satisfied with the first speed?

☆ How did the group work together to plan to reduce the time it took to pass the ball?

☆ Did the group do what it had planned to do?

☆ How many of the members believed the group could beat the "two second" record?

☆ Did it help or hinder to be competing against a record time?

☆ In what ways does this remind you of your personal or group goals in your everyday life?

Part 2

☆ Did people make or exceed their estimated goal?

☆ In real life, how long does it usually take to show significant improvement on an athletic, academic or behavioral goal? (Make the point that improvement or progress toward a goal are often just as important as actually reaching the final goal. People need to learn to use self talk to encourage themselves and affirm their efforts!)

☆ Was there a relationship between believing you could make the goal and actually doing it?

☆ How did individuals plan to improve their performance? (for example, by watching others, by taking a running start, by warming up, etc.)

☆ How did others in the group help or interfere with reaching your individual goal?

☆ Was your goal realistic?

☆ Did it feel risky trying to improve your performance in front of others? Did you feel like your performance was in competition with others even though that was not the focus of the activity?

☆ Do you have some "real life" goals that you are working to meet at this time? If so, what have you learned from these activities that might help you reach those goals more effectively?

HOME PRACTICE

Have students take "Quotable Quotes" Home Practice sheets to complete with their parents. Return for points.

_____'s PERSONAL BEST

Pretend that you are competing in the state long jump competition. Your jump will be successful if both feet clear, but don't touch, the two ropes.

I think my longest jump will be _____ feet.

My actual jump was _____ feet.

Things I can do to maintain my distance or improve it are:

_____

- -

_____'s PERSONAL BEST

Pretend that you are competing in the state long jump competition. Your jump will be successful if both feet clear, but don't touch, the two ropes.

I think my longest jump will be _____ feet.

My actual jump was _____ feet.

Things I can do to maintain my distance or improve it are:

_____

Name _____ # "Quotable Quotes"

Dear Parents,
Please read these quotes aloud with your child and select one or two of them that you both like. Comment on how the statement applies to some goal that you or your child are working on. Consider having your child make a poster of their favorite quote to hang in their room.

"It's not if you win or lose, but how you play the game."
☆☆☆

"Progress always involves risk; you can't steal second base and keep your feet on first." by Frederick Wilcox
☆☆☆

"All students can learn and succeed, but not on the same day in the same way." by William G. Spady
☆☆☆

"When the going gets tough, the tough get going."
☆☆☆

"Keep away from people who try to belittle your ambitions. Small people always do that, but the really great make you feel that you too, can become great." by Mark Twain
☆☆☆

"The greater the obstacle, the more glory in overcoming it." by Moli'ere
☆☆☆

"One of the secrets of success is to refuse to let temporary setbacks defeat us." by Mary Kay
☆☆☆

"The person who makes a success of living is the one who sets his goal steadily and aims for it unswervingly." by Cecil B. DeMille
☆☆☆

"Effort only fully releases its reward after a person refuses to quit." by Napoleon Hill
☆☆☆

"When there is a hill to climb, don't think that waiting will make it smaller." by H. Jackson Brown, Jr.

Comments   _____
_____   Parent's Signature
_____
_____

Activity 7.3 - A Tale of Two Boys

EQUIPMENT
"Be SMART" Chart
"SMART Enough to Set Winning Goals" Home Practice sheet
"Take Aim" Home Practice sheet
"A Tale of Two Boys" story sheet

GAME PLAN

1. Introduce the story by noting that the two baseball players in it set goals for themselves. Read the story and discuss.

2. Ask students if they would like to learn a special way (acronym) to remember the guidelines which will help them to set effective goals. Pass out the "Be SMART" Chart and discuss in light of the boys' story. Consider having students underline sections in the story that illustrate parts of the SMART system.

3. Distribute the "SMART Enough to Set Winning Goals" Home Practice sheet. As a group, analyze the effectiveness of the first goal. Then have students work in pairs to complete the second exercise. The rest of the sheet should be completed at home.

4. The group leader should write a goal and have the group analyze that goal for effectiveness by applying the "SMART" principles. The group leader then directs students to complete their own goals on the Home Practice sheets and discuss with parents.

DISCUSSION

☆ Did both boys seem equally motivated to improve?

☆ Why did Schmo have such a difficult time reaching his goal? Did lacking confidence affect his progress?

☆ What were Schmo's priorities? . . . Joe's? . . . the coach's? Did each sacrifice to reach his goals?

☆ How could Schmo have planned more effectively? Remember the old saying: "If you fail to plan, you plan to fail."

☆ Explain how the saying, "Prior planning prevents poor performance" was true in Joe's case. Note that Joe explained his ideas to another person and put them in writing.

☆ Who earned the respect of the coach and team? Is earning respect important to you?

☆ When the "going got tough," what happened to each player?

☆ In what ways are you like Joe? . . . like Schmo?

☆ Name a goal you would like to work on. What is one thing that is so important that you would sacrifice and plan for it? If students are having a difficult time selecting a goal, ask leading questions like: "Is there something in your life that adults always fuss at you about that you wish you could change just so the fussing would stop? Is there some habit you could change?"

HOME PRACTICE

Have students take "SMART Enough to Set Winning Goals" and/or "Take Aim" Home Practice sheets to complete with their parents. Return for points.

SPECIFIC

MEASURABLE

ACCOUNTABLE

REALISTIC

TOTALLY MINE

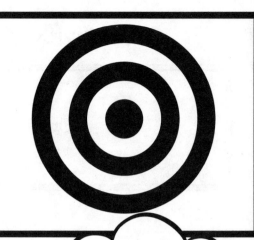

S = You must have a specific goal & a specific plan. **Ask yourself:**

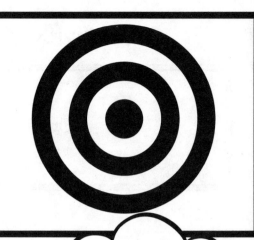
"Do I know exactly what I'm aiming for?" (who, what, when, how often, how long)

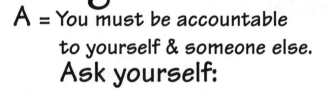
"How can I prove how much or how long I have worked?"

M = You must be able to measure effort. **Ask yourself:**

A = You must be accountable to yourself & someone else. **Ask yourself:**

"Who besides me will I tell about my plan, my progress or the results of my efforts?"

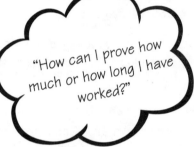
"Is this goal too easy or too hard?"

R = You must be realistic about how much you can do. **Ask yourself:**

T = You must be totally in charge of the things you need control of. **Ask yourself:**

"Is this goal within my control, or does it mainly depend on someone else?"

_____ is S.M.A.R.T. Enough To Set Winning Goals!

Directions: Circle each item on the right (SMART) that describes each goal below.

"I'm gonna bring up all my low
grades next six weeks
& make all A's !"

S pecific
M easurable
A ccountable
R ealistic
T otally Mine

"For the next week, I'm going to ignore my
little sister when she starts
bugging me. I'm going to ask her to
stop & then get up & leave if she doesn't. If I can go
4 days without fighting, I'll be able to have Tom
spend the night on Saturday!"

S pecific
M easurable
A ccountable
R ealistic
T otally Mine

"My goal is to make Charlie be my friend.
I got permission to sit by him
at lunch & asked my mom if he could spend
the night. I'm even bringing
my basketball so he will play with me
at recess."

S pecific
M easurable
A ccountable
R ealistic
T otally Mine

With your parent, select something you want to improve on
& write a personal goal here:

_____

_____

Be sure it's SMART!

S pecific
M easurable
A ccountable
R ealistic
T otally Mine

Name

TAKE AIM!!

Dear Parent(s),

With your child select ONE goal that he or she would like to "aim for" during the next few weeks & complete the information below. Please help your child use the "SMART" criteria to write the goal: **S**pecific, **M**easurable, **A**ccountable, **R**ealistic & **T**otally **T**heirs. This does NOT need to be a short term goal. Many of the biggest challenges your child faces take months of repetition on his part & encouragement & patience on yours! To evaluate **EFFORT** (not perfection), please position your initials on the target below to indicate how close or far away your child is in reference to the goal!

My GOAL is: _____

My <u>EXACT PLAN</u> is:

1. _____ 3. _____

2. _____ 4. _____

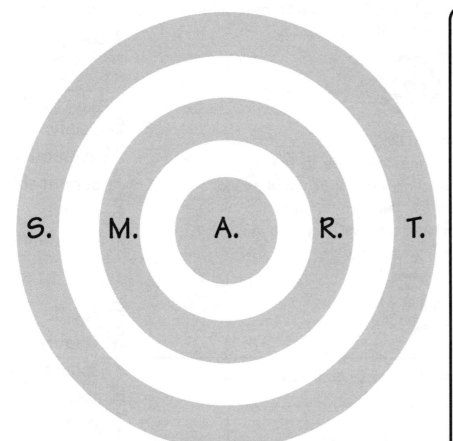

S.   M.   A.   R.   T.

Ways I know I've succeeded:

_____
_____
_____
_____
_____
_____
_____
_____
_____
_____
_____
_____
_____
_____
_____

"A TALE OF TWO BOYS"

Once upon a time, two nine-year old boys joined the same baseball team. Joe and Schmo were both very excited about playing for Coach Brown because his teams always seemed to win. Schmo thought he must be a great player, too, just because he was picked for the team. Joe thought, "Boy, I'm gonna have to do a lot of practicing to keep up with these guys!"

The first day of practice, fifteen players had to run all the way around the practice field three times! Schmo complained because they had to run so much and was secretly wondering why everybody thought Coach was so great . Then they got to practice their batting, catching, pitching and sliding skills. Coach watched every player very carefully and took notes on his clipboard. Before you knew it, practice was over and they hadn't played a single inning!

At the end of practice, Coach blew his whistle and told all the players to join him at the dugout. "Boys, you worked really hard at practice today. How many of you hope we will have a winning season this year?" "I do! I do! I do!" All the boys yelled! They were still excited even after working so hard at practice and being hungry, thirsty and exhausted!

"Boy," said the coach, "am I glad you're excited even though you're tired. By watching you closely, I've figured out which skills you each need to begin practicing if you really want a winning season. Here's your assignments for the skills you'll each need extra work on. I'll be glad to stay after practice any day and help you train. Now, get a good night's sleep. I'll see you at our next practice day after tomorrow."

Joe and Schmo had car pooled to the practice. On the way home, Joe's mom asked how practice had been. "Man, it was AWFUL!" said Schmo. I don't think Coach Brown knows what he's doing. Almost all he had us doing was running and we only had a few turns throwing, catching and batting. I could have done better but I was exhausted from all that running! Then he had the nerve to give me a note saying I need to improve my fielding the most! Duh, he doesn't' know anything; I'm great at catching my dad's pop flies!"

"Joe" his mom asked, "What did you think of practice?"

"Well," he began, "We did run a lot, but I figured the coach was trying to build up our stamina so we could make it through a whole, real game. Coach said I need to work on my throwing. He said dad might have some ideas on how I could do that, and Coach said he'd stay after practice to help. Isn't that great of him?"

"Yes, Joe, it is. Especially since Coach has already put in an eight-hour day at his job before he comes to practice. Sounds like you guys are one of his top priorities. Well, Schmo, here's your stop. Have a good evening and we'll see you on Wednesday."

That evening, Joe spent time with his dad working on a schedule to improve his throwing. He had to take nightly homework, team practice and time to play into account. "Boy," Joe sighed, "I'm going to have a tough time fitting extra practice in with all the things I already have to do! I'm glad you wouldn't let me sign up for karate, too, like I wanted to do. I really wouldn't have had time for it!"

"That's right, son," said his father. You might want to make a chart so you can write down and keep track of what you have done. You can't always do everything you plan to do, but you can keep track of exactly what you have accomplished."

"I'll make sure I do everything I plan because baseball is so important to me! I'll make time!", Joe responded.

By the next morning, Joe had come up with a plan to practice his pitching every day. At breakfast, he showed his plan to his dad who commented, "It looks like you put a lot of thought into this schedule, son. Tell me how you decided on this plan."

"Well, dad, I made a list of my ideas:

practice an hour a day; but then I thought about all I have to do and figured out it just wouldn't work.

practice for a long time once a week; but I realized that if something happened, like it was raining outside that day, I would have wasted a whole week!

keep track on this chart of how many minutes I work out each day.

get one of those practice nets for the backyard that will catch my balls when you're not here to catch 'em for me."

"Those are great ideas, son. I'm really proud of you for thinking of so many ideas and for making a plan to help you practice consistently instead of waiting until the last minute."

When Joe saw Schmo on the school bus later that morning, he asked his friend if he had worked out a practice plan. "Plan? What are you talking about? I don't need no stinkin' plan! My goal is to be the best ball player in the league and I don't need a plan for that! I'm gonna practice till my arm is ready to drop off and get so good that I'll blow all you guys out of the water! Kablooey! Ha!"

Stop here in the story and ask students to predict how the story ends.

Well, to make a long story short, after about three weeks, Joe was showing great improvement in his throwing. Coach Brown was impressed when Joe showed him his daily practice schedule. Because Joe kept track of each date and for how long he had practiced, the Coach could see how much time he had put in. "Joe, do you realize that over the last three weeks you have practiced your throwing for over six hours! And it really shows! Keep up the good work! Next week, you'll be on the starting lineup."

But Schmo was still having big problems with his catching in the field. One day after practice, Coach asked , "Schmo, have you been practicing your fielding?"

"I sure have Coach. I just don't know what's wrong. I think maybe I need one of those new gloves like Larry has. Then I could catch anything. But my mom and dad won't get me one."

"Well, Schmo, I'm sure a new glove would be nice. But, I'm more concerned with whether or not you've put in any extra time."

"Oh gosh, hours and hours! Really! I started out doing almost an hour a day for the first day or so, but then I got busy with this special science project and I went several days without working out at all because of schoolwork and because dad wasn't at home to bat balls for me to catch when I wanted to practice. I figured out I could make up the time over the weekend. I had a special karate tournament that I had to spend extra time at. Dad and I planned to catch up on that weekend, but I got invited to go to Six Flags with my cousin Sam. Then, it rained all day on Sunday. Last week, I had to spend time on my special book report, and then I got sick. Gee, Coach, I want to be the best player on the team; but I just can't seem to find the time to practice! What am I gonna do?" The coach remarked gently, "Schmo, I'm reminded of an old saying: 'If you fail to plan, you plan to fail'."

If you were the coach, how would you answer Schmo?

Joe   Schmo

COACHING TIP:

Consider having group members illustrate different parts of the story. Attach drawings to small pieces of poster board and paste dialogue on the other side to create a flip chart of the story to use with other groups. These characters may be duplicated and added to student drawings.

TIP!!

This week our Objectives included:

☆ You can choose to improve things about yourself; & as you get older, people expect you to be more aware of & be in control of areas in your life that need improvement.
☆ By setting & reaching goals, you can prove yourself capable of making lifestyle changes.
☆ Goals should be specific, measurable, accountable, realistic & "totally within" your control.

"Coach," please be on the lookout for times when I have used these skills at school.

Aiming High!
Goal Setting

High 5's

This week I noticed _____ practicing the skills & ideas in the "Objectives." I've circled on the left the areas I've seen improvement in this week. Below are compliments that "celebrate" his or her good behavior.

_____   _____
Teacher's Signature   Date

- -

This week our Objectives included:

☆ You can choose to improve things about yourself; & as you get older, people expect you to be more aware of & be in control of areas in your life that need improvement.
☆ By setting & reaching goals, you can prove yourself capable of making lifestyle changes.
☆ Goals should be specific, measurable, accountable, realistic & "totally within" your control.

"Coach," please be on the lookout for times when I have used these skills at school.

Aiming High!
Goal Setting

High 5's

This week I noticed _____ practicing the skills & ideas in the "Objectives." I've circled on the left the areas I've seen improvement in this week. Below are compliments that "celebrate" his or her good behavior.

_____   _____
Teacher's Signature   Date

HOME PRACTICE

This week's **"Objectives"** for _Aiming High!_ are:

☆ You can choose to improve things about yourself; & as you get older, people expect you to be more aware of & be in control of areas in your life that need improvement.

☆ By setting & reaching goals, you can prove yourself capable of making lifestyle changes.

☆ Goals should be specific, measurable, accountable, realistic & "totally within" your control.

The home practice on the other side is to help your child apply these skills in "real-life" situations. Please help record your child's ideas. **Your child will receive points in group for returning this completed & signed sheet.**

High 5's

I noticed my child applying ideas from **"Objectives"** learned this week **or in previous weeks**.

Compliments & Comments:

_____

_____

_____

_____

_____   _____
Parent's Signature   Date Due Back

From Your Number ONE FAN

SESSION 8
(Feelings)

GET A GRIP!

CONNECTING TO THE REAL WORLD

The counselor asks students to give examples of pro sports players expressing feelings in helpful and hurtful ways. If time allows, students could share experiencing an intense feeling they had on an actual team they have played with. Ask students:

☆ Is it wrong to feel angry or disappointed when playing on a team?
☆ What happens to the player who uses control over feelings? ...who loses control?
☆ How does it affect the individual player, team, coach or the season performance when a player loses control?
☆ How can you keep an "I can" attitude when you've just made a bad play or your team is losing?
☆ What can you tell yourself to stay "up" and focused?

OBJECTIVES

Students will participate in activities designed to emphasize the following concepts and skills:

All of my feelings are okay.
I can let my feelings show in helpful or hurtful ways.
It causes trouble when I let my feelings out in hurtful ways.
I can choose to share my feelings or keep them to myself.
It's important for me to stay cool when I get upset or angry.

PROCEDURE

Pregame Warmup

☆ As students enter the room, accept "High 5" forms and completed Home Practice sheets.
☆ Tally points using your selected method.
☆ Wearing your coach's hat and whistle, review group rules and point system.
☆ Briefly discuss completed Home Practices from previous week.
☆ Review "Connecting to the Real World" and Objectives.
☆ Introduce the selected activity for the week.

Activities

(choose one or more of the following)

Activity 8.1   Feeling Faces
Activity 8.2   Acting Out Feelings
Activity 8.3   Firecrackers!
Activity 8.4   Bricks in Bags
Activity 8.5   The Fence
Activity 8.6   Stay Cool!

Post Game Commentary

☆ Tally and record individual points gained during group.
☆ Announce housekeeping details (i.e., any change in meeting date and time).
☆ Encourage students to give one another "High 5's" by verbalizing ways in which they have seen each other be especially positive or helpful in group that day.
☆ Give students "High 5" reinforcement sheets to give to their teachers.

EXTENSIONS

High 5's for Teachers
Home Practice Backing for Parents

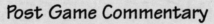

Activity 8.1 - Feeling Faces

EQUIPMENT
Drawing paper
Feelings card game (consider making one of your own or
select a commercially prepared game from among those listed in the bibliography)
"Feeling Faces" Home Practice sheet

GAME PLAN

1. After a general discussion of feeling objectives, have students do a drawing activity. Fold a sheet of blank drawing paper in half ("hamburger style") and draw the outline of a head with ears and neck on the outside and inside of the folded paper. Have students draw themselves as others see them and the feelings others probably perceive. On the <u>inside</u> face, have them draw themselves as they really feel. Invite students to share comments about their drawings.

2. Consider having older students draw a tree with branches and roots thick enough to write words on. Ask that the tree fill the whole page. In the branches, have them note important things in their everyday lives that other people are probably aware of. Then have them imagine that the roots below the ground are hidden and more like the parts of themselves (experiences, feelings, thoughts) that are important but may be unknown to others. Have students comment on their drawings.

3. You may choose to have members create a self-portrait that is then circulated among group members so that each person can add a detail that will make the portrait look more lifelike. Another alternative is to have students draw themselves as they would like to look and feel and then as they really are. Discuss the differences in the pictures.

4. Use a card game to encourage students to identify and express a variety of feelings.

DISCUSSION
☆ Which feelings are comfortable? Which are uncomfortable?
☆ Can you always tell what a person is feeling?
☆ Hold up a specific feeling card and ask if they have ever seen anyone who felt that way.
☆ Holding up the same card, ask if anyone in the group has ever felt that way and why.

HOME PRACTICE
Have students take "Feeling Faces" Home Practice sheets to complete with parents. Return for points.

Feeling Faces

Think of as many feelings as you can & draw what a person's face would look like when they have that feeling. Label the feeling beneath each face. In the center, draw yourself! Show your mom or dad when you're finished.

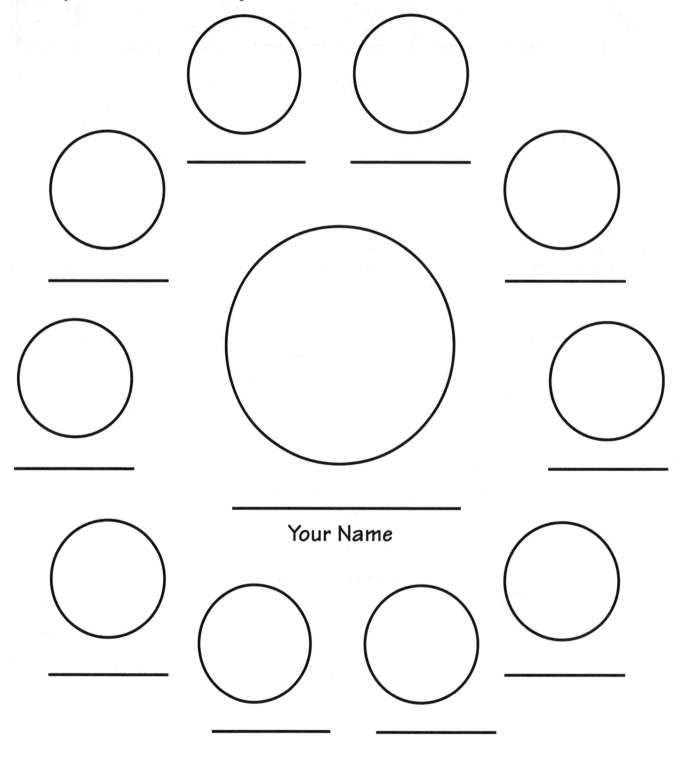

Your Name

Activity 8.2 - Acting Out Feelings

EQUIPMENT

Feeling words on paper strips
Paper bag or container
"If I Were Coach" Home Practice sheet.

GAME PLAN

1. Using a grab bag of feeling words written on slips of paper, have children take turns acting out or describing a situation in which they have experienced that particular feeling.

2. Other members guess the feeling name and can share an experience of their own.

3. Jerry Moe in his book, *Discovery: Finding the Buried Treasure* (see bibliography), suggests that as a student stands up to role-play a feeling, he or she should face away from the group; then, have the group chant the chorus, "Turn, turn, turn in place, with a feeling on your face."

4. As the group finishes chanting, the child slowly turns around to show the feeling he or she previously whispered to you. Then the group members try to guess the feeling.

5. Once correctly identified, ask the child to share a time he or she experienced that particular feeling. If the group is having a tough time, assist the child in giving some verbal clues.

6. If time allows, have students divide into two groups and do a relay race to write on the board the names of the feelings they brain stormed on their Home Practice sheet.

DISCUSSION

☆ How did it feel when others were able to guess which emotion you were acting out?
☆ Who are some people that you sharing your emotions with?
☆ Which feelings were the easiest for the group members to guess? . . . the most challenging?

HOME PRACTICE

Have students take home "If I Were Coach" Home Practice sheets and complete with parents. Return for points.

If I Were Coach...

Pretend that you are the coach of a famous player who is an incredibly bad sport!
Come up with a positive way to turn this bad sport into a winner each time he "loses it!"

THIS BAD SPORT....

Throws things

Pitches a fit

Yells at other players

Argues with officials & other adults

Refuses to practice

Refuses to follow directions

Tries to bargain his way out of things

Calls people names

Breaks things

Hits, kicks & pushes others

Knocks things over

Says ugly things about himself

WHAT IS YOUR FAVORITE "GOOD SPORT" BEHAVIOR?

On another sheet of paper, draw a player doing it!

WHAT HE OR SHE COULD DO INSTEAD:

☆ 168 ☆

Activity 8.3 - Firecrackers!

EQUIPMENT

Cardboard tube for each child or one large paper wrapping tube
Strips of red, orange and yellow colored construction paper
Tissue paper, glue and string
"I Blow My Stack"
Home Practice Sheet

GAME PLAN

1. Ask each child to write on colored slips of paper things that make them angry. Have them stuff the slips into their tubes and decorate as "firecrackers" or decoratye one large firecracker for the group, covering ends of the tube with tissue paper. (NOTE: We received this idea from one of our field testers, counselor Melanie Vaughn.)

2. Discuss that firecrackers are fun if popped safely, but can be dangerous if handled inappropriately. The group leader then discusses consequences of expressing anger appropriately and inappropriately. Brainstorm ways to handle anger without "blowing up" and causing damage to oneself or others. For each suggestion, measure one inch of string ("fuse"). Students enjoy seeing the fuse get longer. Make the connection between a long fuse and being slow to anger.

3. If time allows, use a game or video listed in the bibliography in this or a subsequent session to reinforce appropriate anger releases.

DISCUSSION

☆ Identify situations in which it is most difficult for students to control their anger.
☆ Have students identify their own "most frequently used" methods for handling anger.
☆ Are the acceptable ways of expressing anger the same for your classroom as at home? If not, explain how they are different.
☆ What would your life be like if you had a "long fuse?"

HOME PRACTICE

Have students take "I Blow My Stack" Home Practice sheets and complete with parents.

COACHING TIP:

Sometimes children referred for having problems with anger have already had adults talk to them about the importance of "controlling their temper." However, if asked directly how they are allowed at home and school to let their anger out, most look "clueless." It is helpful to work with parents and child together to generate a list of acceptable anger releases. Then talk with the child and teacher together to discuss acceptable ways to release "angry energy" at school. Ripping up old newspapers or kicking a ball may not work on school grounds. Taking a break in the room, drawing a picture, taking deep breaths, walking away, substituting a silly word like "broccoli" for curse words or asking to speak with another adult like the counselor, are all possibilities. When given specific strategies, a child can also learn to "measure" success by counting how often these appropriate options were chosen over more troublesome ones.

TIP!!

I Blow My Stack!!

Dyn★mite!

Name _____

WHEN DO YOU WANT TO BLOW YOUR STACK?

Activity 8.4 - Bricks in Bags
(A good introductory or closing activity)

EQUIPMENT

Four to six bricks in a bag or knapsack
Optional: substitute a heavy bowling ball with uncomfortable
Feeling labels taped on and have it in a bowling bag for students to carry around
"Expressing Anger" Home Practice

GAME PLAN

1. Explain that sometimes people tend to carry a lot of things around with them that they really don't need to. Sometimes people learn that it is easier to set their bag full of heavy things down and rest for awhile rather than having to carry it on their backs all day.

2. Explain that sometimes people keep feelings inside of them too, without ever letting anyone know what they are feeling. When this happens, feelings are like real items in a bag; they get to be really heavy if you keep them "inside" and never let them out. One way people can let their feelings out is to talk with someone they trust about their feelings.

3. Allow students to role play by talking about their feelings with you as they carry their sports bag full of heavy "feelings." Bricks can be covered with colored paper and labeled with feelings such as mad, sad, upset, scared, worried, etc. This idea was taken from Jerry Moe, who talked at an inservice about the funny looks he got from airport inspectors when he would get on a plane carrying his backpack full of rocks painted and labeled with feelings.

DISCUSSION

(Following the activity, use one or all of these questions to process.)

☆ Ask students if they could share a time in their lives when they had a really big problem that they were afraid to talk to anyone about.
☆ How long did they keep their feelings in before they "broke down" and talked about it?
☆ Who are the people that are the easiest for you to confide in?
☆ How do these people react when you speak to them about your private worries?
☆ Have students make a list of the advantages and disadvantages of carrying feelings around inside.
☆ What happens if a person you trust with your private feelings makes fun of you or puts you down? Would it be easy to trust this person again?
☆ How could you react when people share private thoughts and feelings with you that would make them want to talk with you again?

HOME PRACTICE

Have students take "Expressing Anger" Home Practice Sheet to complete with parents. Return for points.

Name _____

THERE ARE LOTS
OF WAYS TO RELEASE
YOUR ANGER.
SOME WAYS ARE
NOT HELPFUL.
In the thought bubble,
LIST SOME ACCEPTABLE
WORDS YOU CAN USE OR
THINGS YOU CAN DO TO
SHOW THAT YOU ARE
ANGRY.

REMEMBER:
Expressing your anger
SHOULDN'T
hurt you,
hurt others,
or damage anyone's stuff.

Look **COOL**:
_____
_____
_____

Think **COOL**:
_____
_____
_____

Act **COOL**:
_____
_____
_____

EXPRESSING ANGER

172

Activity 8.5 - The Fence

EQUIPMENT

One 2x4 board, about 2 feet long, preferably of soft pine
Hammer and several large-headed nails
Optional book: *Andrew's Angry Words*

GAME PLAN

1. Read or summarize Part One of "The Fence" story on the following page..

2. Ask each child in the group to remember a time that they were really angry.

3. One by one, have each child remember that situation in their minds as they drive a nail into the board. (Hold one end of the board and have it on a sturdy surface. make sure other children are out of the way.)

4. Read Part Two of the story on following page.

5. Invite each child to come back and pull out any one nail from the board.

6. Read part Three of the story on following page.

7. After discussing the story, consider reading *Andrew's Angry Words* by Dorothea Lachner and comparing the effects of angry words and nice words on others.

DISCUSSION

(Following the activity, use one or all of these questions to process.)

☆ How did it feel when you were hammering the nail as you tried to feel angry?
☆ How did it feel when you tried to remove a nail?
☆ What kind of "scars" can people leave in real life when they get angry?
☆ When you've lost control and hurt someone by what you have said or done, what can you do to make it better? Will it ever be the same?

HOME PRACTICE

Have students take "Feeling Hot But Staying Cool" and/or "Great Ways to Keep My Cool" Home Practice Sheets home to complete with parents. Return for points.

THE FENCE

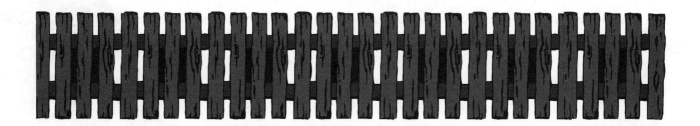

Part One: There was a little boy with a bad temper. His father gave him a bag of nails and told him that every time he lost his temper, to hammer a nail in the back fence. The first day the boy had driven 37 nails into the fence. Then it gradually dwindled down. He discovered it was easier to hold his temper than to drive those nails into the fence. Finally the day came when the boy didn't lose his temper at all.

Part Two: The boy proudly told his father that he had held his temper for over a week! His father suggested that the boy now pull out one nail for each day that he was able to hold his temper. The days passed by and the young boy was finally able to tell his father that all the nails were gone.

Part Three: The father took his son by the hand and led him to the fence. he said, "You have done well, my son; but look at the holes in the fence. The fence will never be the same. When you say things in anger, they leave a scar just like this one. When you lose your temper and hurt others, it doesn't matter how many times you say I'm sorry, the wound is still there. A verbal wound can hurt as bad as a physical one.

⭐ 174 ⭐

FEELING HOT BUT STAYING COOL!

Dear Parent(s),

Please talk with your child about what they get angry about at home and school. Put a check by all the items that he or she mentions and add any others that are discussed.

_____	Being hurt by someone.
_____	Someone tattles to get you into trouble.
_____	You are interrupted.
_____	Someone takes or uses your things without permission.
_____	Someone cuts in line.
_____	You want something and are told "no."
_____	Being shoved or pushed.
_____	When someone does not agree with you.
_____	Being left out.
_____	Losing a game or contest.
_____	_____
_____	_____

Please stress that being angry is NOT a bad thing. It's how you express your madness that counts. Help your child write down ways to stay cool.

Look COOL

What do you do with your body?

_____

Think COOL

What thoughts help calm you down?

_____

Act COOL

What are some ways you can let anger out that won;t hurt you, others,or damage stuff?

_____

GREAT WAYS TO KEEP MY COOL!

Dear Parent(s) of _____,

Please take a few minutes and discuss the following questions with your child:

Some things my child gets really frustrated or angry about are:

At home: _____

At school: _____

There are many ways to express anger and frustration that don;t involve yelling, hurting others, destroying property, or hurting yourself. Put a check by any of the following things your chiold has done on a regualr basis. Put a star by things you are willing to "coach" and encourage him or her to try.

_____ Hit a pillow or punching bag.

_____ Used WORDS to let you know how he or she feels.

_____ Took a "cool off" time to calm down and think.

_____ Did some problem solving.

_____ Counted silently and "used self talk" ("be cool," "no big deal" or "I can handle this.").

_____ Relaxed his or her body.

_____ Took a quick mental vacation to his or her "happy place."

_____ Other: _____

In group this week, we discussed three things we all can do to "get a grip" on strong feelings. Ask your child to demonstrate these three actions!.

Looking COOL   (calming your body down)

Thinking COOL   (thinking aloud)

Acting COOL   (making a wise choice)

⭐ 176 ⭐

Activity 8.6 - Stay COOL!

EQUIPMENT

Paper bag and pencils and slips of paper to write on
Sunglasses
Optional: *Be Cool* videotape series (see bibliography)

GAME PLAN

1. Explain that people show anger in three main ways: being COLD, HOT, or COOL. (This idea is described well in James Stanfield's Be Cool video series that provides an excellent variety of videotapes and handouts for children in lower, middle or upper elementary on dealing with your own anger, reacting to others who are angry, or behaving inappropriately).

2. Demonstrate what **being cold** looks like: giving up (pouting, crying, looking down, timid body language). Then demonstrate what **being hot** looks like: blowing up (arguing, talking loudly, threatening. tense body language). Finally demonstrate **being cool** as the best way to respond when angry, (looks like taking time to stop and relax, having a calm body language, talking to oneself about choices, and communicating wants and needs..)

3. Have children dictate "what makes me mad" responses as the group leader records on the paper slips. Put folded slips of paper into a bag or container.

4. Have each student select a slip from the bag. The group leader role plays either a hot or cold response. Have the group identify the type of response. Then "coach" each child through a more appropriate "cool" response. Continue until every child has role-played being cool. For extra fun, have the child wear sunglasses or a cool hat as they are being cool..

DISCUSSION

(Following the activity, use one or all of these questions to process.)

☆ What is your usual way of reacting at home? at school? with friends?
☆ Compare consequences of acting cool, cold and hot
☆ What are some ways that you can remind yourself to stay cool?

HOME PRACTICE

Have students take "Stay Cool" Home Practice Sheet to complete with parents. You may also send "Anger Awareness" or "Ways to Deal With Anger." Return for points.

Stay COOL!

Parents: Please take time this week on an occasion when your child is frustrated or angry to act as a "coach" by talking through and encouraging your child to demonstrate each step below. It will be helpful if you actually do the steps with your child (or even do some thinking out loud for your child's benefit in a situation when you are irritated).

Look COOL

- ☆ Relax your body.
- ☆ Take 3-4 slow, deep breaths.
- ☆ Put on "imaginary sunglasses."

Think COOL

- ☆ Ask yourself: "What might happen if i act COLD or HOT?.
- ☆ Say to yourself: "Be cool! Stay calm!"
- ☆ Decide what you are getting mad or frustrated about.

Act COOL (Help your child say these things aloud in an appropriate way with no pouting, yelling, whining or "attitude")

- ☆ "I don't like it when_____."

- ☆ "I feel _____ because _____."

- ☆ "What I would like is _____."

- ☆ "What can we do if I can't get what I want? (Parents, don;t feel obligated to make a deal that you can't live with. With a younger child, give 2 or 3 options; with an older child, think of options together.)

We practiced this when my child was upset about: _____

My child deserves a compliment for: _____

_____
Parent Signature   Date

ANGER AWARENESS

Write a "Y" for yes in front of each statement that is true of you and a "N" in front of each statement that is not:

_____ 1. I feel mad almost all the time - at myself and/or at other people.

_____ 2. When I get angry I pout, cry or give up.

_____ 3. I say angry or ugly things to others including teachers, friends or parents.

_____ 4. I hit other people when I get mad.

_____ 5. When I get mad, I yell or throw things.

_____ 6. If others don;t agree with me, I get mad at them.

_____ 7. I'm afraid I might lose control when I get mad.

_____ 8. I think that sometimes grownups and other kids let me have my way so I won't get mad.

_____ 9. At home, I sometimes have temper tantrums.

_____ 10. I blame others when I get angry.

_____ 11. When I get angry with somebody, I tell them I'm going to get them back.

_____ 12. It's very hard for me to apologize when I'm angry.

With your group, brainstorm ideas and fill in the blanks below:

Things you get angry about:

_____

_____

_____

_____

What happens when you get angry:

_____

_____

_____

_____

10-12 Time to Chill!!!

7-9   You're "on edge" a bit too often!

4-6   You know how to pick your battles!

1-3   You know how to keep your cool!!

WAYS TO DEAL WITH ANGER

Remember:

☆ Everyone gets angry.

☆ Anger is a normal human feeling.

☆ The ways we EXPRESS anger may be healthy of unhealthy/hurtful.

Some Healthy Ways to Get Rid of Anger:

(Choose the ones that agree with rules at your house or are appropriate in different situations)

☆ Blow into a paper bag - then pop it.

☆ Pound on a mattress.

☆ Play angry notes on a piano.

☆ Rip up old newspapers or magazines.

☆ Pull weeds.

☆ Take a towel & beat on the bathtub.

☆ Give yourself a 10-20 minute time out.

☆ B R E A T H E slowly & deeply.

☆ Talk it out with someone.

☆ Talk to yourself about your feelings; ask yourself why you are mad.

☆ Replace angry thoughts with pleasant ones.

☆ EXERCISE or play a physical game.

☆ Get your hands busy (on clay, draw, paint, punch pillow).

☆ Write in a journal.

☆ Count to distract and calm yourself.

☆ Draw an angry picture.

☆ Pound on clay.

ADD SOME MORE OF YOUR OWN!!

☆ _____

☆ _____

☆ _____

☆ _____

Parents: Put a check by any of the strategies your child uses to express anger. Add any other great strategies used successfully at home.

This week our Objectives included:

☆ All feelings are okay. People can show their feelings in helpful or hurtful ways.
☆ Letting feelings out in hurtful ways causes trouble.
☆ There are people with whom it's safe to share your feelings.
☆ It's important for me to stay cool when I get upset or angry.

"Coach", please be on the lookout for times when I have used these skills at school.

Get A Grip!
Feelings

High 5's

This week I noticed _____ practicing the skills & ideas in the "Objectives." I've circled on the left the areas I've seen improvement in this week. Below are compliments that "celebrate" his or her good behavior.

_____   _____
Teacher's Signature   Date

- -

This week our Objectives included:

☆ All feelings are okay. People can show their feelings in helpful or hurtful ways.
☆ Letting feelings out in hurtful ways causes trouble.
☆ There are people with whom it's safe to share your feelings.
☆ It's important for me to stay cool when i get upset or angry.

"Coach", please be on the lookout for times when I have used these skills at school.

Get A Grip!
Feelings

High 5's

This week I noticed _____ practicing the skills & ideas in the "Objectives." I've circled on the left the areas I've seen improvement in this week. Below are compliments that "celebrate" his or her good behavior.

_____   _____
Teacher's Signature   Date

HOME PRACTICE

This week's **"Objectives"** for _Get a Grip!_ are:

☆ All feelings are okay. People can show their feelings in helpful or hurtful ways.
☆ Letting feelings out in hurtful ways causes trouble.
☆ There are people with whom it's safe to share your feelings.
☆ It's important for me to stay cool when I get upset or angry.

The home practice on the other side is to help your child apply these skills in "real-life" situations. Please help record your child's ideas. **Your child will receive points in group for returning this completed & signed sheet.**

High 5's

I noticed my child applying ideas from **"Objectives"** learned this week **or in previous weeks**.

Compliments & Comments:

_____

_____

_____

_____

_____   _____
Parent's Signature   Date Due Back

From Your Number ONE FAN

DON'T JUMP THE GUN!

CONNECTING TO THE REAL WORLD

The group leader asks students to think of an important strategy that athletes use to win races - in track, biking, swimming, skiing, motocross racing, etc. Challenge the idea that speed is the only thing to consider. Suggest that speed must be tempered with appropriate pacing and patience which may require restraint. Consider a downhill skier not winning if they have time deducted for knocking down a flag. What happens to a marathon runner going 26 miles if they expend too much energy in the first few hours of the race? Discuss other situations in life in which it's important to slow down and be patient and pace yourself. Be sure students include items like taking criterion referenced exams, reacting when provoked, when in a danger zone, or when doing lengthy assignments. Knowing how far you have to go, when to back off, how far to push (an issue), when to stop (boundaries), how risk taking to be, and how fast or slow to go are all skills that help us to "go the distance" in the race of life.

OBJECTIVES

Students will participate in activites designed to emphasize the following concepts and skills:

It helps me to stop and think before overreacting because
what I say and do affects others.
I can "count to ten" to help me stop and think before I act.
I can practice thinking ahead about what will happen next (consequences).
Doing things at the right pace is important.

PROCEDURE

Pregame Warmup

☆ As students enter the room, accept "High 5" forms and completed Home Practice sheets.
☆ Tally points using your selected method.
☆ Wearing your coach's hat and whistle, review group rules and point system.
☆ Briefly discuss completed Home Practices from previous week.
☆ Review "Connecting to the Real World" and Objectives.
☆ Introduce the selected activities for the week.

Activities
(choose one or more of the following)

Activity 9.1   Group Juggle
Activity 9.2   "The Spit Wad" Story
Activity 9.3   Pacing
Activity 9.4   Game Playing
Activity 9.5   Controlling Yourself

Post Game Commentary

☆ Tally and record individual points gained during group.
☆ Encourage students to give one another "High 5's" by verbalizing ways in which they have seen each other be especially positive or helpful in group that day.
☆ Announce housekeeping details (any change in meeting date and time).
☆ Give students "High 5" reinforcement sheets to give to their teachers.

EXTENSIONS
High 5's for Teachers
Home Practice Backing for Parents

Activity 9.1 - Group Juggle

(Use anytime as an introductory or closing activity)

EQUIPMENT

Items to be tossed and juggled among group members.
These could include bean bags, soft balls, a rubber chicken,
small stuffed animals; the funnier the items, the better.

GAME PLAN

1. Select four to five soft items for the group to "juggle." Have group members stand in a circle. The leader covers "the rules":
   a. Call the name of a person across from you BEFORE YOU THROW.
   b. As play progresses and an item goes around the circle and is thrown to you again, <u>always throw the item to the same person across from you</u> (after you have called their name).
   c. After you've thrown the item to the first person, that person repeats a & b and this continues until all in the circle have caught the object once. The last person to catch the item throws it back to the group leader.

2. Practice several times aiming for fast pace and few drops!

3. When the group has shown some improvement, add a second item while the first item is still being tossed. You can work up to three to five items over time. Comment positively on group progress! This is a good activity to end sessions with!

Note: This "adventure-based" activity can be found in *Cowstails and Cobras II* (see bibliography) and is probably one of the all-time favorites of the kids. Repeat the activity in other sections to note improvement in their control and awareness of others.

DISCUSSION

☆ Was there anything that a person did to make it easier for you to catch the item?
☆ How did it feel for the group to be successful?
☆ What happened when someone threw it too fast or too high? How did it feel then?
☆ What happened when someone wasn't keeping pace? Does this ever happen in class or at home?
☆ How did you balance the "need for speed" with the accuracy required for successful catches?
☆ How is this game like things that happen in the classroom or at home? (for example, when you are expected to do several things at once, when you have to change activities quickly, or when you depend on others to do their part).

HOME PRACTICE

(None)

Activity 9.2 - "The Spit Wad" Story

GAME PLAN

1. Read aloud the story of "*The Spit Wad*."

2. Allow three group members to stand up and act out the story parts of the boy, teacher and voice of his conscience. It is easier for students to find their places if you give each child a script with his or her individual part highlighted. In some groups, all members want to take turns repeating the role play.

3. This activity tends to be short, so consider extending it if discussion is not lengthy by having the group create a cartoon strip together before doing their individual stories at home.

DISCUSSION

☆ Think of a time when you acted before thinking. What happened?
☆ Did you feel a lot like Henry in the story? What other feelings did you experience?
☆ How might others feel if you act before thinking?
☆ Did you "learn your lesson" from your mistake, or did it happen again and again?
☆ What are some ways that you could remind yourself to think things over before acting?

HOME PRACTICE

Have students take "*The Importance of Timing*" Home Practice sheets and create a cartoon strip showing a character acting before he or she thinks and the feelings and consequences that occur. Encourage students to work with their parents on this activity. Consider doubling the points when it is returned since this is a very difficult, creative activity.

"THE SPIT WAD"

(Adapted from "*The Paper Airplane*" from FEELINGS by Aliki)

Conscience:	**Yo, I'm your conscience. You gotta listen to me! You'd better not throw that spit wad!**
TEACHER:	HENRY, WERE YOU THE ONE WHO MADE THIS GROSS MESS?
Conscience:	**I told you so!**
Henry:	I got snagged!
Conscience:	**Bet you feel really stupid!**
Henry:	My face is all red!
TEACHER:	COME UP HERE TO MY DESK IMMEDIATELY!
Conscience:	**I bet you're really embarrassed now!**
Henry:	I should have thought about what would happen if I did it.
Conscience:	**Now you're sorry, huh? Huh?**
Henry:	What's my mom gonna say if she finds out?
Conscience:	**Feeling guilty now? Maybe a little scared?**
Henry:	Is she gonna call my dad?
TEACHER:	YOU'VE BEEN WARNED ABOUT THIS BEFORE!
Conscience:	**Bet you're humiliated, 'cuz all the kids are listening to this.**
TEACHER:	YOU KNOW THERE ARE CONSEQUENCES FOR THIS KIND OF BEHAVIOR!
Conscience:	**I'll bet you're sorry now!**
Henry:	Boy, AM I sorry now!
TEACHER:	YOUNG MAN, NEXT TIME YOU'D BETTER THINK ABOUT THE TROUBLE YOU'LL GET INTO BEFORE YOU BLOW IT!
Conscience:	**He's learned his lesson!**
Henry:	NOTHING is worth this!!!

The Importance of Timing

Name _____

With a parent, brainstorm a situation in which timing is important. Then create a cartoon strip showing a character who acts before thinking. Show some of the feelings & consequences that occur.

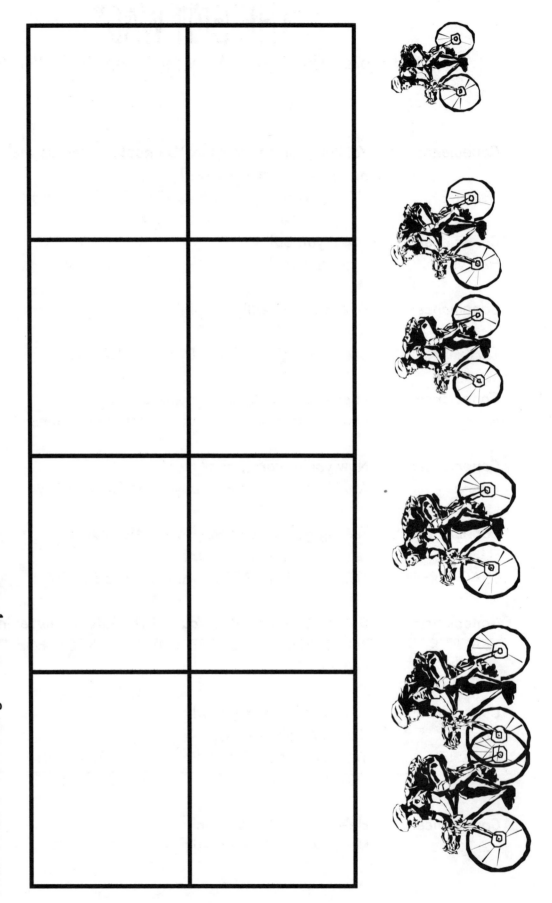

Activity 9.3 - Pacing

EQUIPMENT
Pictures showing a variety of family and school situations
such as eating a meal, running a race, shopping, doing paperwork etc.
Charts of "Slow," "Medium" and "Fast"
"Going the Distance" Home Practice sheet

GAME PLAN

1. Show pictures and describe situations in which it would be appropriate to do things at a fast or slow or medium pace. You may use the charts included as samples and list other things brainstormed by the group on these sheets.

2. Then have the group practice speaking, writing, or lining up at different speeds.

3. Compare and comment on any differences in rates between group members that you or the students noticed.

4. As a group, estimate the passage of various amounts of time (thirty seconds, one minute). Then ask students if one minute seemed to be a longer time than they expected it to be.

5. Discuss the meaning of punctuality and how one's understanding of time helps one to be more punctual.

DISCUSSION

☆ Give three specific sports examples that demonstrate the importance of pacing or timing.
☆ Which is more difficult for you to do: speeding up or slowing down in various activities?
☆ How does it feel when someone around you is faster or slower at a particular activity?
☆ What does your being late mean to a friend who is waiting for you?
☆ How is this different from keeping your teacher waiting?
☆ How do you feel when you are kept waiting by others?
☆ Do you agree with the idea that activities have optimum speeds at which to be done depending on the situation?
☆ Has "speeding up" ever caused a problem for you at school? (for example, rushing through paperwork, running in the halls, starting an assignment before all the directions were given).

HOME PRACTICE

Have students take "Going the Distance" Home Practice sheet to complete with their parents. Return for points.

eating
with
a friend

setting
the table

dialing
long distance

reading

lining
up

SLOW

walking
inside

carrying
books

drawing

doing
homework

painting a
picture

MEDIUM

Carrying a drink or plate

writing

taking a break

writing down a phone number

bike riding

eating

juggling balls

going to an appointment

keeping up with a schedule

getting a surprise ready

FAST

getting dressed

going around the world

eating

answering the phone

Going the Distance!

_____
Name

☆ Write 3 things you usually do at just the right pace:

_____

_____

_____

☆ Write 1 thing you usually *do too quickly!*

_____

☆ With your parent, write suggestions that would help you to practice slowing down this activity:

_____

_____

_____

☆ What is one thing you usually *do too slowly?*

_____

☆ With your parent or teacher, write suggestions that would help you to increase your speed while doing this activity:

_____

_____

_____

Activity 9.4 - Game Playing (lengthy!)

EQUIPMENT

Stop, Relax, Think Game or the *Social Skills Game* (see bibliography)
or a counselor-made game emphasizing impulse control
"Goalie Technique" handout

GAME PLAN

1. Consider spending two group sessions on this topic, emphasizing objectives before playing the game. *The Stop, Relax, Think game is most appropriate for first through third graders, and the Social Skills Game for older children.*

2. Before playing the game, describe and practice the self-monitoring *"Goalie Technique"* on the following handout*. Describe situations in which an adult could give a visual or verbal prompt. In response to this prompt students should pull in their arms and legs, look all around to see what's happening, and ask themselves what they are supposed to be doing at that time. (This is a skill that is best learned if you apply it consistently in subsequent sessions and encourage teachers and parents to use it as well!)

3. Play the game you have chosen. During the second group session, focus on the *"Don't Jump the Gun!"* concept of controlling impulses by using the handout. Sometimes we react quickly without thinking. But just as in a race, if you "jump the gun" by starting before the signal, you could get off to a "false start," waste energy and have to begin again. Sometimes there's even a penalty involved! In real life, as in sports, it pays to stop and think before you act. In the situations below, tell how reacting impulsively ("jumping the gun") could cause problems. Then discuss the best ways to respond.

   ☆ At recess, somebody runs into you.
   ☆ When the teacher says to line up, you and a classmate both rush to the front of the line.
   ☆ You know the answer, and even though it's not your turn, you want to say it.
   ☆ Your brother teases you or comes into your room without asking.
   ☆ Mom or dad tells you to redo your homework because it's too messy.

DISCUSSION

☆ What was something we talked about during the game that is important to remember?
☆ When at school, home, or in the neighborhood, would the *"Goalie Technique"* be helpful?
☆ Who might remind you to use this technique?
☆ What does it take to make the best choice in a tricky situation?(stop & think, ask "what if")
☆ Have your folks share a time when they had problems because they jumped the gun. Then have them tell about a time they were successful at "not jumping the gun" with a problem.
☆ Ask your parent to notice times this week when you really stop and think before acting or reacting.

HOME PRACTICE

Have students take the *"Don't Jump the Gun"* Home Practice sheet to complete with parents. Return for points. (If you divide this activity into two sessions, have students take home *"Goalie Technique"* to role play and discuss with their parents the first week.)

*an adaptation of Arthur Robin's *"turtle technique"* as used by Russell Barkley

Name _____

Note to Coaches:
(parents & teachers)

This can be a useful technique for helping children regain control using minimal reminders.

Sign below if you & your child have practiced this technique this week.

_____
Parent's signature

 # "Goalie" Technique

☆Listen for a cue word or signal from an adult.

☆Pull in your arms & legs.

☆Look all around to see what's happening.

☆Ask yourself, "What am I supposed to be doing?"

☆ 195 ☆

Don't Jump The Gun!

ON YOUR MARK...

Be alert! Assess what's going on & stay calm

GET SET:

Think about all your choices & consider consequences.

GO !

Act on your choice & maintain a positive attitude!

☆☆☆

Please have your child explain these 3 steps to you

Think about a typical week. Help your child to identify one situation in which he or she used these 3 steps effectively:

_____

_____

_____

Please discuss with your child & record a situation in which it is currently difficult for him or her to use these skills.

_____

_____

_____

Give your child an example of a situation when they have shown improvement in "not jumping the gun" as they have grown & matured.

_____

Please share a personal example with your child in which you really had to learn how to apply the "On Your Mark, Get Set, Go!" principle.

⭐ 196 ⭐

Activity 9.5 - Controlling Yourself

(Divide #1, 2, 3 into three separate sessions if you think students need more reinforcement.)

EQUIPMENT

Cardboard remote control for each child
Markers or small stickers
A copy of *Hunter & His Amazing Remote Control**

GAME PLAN

1. Ask how many in the group know how to use a remote control. State that it's fun being able to know what buttons to push and it saves a lot of time. It allows you to make decisions quickly and can prevent you from being on the wrong station at the wrong time. Tell the group that for the next few weeks we'll be learning to work with a different kind of remote control with the following buttons:.

Channel Changer	Filtering out distractions
Pause	Stopping to think, relax and create a plan
Fast Forward	Thinking before acting
Rewind	Shifting focus from a mistake to a better way to do things
Slow Motion	Slowing down and managing stress
Coach	Seeking help to solve problems
Zapper	Recognizing and rejecting negative thinking
Way to Go	Using positive self-talk

Read or summarize pp. 1-13 of the story that addresses filtering out distractions and taking time to relax. Choose from *Creative Coaching* activities: Spotlight Activity 3.1, Activity 10.1 or 10.2, Activity 1.5, or associated activities from *Hunter and His Amazing remote Control*.*

2. Read or summarize pp. 14-23 of the story to cover thinking before acting and rethinking mistakes as well as slowing down instead of overreacting. Choose from *Creative Coaching* activities: Activity 10.1 or 10.2, create a "mistakes" list and role-play "rewind" solutions, or select associated activities from *Hunter and His Amazing Remote Control*.*

3. Read or summarize pp. 24-32 of the story to cover seeking help, rejecting negative thinking, using positive self-talk, and to review all previous buttons. Choose *Creative Coaching* activity: 9.1 Group Juggle or select associated activities from *Hunter and his Amazing Remote Control*.*

DISCUSSION

☆ What new buttons did we hear about today? Color them in or add a sticker to them.

☆ When did you use one of these buttons during the last week? Did you miss an opportunity to use a button?

☆ When did you see someone else in your family or classroom use one of these buttons?

☆ How can you remind yourself to use these buttons every day? (Give specific ideas: keep remote on desk, memorize it & keep it in your head, write it on the inside of your hand, etc.)

HOME PRACTICE

Use pages that accompany activities from Creative Coaching or Hunter and His Amazing Remote Control* with the Home Practice backing.

*This book is an unique, cognitive-behavioral approach to teaching self-control. Using the buttons on their "remote controls" can help them to improve self-monitoring, impulse control, and self-confidence. The book contains an activity guide and storybook section.

Don't Jump The Gun!
Impulsivity

High 5's

This week our Objectives included:

☆ Instead of overreacting, stop & think because others are affect-ed by what you say & do.
☆ Stopping to **"count to ten"** before acting gives a person time to think things out.
☆ It is important to practice think-ing ahead about consequences.
☆ It is important to recognize the best pace at which to do certain activities.

"Coach", please be on the lookout for times when I have used these skills at school.

This week I noticed _____ practicing the skills & ideas in the "Objectives." I've circled on the left the areas I've seen improvement in this week. Below are compliments that "celebrate" his or her good behavior.

_____   _____
Teacher's Signature   Date

- -

Don't Jump The Gun!
Impulsivity

High 5's

This week our Objectives included:

☆ Instead of overreacting, stop & think because others are affect-ed by what you say & do.
☆ Stopping to **"count to ten"** before acting gives a person time to think things out.
☆ It is important to practice think-ing ahead about consequences.
☆ It is important to recognize the best pace at which to do certain activities.

"Coach", please be on the lookout for times when I have used these skills at school.

This week I noticed _____ practicing the skills & ideas in the "Objectives." I've circled on the left the areas I've seen improvement in this week. Below are compliments that "celebrate" his or her good behavior.

_____   _____
Teacher's Signature   Date

HOME PRACTICE

This week's **"Objectives"** for _Don't Jump The Gun!_ are:

☆ Instead of overreacting, stop & think because other are affected by what you say & do.
☆ Stopping to **"count to ten"** before acting gives a person time to think things out.
☆ It is important to practice thinking ahead about consequences.
☆ It is important to recognize the best pace at which to do certain activities.

The home practice on the other side is to help your child apply these skills in "real-life" situations. Please help record your child's ideas. **Your child will receive points in group for returning this completed & signed sheet.**

High 5's

I noticed my child applying ideas from **"Objectives"** learned this week **or in previous weeks.**

Compliments & Comments:

_____

_____

_____

_____

_____   _____
Parent's Signature   Date Due Back

From Your Number ONE FAN

SESSION 10
(Relaxation)

TAKING A BREATHER

CONNECTING TO THE REAL WORLD

Great athletic or academic performance depends on knowing when and how to relax mentally and physically. For anyone to deal successfully with the stress of many things to do or of competing under performance pressures, they must be able to clean out their mental clutter, relieve their anxieties, and focus on the task at hand. Bernie Siegel explains that relaxation doesn't mean falling asleep in front of a tv set or unwinding with friends. It is a quieting of mental activity and withdrawal of body and mind from external stimulation, a way of "erasing the blackboard" of all mundane concerns in preparation for contacting deeper layers of the mind.

⭐ 201 ⭐

OBJECTIVES

Students will participate in activites designed to emphasize the following concepts and skills:

It is easier to pay attention, work, and perform when I am relaxed.
I can learn ways to help my body and mind relax.
"Staying still" and relaxed keeps me from distracting myself and others.

PROCEDURE

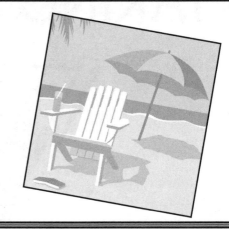

Pregame Warmup

☆ As students enter the room, accept "High 5" forms and completed Home Practice sheets.
☆ Tally points using your selected method.
☆ Wearing your coach's hat and whistle, review group rules and point system.
☆ Briefly discuss completed Home Practices from previous week.
☆ Review "Connecting to the Real World" and Objectives.
☆ Introduce the selected activity for the week.

Activities

(choose one or more of the following)

Activity 10.1 Breathing
Activity 10.2 Guided Relaxation

Post Game Commentary

☆ Tally and record individual points gained during group.
☆ Encourage students to give one another "High 5's" by verbalizing ways in which they have seen each other be especially positive or helpful in group that day.
☆ Announce housekeeping details (any change in meeting date and time).
☆ Give students "High 5" reinforcement sheets to give to their teachers.

EXTENSIONS

High 5's for Teachers
Home Practice Backing for Parents

Activity 10.1 - Breathing
(best for primary students)

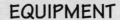

EQUIPMENT

Pencils, crayons or markers and paper for each student
Small piece of sponge for each student
Solution of bubbles and wand
"Take a Breather" Home Practice sheet.

GAME PLAN

1. Explain to the group that today we are going to practice how to know the difference between what your body feels like when it is tense and when it's relaxed.

2. Give each student a small piece of pliable sponge and ask them to squeeze and hold it tightly by tensing their whole arm and fist. Have students hold the pressure for a count of ten.

3. Ask students to unfold their fists slowly and to describe how tensing and relaxing felt.

4. Practice tensing and relaxing other muscles (shoulders, legs, face, etc.)

5. Explain that muscles in our bodies work best when they have both relaxing and tensing times. Using a bubble wand and solution, demonstrate the effects of a rapid burst of air and of a more controlled, slow breath of air. Ask students to notice which breath produced the longest lasting bubble.

6. Allow each student (one at a time) to blow a bubble with a slow, controlled breath. Use your best judgment about making this an inside or outside activity, but be sure to set clearly defined behavioral limits.

7. Have students demonstrate slow, controlled breathing without bubbles.

NOTE: We learned about this activity from a participant who attended one of our first workshops. (Unfortunately, we forgot to get her name!)

DISCUSSION

☆ What makes it easy to relax your muscles and breathe slowly and deeply?
☆ What is the most difficult part about relaxing muscles and breathing slowly and deeply?
☆ When could you use these ideas at school? . . . at home? (include going to bed at night, right before a test, during a competition, when faced with an overwhelming job or task, when time is running out, etc.)

HOME PRACTICE

Have students take "Take a Breather" Home Practice sheet to complete with their parents. Return for points.

Take A Breather

Dear Parent(s),

In each column below, please list some of your favorite ways to relax. Please identify & discuss situations in which you think it's important to relax. If your child enjoys doing art work, ask him to use another sheet of paper to draw himself in a safe, relaxing place.

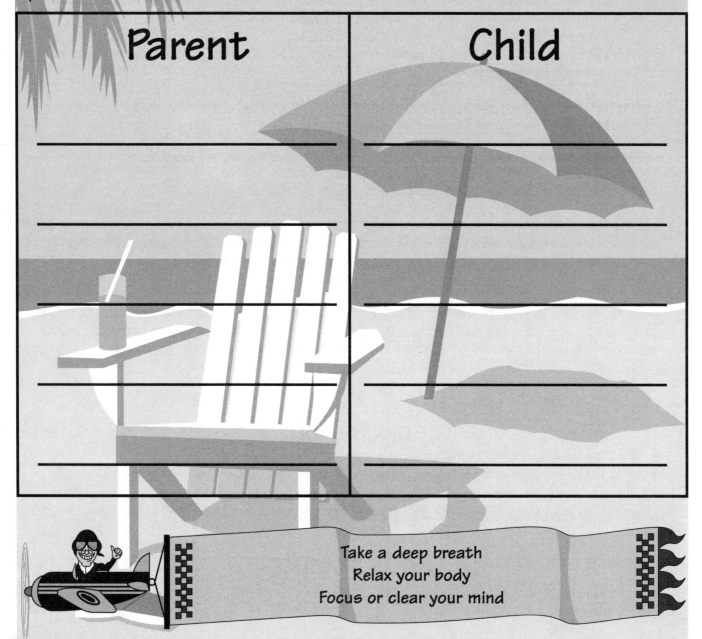

Parent	Child

Take a deep breath
Relax your body
Focus or clear your mind

Activity 10.2 - Guided Relaxation
(best with intermediate ages)

EQUIPMENT
"Times It's Important to Relax!" *"Ways to Relax"*
Tape of soothing music
Script of *"The Hot Air Balloon Ride"*
"Don't Crash Under Pressure" activity sheet
"Exercise Helps Body"
"Take a Breather" Home Practice sheet

GAME PLAN

1. After you have discussed the Connecting to the Real World and the objectives, ask students to think of times when they felt pressure anxious or tense. Have the group brainstorm "times it's important to relax" and list on the board. (See *"Ways to Relax"* and *"Times It's Important to Relax"* for ideas.)

2. Explain that we can learn strategies to help relax our minds and bodies. Discuss things students do already to calm down. As you list on a board or chart, have students complete the activity sheet *"Don't Crash Under Pressure."*

3. Say: Today, we are going to practice relaxing our minds and our bodies. Learning to breathe deeply and slowly helps all of the muscles of your body to get plenty of oxygen. Quietening your mind keeps it from "racing." Tell students to take a deep breath, hold it for a count of four (while the group leader counts orally), and slowly release breath for a count of four. Encourage students to breathe deeply using their diaphragms instead of relying upon shallow, upper chest breathing.

4. Ask students to either put their heads down on a table or to stretch out on the floor in a comfortable position. Play soft music while you tell a story that will help their minds relax. Ask them to keep their eyes shut in order to imagine what you are describing. Stress that it is important to be totally silent in order to avoid distracting others. The group leader then softly and slowly reads the story of *"The Hot Air Balloon Ride"*. (If students are not capable of being quiet for the few minutes the tape is playing, don't be discouraged - just forego the activity.)

DISCUSSION

☆ Invite students to describe their safe place. What made it easy or difficult to relax?

☆ When might you use this specific technique? (i.e.. at bedtime or when trying to calm down after being upset).

☆ How could this be adapted for use during the day at school?

☆ Explain that doing this activity was only one way to handle stress. Another way is to exercise regularly, and by doing so, a person's body actually gets healthier. Refer to the sheet *"Exercise Helps Body."*

☆ Share the story *"True Heights"* by David Naster as given in *Chicken Soup for the Soul, III* (see bibliogrphy).

HOME PRACTICE

Have students take *"Take a Breather"* Home Practice sheet to complete with their parents. Return for points.

TIMES IT'S IMPORTANT TO RELAX:
(Here are some ideas our groups came up with!)

☆ Before going to bed
☆ When you're grumpy
☆ After a hard day
☆ When parents get home from work & are tired
☆ When you're afraid something is going to hurt
☆ When you stress out because of too much homework
☆ When you're trying to remember
☆ At a rest time or time to stop
☆ After a lot of exercise
☆ When it's time to wait
☆ When you are sick

WAYS TO RELAX:
(More ideas from our groups!)

☆ Read
☆ Take deep breaths
☆ Watch TV (like cartoons) or a video or play video games
☆ Take a mental vacation
☆ Float in the pool
☆ Lay on your bed or on grandma's bed
☆ Ride your bike
☆ Play baseball
☆ Lay down with a favorite blanket
☆ Put your feet up where it's cool
☆ Play with your pet
☆ Exercise (see page 210 Exercise Helps The Body)

The Hot Air Balloon Ride - A Relaxation Exercise

One way in which children can learn to relax is to take their imaginations on a special ride. This is also a good activity to use with children whose parents report that the child is having a hard time falling asleep at night. Use this in small groups that are discussing how to handle stress. Let students stretch out if possible in a comfortable spot, dim the lights and turn on soft, "mood" instrumental music, ask students to close their eyes and get in a relaxed position. Then in a soft, slow voice, begin to tell this story:

"Imagine you are in a dark room. It is a safe place and you are feeling very comfortable. Suddenly, you realize a door has opened at one end of the room and through the door is floating toward you a beautiful hot air balloon. Imagine what color it is. Imagine that as the balloon is coming closer to you, it is growing larger and larger.

You look up and notice that the ceiling of the room has opened up and you can see the sky. You realize that the balloon is big and strong enough for you to climb in and that you can take a ride. So you climb on the balloon and feel it slowly, slowly rising up, up, up into the sky. Imagine flying through the sky on your balloon! Feel the breeze on your face. Imagine everything you see. Is it a night sky with stars and a bright moon? Or is it a daytime sky with clouds and the sun?

You feel so comfortable and relaxed as you fly gently through the sky. As you look down, you notice a beautiful meadow below. Imagine the wind blowing the grass on the ground. You notice many beautiful wildflowers growing in the meadow. Do you see any animals playing below? The meadow looks so relaxing that you wish you could stop and play there, but the balloon is taking you farther and farther.

As you look ahead, you see a mountainside coming closer. As you grow close to the forest there, you take a deep breath and you can smell the evergreen trees in the forest. You see a bubbling stream flowing over the rocks and hear the sound of the water in the stream. You notice animals drinking from the stream. It is so cool and refreshing there that you wish you could stop and stay awhile, but the balloon is taking you higher and higher.

Soon, you see a beautiful rainbow ahead and you feel your body tingle as you pass through it on the balloon. You feel like you are heading to a favorite place; and, you are. You have arrived at the place that is most special to you in the whole world! As your balloon lets you down to the ground, you realize you can climb off and stay a while in this special place. You can imagine yourself alone there, or you can imagine someone else there to share your relaxing spot with you. I am going to be very quiet for a few moments while you imagine yourself in your own special place.

(A one to two minute pause is usually enough; use your judgment)

You would like to stay in your favorite spot for a long time. But your balloon has returned and you realize you must now leave. But you know that you can return here in your imagination anytime you would like. You say goodbye to anyone who might have been there with you, and climb carefully into your hot air balloon. Slowly, slowly, your balloon rises into the air. You feel the breeze blowing softly on your face.

And as you begin your journey back, back, back through the rainbow, you feel your skin tingle. Back, back over the mountainside where you can still hear the babbling brook and smell the trees in the forest. Back, back through the peaceful meadow with the grasses blowing in the breeze. And finally, back to the room where you began. The balloon slowly descends into the room, and you climb off. It floats away, getting smaller, and going through a door. As the door closes, you are once again in the safe, dark room feeling rested and relaxed. When you are ready to rejoin the group, open your eyes and sit quietly until all are ready.

Don't Crash Under Pressure!

Think of some things that could be done or said to relieve some of the pressure in this situation!

Think of some things that could be done or said to relieve some of the pressure in this situation!

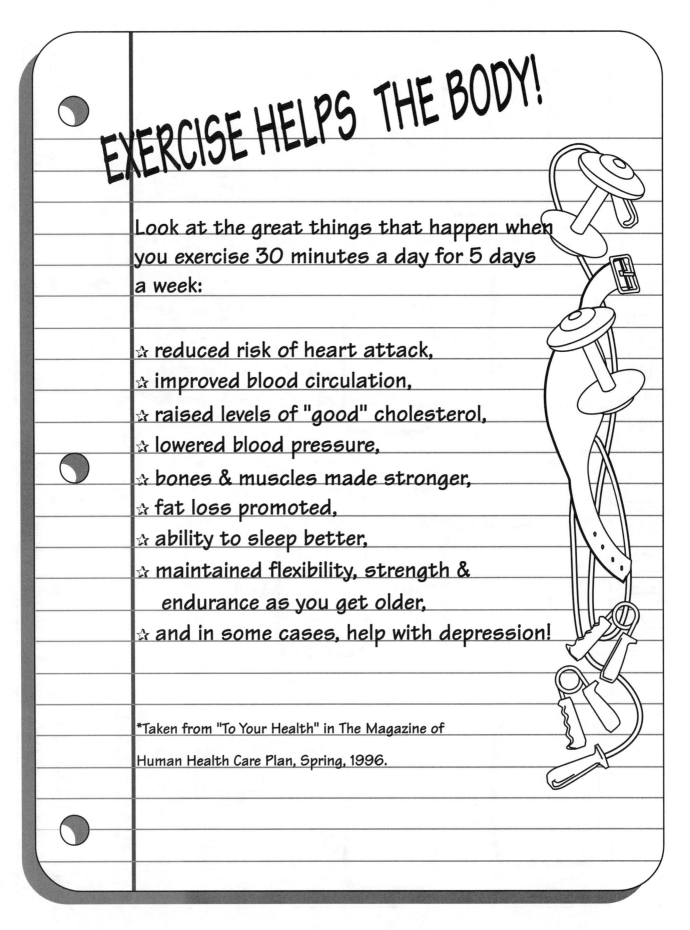

EXERCISE HELPS THE BODY!

Look at the great things that happen when you exercise 30 minutes a day for 5 days a week:

☆ reduced risk of heart attack,
☆ improved blood circulation,
☆ raised levels of "good" cholesterol,
☆ lowered blood pressure,
☆ bones & muscles made stronger,
☆ fat loss promoted,
☆ ability to sleep better,
☆ maintained flexibility, strength & endurance as you get older,
☆ and in some cases, help with depression!

*Taken from "To Your Health" in The Magazine of Human Health Care Plan, Spring, 1996.

Taking A Breather
Relaxation

This week our Objectives included:

☆ It is easier to pay attention, work, & perform when relaxed.
☆ It is possible to learn ways to help one's body & mind relax.
☆ When you stay still & relaxed, you are more able to focus & are less distracting to others.

"Coach," please be on the lookout for times when I have used these skills at school.

High 5's

This week I noticed _____ practicing the skills & ideas in the "Objectives." I've circled on the left the areas I've seen improvement in this week. Below are compliments that "celebrate" his or her good behavior.

_____   _____
Teacher's Signature   Date

- -

Taking A Breather
Relaxation

This week our Objectives included:

☆ It is easier to pay attention, work, & perform when relaxed.
☆ It is possible to learn ways to help one's body & mind relax.
☆ When you stay still & relaxed, you are more able to focus & are less distracting to others.

"Coach," please be on the lookout for times when I have used these skills at school.

High 5's

This week I noticed _____ practicing the skills & ideas in the "Objectives." I've circled on the left the areas I've seen improvement in this week. Below are compliments that "celebrate" his or her good behavior.

_____   _____
Teacher's Signature   Date

HOME PRACTICE

This week's **"Objectives"** for _Taking A Breather!_ are:

☆ It is easier to pay attention, work, & perform when relaxed.
☆ It is possible to learn ways to help one's body & mind relax.
☆ When you stay still & relaxed, you are more able to focus & are less distracting to others.

The home practice on the other side is to help your child apply these skills in "real-life" situations. Please help record your child's ideas. **Your child will receive points in group for returning this completed & signed sheet.**

High 5's

I noticed my child applying ideas from **"Objectives"** learned this week **or in previous weeks.**

Compliments & Comments:

_____

_____

_____

_____

_____   _____
Parent's Signature   Date Due Back

From Your Number ONE FAN

SESSION 11
(Communication)

GETTING THE SIGNALS STRAIGHT

CONNECTING TO THE REAL WORLD

Just as in a football game, where there are plays that either get yardage or lose ground, there are also helpful and harmful ways of communicating with others. Some ways we communicate with others are verbal, just like when the quarterback calls an audible play at the line. Some ways are nonverbal, just like when the referee signals a penalty or first down with flags or hand motions. Sometimes people may even get thrown out of the game for communicating poorly in an unsportsmanlike way. Do people ever get in trouble at school or at home for communicating poorly?

OBJECTIVES

Students will participate in activites designed to emphasize the following concepts and skills:

I communicate with my face, my body and my words.
I can communicate better with others when I watch their "body language."
It is easier to communicate when I can look at the person who's talking and can ask them questions.
I can make comments without blaming or accusing others.
I can ask for what I want or need in a positive way.
I can show responsibility for my feelings by using an "I" message.

PROCEDURE

Pregame Warmup

☆ As students enter the room, accept "High 5" forms and completed Home Practice sheets.
☆ Tally points using your selected method.
☆ Wearing your coach's hat and whistle, review group rules and point system.
☆ Briefly discuss completed Home Practices from previous week.
☆ Review "Connecting to the Real World" and Objectives.
☆ Introduce the selected activity for the week.

Activities

(choose one or more of the following)

Activity 11.1 Gestures, Postures and Facial Expressions
Activity 11.2 Back-to-Back
Activity 11.3 Verbal Communication Strategies
Activity 11.4 "I" Messages

Post Game Commentary

☆ Tally and record individual points gained during group.
☆ Encourage students to give one another "High 5's" by verbalizing ways in which they have seen each other be especially positive or helpful in group that day.
☆ Announce housekeeping details (any change in meeting date and time).
☆ Give students "High 5" reinforcement sheets to give to their teachers.

EXTENSIONS

High 5's for Teachers
Home Practice Backing for Parents

Activity 11.1 - Gestures, Postures & Facial Expression (lengthy activity)

EQUIPMENT
Scarf

Pictures or photos of faces showing different expressions (include some sports figures)
"Sending and Receiving Feelings" card game
(cut cards out, attach appropriate backings and laminate for durability)
(Optional: *Helping the Child That Doesn't Fit In* emphasizes the importance of teaching nonverbal communication skills,
offers additional suggestions for children's activities and tips for parents.)
"Offense Meets the Defense" Home Practice sheet

GAME PLAN
(divide into two sessions if you feel students need more reinforcement)

1. Explain that people use words, tone of voice, gestures, posture and facial expressions to communicate with others. Define *nonverbal communication* as sending messages to others through facial expressions, gestures and postures. Define *gestures* as communication involving the use of hands, arms and fingers which add understanding or meaning to our verbal communication. Define *posture* as a body position involving most or all of one's body that could include combinations of torso, hand, arm, foot and head positions.

2. Ask students what would happen if a listener paid attention only to the words being used. Demonstrate by covering your face with a scarf or book as you talk. Remove the barrier and repeat the same phrase sharing your facial expression and ask if anyone changed their mind about your intent once they had seen your face.

3. Ask students to recall previous lessons on feelings. Explain that the group will be focusing on how to improve communication with others, especially by noticing others' facial expressions and therefore, their feelings.

4. Show photos of people's faces (use pictures or drawings if photos are not available). Ask students to guess how these people are feeling and what they might be thinking. Ask them if they were actually with the person in the photo, how would they respond to them.

5. Stress how important it is to use appropriate gestures and posture to communicate with people. Nonverbal messages are often stronger than verbal, especially when "the message" seems mixed; that is, when your face says one thing and your words say another. Have students guess gestures that illustrate:

STOP - hand held up	CEASE COMMOTION - hands palm down at waist level
GET AWAY - arm outstretched, hand up	
YES - Nodding	I MEAN BUSINESS - hands on hips
NO - shaking head; wagging finger	YOU'D BETTER LISTEN - pointed finger
NERVOUS/IMPATIENT - tapping foot	I GIVE UP - arms to side and up
RESISTANCE - arms crossed	I DON'T KNOW - shrug
GOODBYE - wave	

Ask students to come up and demonstrate with other examples and let others guess what the gestures mean (examples could include clapping, "yes!," victory, come on, etc.). Then, if time allows, have them play the "Sending and Receiving Feelings" card game.

DISCUSSION

☆ Share a time when you could tell what people were feeling by the look on their faces.

☆ Tell about a time when you couldn't figure out what your teacher's facial expression meant.

☆ Could a person have more than one feeling at a time? Discuss examples.

☆ Have you ever been misunderstood when you expressed a feeling in body language alone?

☆ Tell about a time when you misunderstood somebody else's body language.

☆ Which helps you to understand someone better, their body language and the look on their face or the words they use? Give a specific example.

☆ Which are most challenging to understand - nonverbal signals from other kids or from adults?

☆ How does it help communication if two people are each aware of how the other is feeling?

HOME PRACTICE

Have students take home "Offense Meets the Defense" Home Practice sheet in which students cut out and paste on magazine pictures of people that illustrate various facial expressions, gestures and postures. Invite help from parents and return for points.

SENDING AND RECEIVING FEELINGS
DIRECTIONS FOR CARD GAME

Divide cards into three stacks:

Send/Receive Stack   Feelings Stack   Body Language Stack

The player to be "it" draws a Send/Receive card from the stack. The player shows only this Send/Receive card to others; all other drawn cards are kept face down. If a Send card is selected, then the player selects a Feeling card and a Body Language card to act out. The player to the right "Receives" and guesses what is being acted out. (Student supplies a feeling word with a blank card.)

If the player to be "it" selects a Receive card, the player to the left acts as the Sender and gets to select a Feeling card and a Body Language card to act out. "It" then guesses what feeling is being "sent."

Play continues until all have had a chance to act out or receive or until time is up.

Confident	Enraged	SEND
Depressed	Frightened	RECEIVE
Excited	Proud	SEND
Embarrassed	Lonely	RECEIVE

FEELINGS	FEELINGS	SEND/RECEIVE
FEELINGS	FEELINGS	SEND/RECEIVE
FEELINGS	FEELINGS	SEND/RECEIVE
FEELINGS	FEELINGS	SEND/RECEIVE

(Card Backings)

POSTURE	Bored	Angry
FACIAL EXPRESSION	Nervous	Happy
HANDS	Shy	_____
GESTURE	Sad	_____

FEELINGS	FEELINGS	BODY LANGUAGE
FEELINGS	FEELINGS	BODY LANGUAGE
FEELINGS	FEELINGS	BODY LANGUAGE
FEELINGS	FEELINGS	BODY LANGUAGE

(Card Backings)

Offense Meets

Name _____   Parent signature: _____

Cut out & paste magazine pictures of faces in the circles. For extra points, find pictures that show gestures & postures (body language). Paste these in the center! Find as many different pictures as you can!

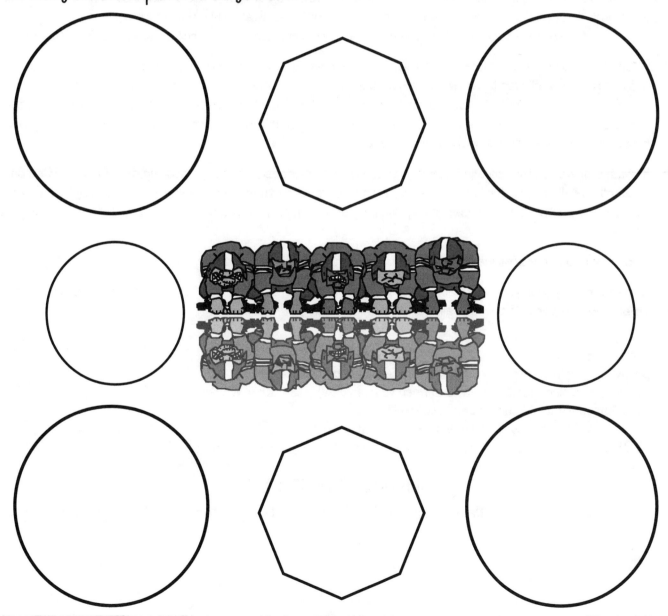

Activity 11.2 - Back to Back

(for intermediate age)

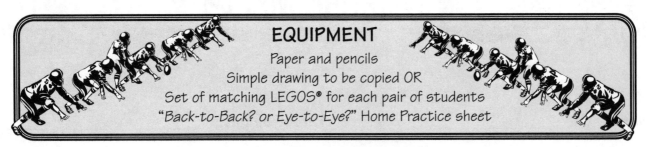

EQUIPMENT
Paper and pencils
Simple drawing to be copied OR
Set of matching LEGOS® for each pair of students
"Back-to-Back? or Eye-to-Eye?" Home Practice sheet

GAME PLAN

1. Have students sit back-to-back in pairs or triads and ask one student to do a simple drawing as he or she gives oral directions to the other student(s) as to how to duplicate this picture on their own paper. (You may want to give a prepared drawing to the first student and have him or her just describe the picture.)

2. When giving verbal descriptions, the student may not name any items but can describe how things look so the others can duplicate the drawing. Other students are not allowed to ask any questions during the first round. After a few minutes, allow students to begin asking questions. After about five minutes, have students share drawings and discuss. Then do another round in which students reverse roles in giving and receiving directions with and without questions.

3. If you are able to secure enough building blocks, give each pair of students a matching set of blocks. Have one student give directions for how to assemble the blocks. The student may ask if his or her partner understands. The partner can only respond by clapping once if directions are understood and twice if not understood.

4. During the next round, students reverse roles in giving and receiving directions.

5. Consider having younger students sit face-to-face in front of building blocks to help them compare or contrast how effective it is to maintain eye contact when communicating.

DISCUSSION
☆ What helped you to follow directions? (listening, paying attention)
☆ Was it easier to follow directions when you could ask questions? Why or why not?
☆ What made it difficult to be successful?
☆ How is this activity like following directions at school? . . . at home?
☆ What are the benefits of having good eye contact when listening to directions?

HOME PRACTICE
Have students take "Back-to-Back? or Eye-to-Eye?" Home Practice sheets to complete with their parents. Return for points.

Back-to-Back?
or
Eye-to-Eye?

In our All-Stars Group this week, pairs of students sat back-to-back while one child gave oral directions for the other to follow. The person receiving the directions could not ask questions, but communicated by clapping (one clap indicated that they understood, two claps signaled confusion). We learned a lot !

This week, I'd like for you to explore the concepts listed on the Home Practice sheet with your child in a different way by following the directions below:

☆ Select an activity that is not routinely done by your child. This should be an activity that requires him or her to rely solely on your verbal directions.
   Be sure to sit or stand back-to-back.
   Some possibilities are:
   ° draw (back-to-back) a particular object without naming it
   ° make instant pudding or Jello®
   ° wrap a package
   ° use blocks, beads, etc. to make a pattern or structure

☆ Check for understanding after each step of the directions are given. You may choose to use the clapping or one word responses to the question, "Do you under stand?"

☆ Halfway through the directions, stop, turn to face each other & check on progress. Now, position yourself so that you can see each other & finish giving directions to allow your child to complete the task. For fun, you can reverse roles!

☆ Take a few minutes & discuss the following things:
   How did you feel as the direction giver? As the receiver? What made it difficult to be successful? What helped? What are the benefits of eye contact? What did you learn about the way you communicate?

   _____

   _____

   _____

   Student Name _____ **Parent Signature:** _____

Activity 11.3 - Verbal Communication Strategies

EQUIPMENT

Communication role plays
Crayons or highlighters
"Flag on the Play" activity sheets
Yellow referee flags and whistles (optional)
"Instant Replay" Home Practice sheets
Tangible rewards (stickers or candy)

GAME PLAN

1. Ask students to think of an unnamed person in their class that they usually seem to enjoy talking with. Ask what it is that makes that person easy to communicate with. List ideas on the board or on a poster (they listen without interrupting, let others have time to talk, speak clearly, speak respectfully, stick to the point).

2. Now ask students to think of a time when they became really frustrated or angry when trying to communicate with someone. Explain that today in group, they will listen to examples of ineffective communication, decide what is happening in the situation and brainstorm ways to improve the specific situation.

3. Explain that students will participate in a role play with you. The "ineffective communicator" role should always be played by the group leader.

4. Distribute the *"Flag on the Play"* activity sheet with flags (and optional whistles). Explain that as observers watch each role play, they are to "toss the ref's flag" (and blow their whistles) when they figure out what "foul" in communication is going on. As the role playing student does an "instant redo" of how the communication could be done more effectively, students can color in the appropriate flag on their handout. (The flags and whistles may seem a bit of unnecessary silliness. But having a concrete focus helps to set firmly into memory the concepts discussed. Making mental connections .... building neural pathways.... who knows?)

5. Continue this process until all children have had an opportunity to role play effectively.

NOTE: Even though students generally love gaining negative attention by playing the "bad guy" roles, research shows that it is not healthy for them to do so. Consider offsetting this appeal by tangibly rewarding the more difficult task of communicating appropriately during the "replays." As each child communicates effectively in the repeated role play, consider giving a "SCORE®" candy bar, football player's card or other incentive.

DISCUSSION

☆ What are some key things to remember if you want to be a pro at communicating?
☆ How do you feel when people commit communication fouls with you?
☆ Which communication foul tends to upset you the most?
☆ How do people feel when you commit communication fouls?
☆ What usually happens to the conversation when communication fouls occur in real life?

HOME PRACTICE

Have students take *"Instant Replay"* Home Practice sheets to complete with their parents. Return for points.

Talking Too Little

Jake: (Calls friend on phone) "Hey, Sam, can you come over to play soccer in a little while?"

Sam: "Maybe."

Jake: "A whole bunch of us guys are gonna meet at the field behind school. How about you round up some kids from your street too?"

Sam: "Nah."

Jake: "Why not? Don't you want to play?"

Talking Too Much

Lakeshia: "Ooh, we saw a cool movie this weekend!"

Dennis: "Yeah, I saw this, umm, video with all these guys, and uh, they were dressed in these special suits, and uh, that let their skin breathe while they walked through this fiery pit on the planet Zenon. And then, uh, they were battling these, these really awful, gross creatures covered with zits and slime that melted anything that, like, touched them."

Lakeshia: "Sounds like your kind of film. Well, any way, I wanted to tell you about the movie we saw."

Dennis: "But I didn't tell you about the man-eating plants. One of the good guys got tripped and landed in the middle of these really um, huge, gross plants that ate his guts and then spit out his bones. It was cool. But, but, the best part was near the end when the gross creatures started melting the plants and it looked like, uhh, you know, that acid stuff dripping everywhere!"

Lakeshia: (hearing the recess whistle says) "Yeah, well, it's time to go in."

COMMUNICATION ROLE PLAYS

Select the most appropriate role plays for your group or create your own. Make two copies of each dialogue, cut up & paste on index cards.

Not Listening

Ann: "This Indian village project is going to be really fun! What tribe do you like best, Javier? . . . Javier?"

Javier: "Huh?"

Ann: "I asked you which tribe of Indians you wanted to vote for."

Javier: "Why are we voting?"

Ann: "Weren't you listening to the teacher?"

Interrupting

Lee: "Hey, did you see us playing at recess? I was running really fast and . . . . "

Jamie: "Look at this rock I found out there. I found it by the big tree."

Lee: "Yeah, that's neat; well, anyway, while we were chasing the girls, Steve got stuck ..."

Jamie: "I know Steve; he's the guy in Mrs. Hooper's class."

Lee: "Duh! Well, he was chasing Melanie and the funniest thing happened. . . ."

Jamie: "Is Melanie the girl with the long brown hair?"

Lee: "Never mind!" (and walks off disgustedly)

Bragging

Ron: "My dad bought me this really cool video game!"

Steve: "So, I'm getting a virtual reality game for my birthday. Only my best friends are gonna get to play."

Ron: (refusing to be hooked, says) "Cool . . . I'll bet you're really excited!"

⭐ 226 ⭐

Rude or Gross

Alex: "Hey, look!" Chocolate milk and lasagna mixed together look like throw-up. Want some?"

Natalie: "I'd rather look at someone who knows how to eat!" (turns calmly and talks to another friend, ignoring Alex)

Alex: "Can't take it, huh?"

Natalie: "This looks like the last time I'm sitting near you!"

Cut-downs

Carlos: "Hey, shorty! You're so short, you have to look up to see the floor!"

Joe: (Stops, thinks & then says) "You know, every time you're having a hard day, you always find somebody to take it out on."

Carlos: "Oh, yeah, you're not only short, you're stupid too!"

Joe: (Rolls eyes & says) "I'm not sticking around to listen to you" (as he walks off).

Blaming

Sue: "I'm so mad at you! I have to miss recess today and it's all your fault!"

Maria: "What do you mean? I didn't do anything!"

Sue: "Yes, you did! You kept making so much noise that I couldn't think and I didn't get my work done and now I have to stay in and finish this dumb work!"

Maria: "I'm sorry you feel that way. You never said anything to me, so I didn't know I was bothering you."

Flag on the Play

_____
Name

Color in the penalty flag for each unsportsmanlike example you've seen role-played today!

INTERRUPTING

BRAGGING

PUTTING DOWN

BLAMING

NOT LISTENING

TALKING TOO MUCH

TALKING TOO LITTLE

GROSS OR RUDE

Instant Replay

_____
Name

With your parent, change each communication foul on the left to a more "sportsman like" response.

Talks too much   _____

Talks too little   _____

Talks too fast   _____

Talks too slow "and, uhhh..."   _____

"Like"   _____

Talks without listening to others   _____

Interrupts others   _____

Blames others   _____

Calls people names (being rude)   _____

Gets bored & changes subject
being discussed   _____

_____
Name one that's been left out that
bothers you!

One thing my child did to communicate well this week is:

_____

Activity 11.4 - "I" Messages

EQUIPMENT

"I" Message formula chart
"Blaming You-Messages" activity sheet
Situation Prompts cards
"I Can" Home Practice sheets

GAME PLAN

1. Ask students if they have ever seen an animal "cornered." Ask them to explain the concept of "backing some one into a corner" and what types of talking and behaving tend to make people feel defensive. Explain that many years ago people figured out how to communicate unpleasant news in a way that wouldn't "back people into a corner."

2. Show the "I" Message formula on the board or on a poster and demonstrate how you would use it in an actu-al group situation. Include examples of giving both positive and negative thoughts with an "I" Message. For example, "Jose, I feel really glad when you always remind me that group is about to be over because then I can make sure to get everyone's points recorded before it's time to go!" or "Jane, I feel really irritated when you continue to tap your pencil because I can't concentrate when there is so much noise in here. Please stop."

3. Have students restate the "Blaming You-Messages" on the following activity sheet into an "I" Message for-mat. The group leader may choose to write these on index cards, on the board or enlarge the sheet to poster size.

4. Divide the group into two teams. Team A takes a turn reading the situation prompt (swings at recess) and the group leader makes an aggressive or inappropriate statement to which the other Team B responds with an appropriate "I" Message. Repeat with Team B reading prompt and Team A creating the "I" Message. Continue until each team has had several turns. It is okay for team members to confer and give a coopera-tively derived group statement. Give one to three points for good to great responses and consider giving an immediate tangible reward at the end of the game.

DISCUSSION

☆ Can you think of a time this week when you could have used an "I" Message at school? . . . . . . .at home?
☆ Have you ever noticed anyone talking in this way before?
☆ Do you think using an "I" Message would reduce the number of arguments a person got into?
☆ What are some of the other benefits of using "I" Messages?
☆ Do you think that using an "I" Message will feel comfortable or uncomfortable the first few times you try it? Why?
☆ How could you encourage yourself to practice this new skill?

HOME PRACTICE

Have students take the "I Can" Home Practice sheets to complete with their parents. Return for points.

"I" MESSAGES

1. I feel...	2. ...when you...	3. ...because...	4. So...
mad	say it's time for a test		-Can we talk?
calm	tease me		-Please stop.
upset	rush me		-I'm going to...
happy	compliment me	...I think you are trying to get even with me.	-How can we work this out?
proud	say it's my fault		
scared	ask me to write things down	...it hurts to have a friend do that.	-Please _____ instead.
worried	make me do something over		
relieved	tell me to do 3 things at once	...it makes me think you don't like me anymore.	-What can we do about this?
excited	ask me to do chores before TV		
jealous	don't listen to me	...it makes me think that what I say is not important.	-Are you willing to try & work this problem out?
nervous	aren't fair to me		
anxious	interrupt me	...I get confused.	
confused	listen to me		
miserable	help me	...I think I can do a great job.	
frustrated	read to me	...I think that nothing I can do pleases you.	
aggravated	yell at me		
embarrassed	play with me		

Blaming You Messages

_____
Name

Using these "Blaming You" messages as a start, turn each one around into a more appropriate "I" Message.

You didn't give me enough time to finish.

_____

Nobody understands this homework!

_____

You never gave me a turn!

_____

When you don't know the rules, how can you be out?

_____

He makes me so mad!

_____

But, everybody was talking in the cafeteria!

_____

You're not fair! (It's not fair!)

_____

You think you know everything! You're so bossy!

_____

Mom, you love him best!

_____

You always think I have to be PERFECT!

Situation Prompts

Place in line	Swings at recess
Turn at bat	Chores at home
Job well done	Clean-up in classroom
Picking a captain	Got in trouble at home or school
Helped someone	Create your own

 233

I CAN!

PARENTS

Situation: _____

I feel _____

when you _____

because _____

so _____

Brother, sister or teammate

Situation: _____

I feel _____

when you _____

because _____

so _____

TEACHER

Situation: _____

I feel _____

when you _____

because _____

so _____

This week our Objectives included:

☆ Communication includes words, facial expressions & body language.
☆ People communicate more effectively when they notice others' body language.
☆ It's easier to communicate when you maintain eye contact & ask questions.
☆ It's possible to make comments without blaming or accusing others.
☆ It's important to ask for what you want or need in a positive way.
☆ Using an "I" message ("I feel... when...because.") is one way to take responsibility for your own feelings, thoughts & behaviors.

"Coach," please be on the lookout for times when I have used these skills at school.

Getting the Signals Straight! Communication

High 5's

This week I noticed _____ practicing the skills & ideas in the "Objectives." I've circled on the left the areas I've seen improvement in this week. Below are compliments that "celebrate" his or her good behavior.

_____   _____
Teacher's Signature   Date

This week our Objectives included:

☆ Communication includes words, facial expressions & body language.
☆ People communicate more effectively when they notice others' body language.
☆ It's easier to communicate when you maintain eye contact & ask questions.
☆ It's possible to make comments without blaming or accusing others.
☆ It's important to ask for what you want or need in a positive way.
☆ Using an "I" message ("I feel... when...because.") is one way to take responsibility for your own feelings, thoughts & behaviors.

"Coach," please be on the lookout for times when I have used these skills at school.

Getting the Signals Straight! Communication

High 5's

This week I noticed _____ practicing the skills & ideas in the "Objectives." I've circled on the left the areas I've seen improvement in this week. Below are compliments that "celebrate" his or her good behavior.

_____   _____
Teacher's Signature   Date

 235

HOME PRACTICE

This week's **"Objectives"** for *Getting the Signals Straight!* are:

✰ Communication includes words, facial expressions & body language.

✰ People communicate more effectively when they notice others' body language.

✰ It's easier to communicate when you maintain eye contact & ask questions.

✰ It's possible to make comments without blaming or accusing others.

✰ It's important to ask for what you want or need in a positive way.

✰ Using an "I" message ("I feel… when…because.") is one way to take responsibility for your own feelings, thoughts & behaviors.

The home practice on the other side is to help your child apply these skills in "real-life" situations. Please help record your child's ideas. **Your child will receive points in group for returning this completed & signed sheet.**

High 5's

I noticed my child applying ideas from **"Objectives"** learned this week **or in previous weeks.**

Compliments & Comments:

_____

_____

_____

_____

_____   _____
Parent's Signature   Date Due Back

From Your Number ONE FAN

TEAMING UP WITH FRIENDS

CONNECTING TO THE REAL WORLD

There is a difference between "hot dogging it" and being a member of a winning team. While the first keeps a person in the spotlight, the second allows that person to share the spotlight and glory. You've heard it said that winning isn't everything. When it comes to having and keeping friends, it's how you play the game that counts! A good team player respects other people's territory during the game, expects to see disagreements, learns how to compromise with players, meets expectations of referees and coaches, and tries to avoid blowing up because of penalties that occur. Think of some professional sports figures who come to mind when you think of good team players. Also, in professional sports, coaches often use game videos to help players self evaluate their performance so they can do better the next time. Friendship skills in real life take practice too.

 237

OBJECTIVES

Students will participate in activites designed to emphasize the following concepts and skills:

I need to respect other people's space.
Teamwork takes trust and noticing what others need.
Even good friends disagree sometimes.
It is important to learn how to solve conflicts respectfully.
I am a good sport when I communicate, compromise, and cool off before reacting.

PROCEDURE

Pregame Warmup

☆ As students enter the room, accept "High 5" forms and completed Home Practice sheets.
☆ Tally points using your selected method.
☆ Wearing your coach's hat and whistle, review group rules and point system.
☆ Briefly review "Connecting to the Real World" and Objectives.
☆ Introduce the selected activity for the week.

Activities
(choose one or more of the following)

Activity 12.1   Bubbles/Space Invaders
Activity 12.2   Shark Attack
Activity 12.3   Sink or Swim
Activity 12.4   Diving Through Hoops

Post Game Commentary

☆ Tally and record individual points gained during group.
☆ Encourage students to give one another "High 5's" by verbalizing ways in which they have seen each other be especially positive or helpful in group that day.
☆ Announce housekeeping details (any change in meeting date and time).
☆ Give students "High 5" reinforcement sheets to give to their teachers.

EXTENSIONS

High 5's for Teachers
Home Practice Backing for Parents

Activity 12.1 - Bubbles/Space Invaders

EQUIPMENT

Jar of bubble solution with wand
"Staying in Your Lane" Home Practice sheet

GAME PLAN

1. Select one student to demonstrate blowing a big bubble as he or she possibly can. As the bubble is blown, the group leader suddenly pops the bubble, invading the child's "space." The group leader apologizes and the group leader invites the child to try again, promptly popping the bubble again.

2. Discuss with the child how it felt when the bubble was popped. Ask what the student would have done if the group leader had been another kid who did that. Point out that popping the bubble is one way of "invading" another person's space without permission. Conclude by letting the same child complete a bubble without any interference and share how it felt.

3. Extend discussion to include the idea that a person who invades your space or is "in your face" is usually one that others don't like to be around for very long. Discuss other ways that people can invade one's space (loud voices, physical roughness, name calling). Expand the metaphor of the bubble by describing everyone having an "invisible" bubble around him or her that represents their personal space.

4. Allow each child to blow a bubble, after having described how much "space" they would like to have. What is their "comfort zone?" For example, do they want people to pop their bubble before it is released from the wand, to stand back and pop the bubble later when it is in the air, or not to pop it at all?

5. Next, explain that there are times when it's okay for a friend to enter your bubble space (i.e., hugs, high fives, when working closely on a project, shoulder to shoulder). But, at other times, you may feel like someone has popped your bubble and entered your space without your permission (i.e., shoving in line, taking something from your desk, standing too close to you, pulling on you to get your attention.)

6. Ask students to role play the following situations to demonstrate "comfort zones."

   ☆ a boy and girl working on a school project in class
   ☆ two people that don't get along well   ☆ or two close friends
   ☆ a teacher correcting behavior   ☆ or a teacher answering a question
   ☆ lining up in the cafeteria   ☆ or playing a board game with a friend

DISCUSSION

☆ How do other people let you know if you're getting too close and invading their space?
☆ How do you let others know?
☆ Is interrupting a person like invading their space?
☆ Suppose you wanted to give a hug to a friend who didn't want to be hugged. What could you do?
☆ Name four or five ways to show that you like someone without "poppong their bubble."

HOME PRACTICE

Have students take *"Staying in Your Lane"* Home Practice sheets to complete with their parents. Return for points.

Staying in Your Lane

When swimmers race, officials make sure they stay in their own space by creating lanes with special ropes in the pool In the bubbles below, write or draw how you could stay in your own lane (that is, recognize & respect limits) with the following people.

brother or sister

mom or dad

neighbor

kid in class

_____
Name

Activity 12.2 - Shark Attack

EQUIPMENT

Eight three-foot lengths of twine or rope, each tied into a loop
Large open space
(Optional) toy helicopter, boat, or Coast Guard rescue flag
"No Man is an Island" Home Practice sheet

GAME PLAN

1. The group leader sets the scene by explaining: "You have been swimming with friends in an area that's suddenly become infested with sharks. But this area also has sandbars where you can stay to avoid danger. The sandbars can also change as the tides move in and out. Your job is stay safe on a sandbar until rescue help arrives. Our goal as a group will be to ensure the safety of all group members."

2. The group leader then arranges loops on the floor, about two to three feet apart if possible, to represent the sandbars. Ask each student to step onto one of the sandbars (or in the loop).

3. Explain that each time you announce, "TIDE'S OUT!" they have to move to another sandbar. Without announcing it, the group leader quietly removes a loop with each tide change. Students may need to be encouraged to share their space creatively to reach their group goal (safety of all members).

4. Keep playing till all members are on one sandbar or until a member is lost. Then, announce that the Coast Guard has arrived to help.

NOTE: This game has been adapted from the interactive group game "All Aboard" that can be found in *Silver Bullets* (see bibliography).

DISCUSSION

☆ If your group was not successful the first time, process and discuss strategies for improvement. Repeat activity and discuss again.
☆ Did anyone get eaten by the sharks? If so, how did that person feel about the group?
☆ What did it take to keep others safe?
☆ What helped you to share your space?
☆ What made it difficult to share space?
☆ Did you feel like your space was being invaded?
☆ Is there anyone in the group you'd like to compliment or thank?
☆ What are some real life situations when it's important to share your space?
☆ What are examples of real life situations when you or another person would not feel comfortable having your space invaded?

HOME PRACTICE

Have students take *"No Man is an Island"* Home Practice sheets to complete with their parents. Return for points.

No Man Is An Island

Please ask your child to describe the activity, "Shark Attack" that we did together in group. Then, discuss & complete the following questions together. All involve understanding when it's appropriate (or not) to share your space or be in close physical contact with others.

Name _____

Name some times when it's ok to work or play with someone in a small space.

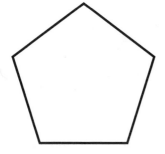   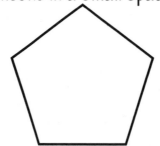   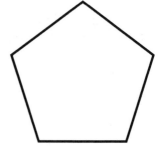

Name some times when people really "need their space"

_____   _____   _____

What are some "signals" that people send to let others know they feel uncomfortable being crowded.
(Please include words, body language & actions they might use)

Which sports activities provide the most individual space?

_____   _____   _____

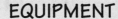

Activity 12.3 - Sink or swim

EQUIPMENT
Ten to twenty empty aluminum cans with one undertow card for each
Blindfold
Overhead marking pen
"Sink or Swim: You Can Count on Me" Home Practice sheet

GAME PLAN

1. As a group, brainstorm a list of things that can cause a friendship to "sink."

2. Record your ideas on each of the undertow cards.

3. Divide the group into pairs and have them decide who will be "A" and who will be "B."

4. Set the scene by explaining that today your group is on an international swim team that's crossing the English Channel. The channel has areas that have dangerous undertows that can pull you under. Some members of the team have experience in successfully swimming this channel. Pretend you're the new man on the team and a dense fog has rolled in. You must now trust your experienced partner to guide you past the whirlpools and undertows. You have a few minutes to discuss strategy before crossing. You will be blindfolded (in the fog) and your guide will stand across the channel giving directions out loud to help you swim and not sink. The rest of the team will watch carefully to make sure you are safe.

5. The group leader then arranges the empty aluminum cans "in the channel" (on the floor) and balances on top of each can an undertow card upon which has been written a danger to friendship.

6. Explain that the "A" partner will be the first swimmer and "B's" the first guides.

7. Blindfold the first "swimmer" and place their partner at the other end of the obstacle course. The goal is to cross as safely as possible by avoiding the undertows of friendship (i.e., by not tipping the can).

8. Consider developing a system for "partial credit" of a one, two, or three rating if few cans are tipped.

9. When all "A" swimmers have crossed, reverse roles and let "A's" become guides as "B's" swim across.

NOTE: This activity is adapted from "Minefield" from Silver Bullets (see bibliography).

DISCUSSION
☆ Did it seem like the swimmer trusted the guide?
☆ What did the guide do that helped? (focus on evidence of awareness and sensitivity)
☆ What else could the guide have done to communicate more clearly?
☆ What are some real life situations in which it helps to trust and depend upon a friend?
☆ What things can happen to interfere with trust?
☆ Depending on time allowed and eagerness of the group, you may choose to do most of the debriefing after all the swimmers have crossed, or you may choose to do so after each crossing.

HOME PRACTICE

Have students take "Sink or Swim - You Can Count on Me" Home Practice sheets to complete with their parents. Return for points.

Sink or Swim: You Can Count on Me

_____
Name

Things I trust
my **dad** to do:

_____

_____

_____

_____

Things I trust
my **mom** to do:

_____

_____

_____

_____

The **friend** I trust
most is:

_____

because:

_____

_____

_____

Things I trust my
teacher to do:

_____

_____

_____

_____

People know that I can be trusted when I
(keep private things private, do what I say I will do, tell
the truth, respect people's property, do my part, etc.)

_____

_____

_____

_____

_____

_____

_____

Trust is important
because:

_____

_____

_____

_____

D
A
N
G
E
R

UNDERTOW

CAN
CAUSE
A
FRIENDSHIP
TO SINK!

D
A
N
G
E
R

UNDERTOW

CAN
CAUSE
A
FRIENDSHIP
TO SINK!

Activity 12.4 - Diving through Hoops

EQUIPMENT

Hula hoop
Stop watch
"Diving Thru Hoops" Home Practice sheet
"The Value of Game Playing" Parent handout

GAME PLAN

1. Explain that today we will pretend to be an aquatic team whose goal is to learn how to dive through hoops without losing a single team member. Join with group members to form a circle. Hold hands and place a hula hoop over your arm and ask how many think the entire team can pass through this hoop without breaking hand contact.

2. If a team member gets "lost" (breaks hand contact), the group will have to start over. After the hoop has passed completely around the circle successfully, give the group positive feedback and/or solicit possible comments from members.

3. Challenge the group to guess how quickly (within a matter of seconds or minutes) the whole group could "dive through" the hoop. Have group reach a consensus on a time goal.

4. Use a stopwatch or second hand on clock to time the group.

5. Celebrate reaching goal. Elicit strategies for continued improvement and repeat if possible.

DISCUSSION

☆ During a game, there are many different ways for each player to respond to those around him or her.
☆ Have students brainstorm some of these different ways and list on board and discuss (using the "Diving Thru Hoops" Home Practice sheet as a guide if necessary).
☆ Which items listed on the board did the group actually do?
☆ What helped the team be successful? What did people say or do to encourage one another?
☆ Is there someone in the group you would like to compliment for their good sportsmanship?
☆ Were there any ways in which teamwork could have been better?
☆ Did we "lose" any players?
☆ Another way that a team can lose a player is if a member gives up and quits trying because they feel left out, discouraged, or put down. Did this happen in our group today? (If it did, encourage apologies and acceptance of apologies using "I" Messages).
☆ Has this ever happened in a group you've been in before?
☆ What responsibilities do you as a group member have to the team?

NOTE: This activity has been adapted from "Hula Hoop Pass" (Adventure Based Resource Index System, #825). You can have students play common games (like cards, dominoes, or checkers) and make a "Conflict" card to pull out if a problem arises. Explain that you will observe to see how students resolve the conflict using positive teamwork. Resolutions will be discussed when the game is completed.

HOME PRACTICE

Have students take "Diving Through Hoops" Home Practice sheets to complete with their parents. Return for points. Also send home to parents the handout, "The Value of Game Playing."

Diving Through Hoops!

From the list, find the ways an Olympic-quality athlete chooses to act when on a team. **Write them in the Olympic circles.**

NOTE TO PARENTS:

Play a game with your child this week & put a star by all the positive ways he or she chooses to behave while playing!

Blame
Fight
Explain
Apologize
Cool Off
Back Off
Talk Calmly
"Hog" the Equipment
Knee-jerk Reactions
Use Healthy Humor
See Only One Point of View
Let Others Have Their Way
Keep Focusing on Hassle
Insist on Your Own Way
See Other's Point of View
"Me First" Attitude
"Let Go of Hassle"
Stop & Think
Yell at Others
Be Sarcastic
Compromise
Get Angry
Take Turns
Face Off

_____
_____

THE VALUE OF GAME PLAYING

One of the hallmark characteristics of children with ADHD is their marked immaturity in game situations. Their lack of impulse control, excitability, and tendency to overreact quickly can turn a board game into a battlefield. Peers and siblings often do not tolerate such behaviors for very long. So, it is important that parents take the time to strengthen their child's ability to interact with others in a game format. With computerized games so popular today, children may be missing out on playing simpler, more interactive games. Of which games do you have the fondest memories? You learned a lot about yourself and how to get along with others when you had to deal with friendly competition and challenges. Some lessons were more subtle - how to be a gracious winner or loser, or how to read the looks on other players' faces. It wasn't all just about winning.

Children with ADHD can learn many skills from the issues and themes that arise during the process of playing games. For instance, all games require players to follow or operate within certain boundaries. Being able to live within the boundaries of set rules is a critical lesson we all must learn. Honesty, a sense of fair play, persistence, the ability to accept disappointing "set backs," a sense of compassion or empathy for the loser, and the ability to put winning into perspective are all character traits that gradually emerge as players increase in mature. There are other practical lessons to be learned from successful game playing: the importance of listening to and following directions, the need to pay attention to the order of play, and the art.. The critical skill of learning to express feelings appropriately (from anger to excitement) can be refined in the arena of interactive games.

Before you jump into the potential maelstrom of playing games with your child, take time to plan your own strategies. Consider these helpful "coaching" hints:

1. Play a game with your child many times before you can expect him or her to play it successfully with another child. Coach and cue behaviors until your child is more confident with skills.

2. Have your child get to the point where he or she can tell you the rules in their own words.

3. Set behavioral ground rules for play and have a plan for how to handle blatant disregard for the rules. Verbalize your own discomfort if your child shows anger inappropriately during play.

4. At first, set short time limits. Children with ADHD tend to want to quit immediately when they see that they are not going to win. Lengthen times gradually so as not to set them up for failure.

5. De-emphasize the winning and losing of games; stress enjoy the time together .

6. Compliment sportsmanlike conduct! Make additional suggestions if needed.

7. Model constructive ways to cope with making mistakes and expressing disappointment.

8. Don't always let them win - life is not that way. Don't always beat the socks off them because life shouldn't be that way either.

9. After the game, talk about what you both liked, what was frustrating and how you'd play it differently the next time.

10. When your child begins to mature, allow him to ask a friend to play with both of you. Be ready to "step in" and call for a time out or ending the game if needed. Good luck as you and your child engage one another on the playing field!

This week our Objectives included:

☆ It is important to respect others' space.
☆ Teamwork requires trusting others & being aware of their needs.
☆ Even good friends will disagree at times.
☆ It is important to learn how to solve conflicts in respectful ways.
☆ A good sport communicates well, compromises, & cools off before reacting.

"Coach," please be on the lookout for times when I have used these skills at school.

Teaming Up With Friends!
Friendship

High 5's

This week I noticed _____ practicing the skills & ideas in the "Objectives." I've circled on the left the areas I've seen improvement in this week. Below are compliments that "celebrate" his or her good behavior.

_____   _____
Teacher's Signature   Date

This week our Objectives included:

☆ It is important to respect others' space.
☆ Teamwork requires trusting others & being aware of their needs.
☆ Even good friends will disagree at times.
☆ It is important to learn how to solve conflicts in respectful ways.
☆ A good sport communicates well, compromises, & cools off before reacting.

"Coach," please be on the lookout for times when I have used these skills at school.

Teaming Up With Friends!
Friendship

High 5's

This week I noticed _____ practicing the skills & ideas in the "Objectives." I've circled on the left the areas I've seen improvement in this week. Below are compliments that "celebrate" his or her good behavior.

_____   _____
Teacher's Signature   Date

HOME PRACTICE

This week's **"Objectives"** for _Teaming Up With Friends!_ are:

☆ It is important to respect others' space.
☆ Teamwork requires trusting others & being aware of their needs.
☆ Even good friends will disagree at times.
☆ It is important to learn how to solve conflicts in respectful ways.
☆ A good sport communicates well, compromises, & cools off before reacting.

The home practice on the other side is to help your child apply these skills in "real-life" situations. Please help record your child's ideas. **Your child will receive points in group for returning this completed & signed sheet.**

High 5's

I noticed my child applying ideas from **"Objectives"** learned this week **or in previous weeks.**

Compliments & Comments:

_____

_____

_____

_____

_____   _____

Parent's Signature   Date Due Back

From Your Number ONE FAN

THE LIFELONG TREK - GOING THE DISTANCE

CONNECTING TO THE REAL WORLD

During our time together, we've discussed many connections to the real world. Again, who are those players we've really been talking about each week? Us, of course, and we are still playing this important game of "Life." We continue to experience winning plays and painful defeats. We're still in training to improve on our personal bests in many areas of our lives. We're still valuable players on our school, sports, friends, family and church teams. We are discovering that some of our best coaches are teachers, parents, doctors, and friends who will help us find structure in our lives.

As we have gotten to know ourselves and others better in our group activities, we have been able to recognize our own and others' strengths and limitations. Now, when we are unhappy with our personal performance in an area, we know that we can choose to either make excuses and give up or make a plan to change. It's an on-going challenge to accept ourselves and each other.

We have been discovering some of the abilities we were born with and have worked to develop and practice other skills like: handling feelings, listening, paying attention, controlling impulses, relaxing, communicating clearly, cooperating with others, and setting goals for ourselves. As we "go the distance" on this lifelong trek, we need to take the opportunity to learn as much as we can about all parts of ourselves, including what it's like to have ADHD. As we gain insight, we'll know ourselves better and be able to capitalize on our strengths and compensate for things that hold us back. But most of all, we must remember that winning in life means never giving up.

OBJECTIVES

Students will participate in activites designed to emphasize the following concepts and skills:

Learning about how I think, feel, and act is one way that I and others with ADHD
maintain a healthy perspective as we work toward success in our lives.
I have personal characteristics that can be positive or negative depending on how and
within what situations I use these traits.
It is important to know about ADHD without using it as an excuse.
Believing in myself and being persistent may be one of the most important abilities I have.
I can learn to work with others in a group to accomplish many tasks.

PROCEDURE

Pregame Warmup

☆ As students enter the room, accept "High 5"
forms and completed Home Practice sheets.
☆ Tally points using your selected method.
☆ Wearing your coach's hat and whistle, review
group rules and point system.
☆ from previous week.
☆ Review "Connecting to the Real World" and
Objectives.
☆ Introduce this week's activity.

Activities

(choose one or more of the following)

Activity 13.1   Doctor's Visit
Activity 13.2   Famous Flops

Post Game Commentary

☆ Tally and record individual points gained during game. Distribute final rewards.
☆ Encourage students to give one another "High 5's" in written form.
☆ Announce details about group ending celebration activity if one is planned.
☆ Have students make thank-you notes to teachers & parents for all the "High 5's" they completed!

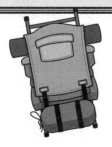

EXTENSIONS

High 5's for Teachers
Home Practice Backing for Parents

Activity 13.1 - Doctor's Visit

GAME PLAN

1. Consider arranging for a medical expert in the area of ADHD to come and speak with group members. Give the students an opportunity to share what they have learned in the group and ask the doctor to do a brief overview of ADHD and be prepared to answer questions students may have. (Touch base with parents to see if they are comfortable having their child attend this activity. If some students are not included, consider scheduling it at an alternate time, like lunch).

2. If you are unable to have a speaker, refer to the "*I've Got What?*" dialogue sheet for information to share. Have students draw questions from a bag that you as an "expert" answer, or for younger children, you may want to use a child and adult puppet to role play a child's visit to the doctor's office.

3. As a closing activity, select one of the inspirational stories mentioned in the equipment list (or choose one of your own favorites) to share with the group.

DISCUSSION

☆ What was something new that you learned today from our visitor (puppet or real doctor)?
☆ Have you ever known anyone who has overcome obstacles like the ones described in the story we've shared today?
☆ How can reading about other people and their experiences be helpful to us?
☆ Have you ever heard someone use ADHD as an excuse?
☆ How do other people react when someone is making excuses?
☆ What is the difference between an excuse and an explanation? (Emphasize that using an explanation too frequently turns into excuse making…)
☆ Emphasize that explanations, although truthful and valid, don't eliminate consequences. (A stretched muscle may explain why you didn't make it to second base, but you're out just the same!)

HOME PRACTICE

Have students take "*Excuses or Explanations*" Home Practice sheet to complete with parents. Return for points (if this is not going to be your last session).

EXCUSES OR EXPLANATIONS?

Sometimes, people make mistakes or don't do what others expect of them. When you "mess up," do you try and give an "excuse" for your choices or behavior, or do you accept responsibility for your actions, while possible giving an "explanation" of what happened. There is a subtle difference between the two responses. For each statement below, write in the blank whether you think the person is offering an **EXCUSE** or an **EXPLANATION**.

_____ "Everybody else was doing it!"

_____ "I thought it was finished."

_____ "My medicine ran out."

_____ "I had to go to the doctor's office."

_____ "I didn't hear the directions."

_____ "I don't feel good, so I can't do _____."

_____ "I forgot...."

_____ "I did it, but it got lost."

_____ "I forgot because I didn't write it down."

_____ "I didn't spend much time on the project."

_____ "You never told me to do that."

_____ "I'm busy; I'll do it later."

Make up an example of an excuse someone might give:

_____
_____.

Give an example of an explanation someone might give.

_____
_____.

Note to Parents: Please discuss with your child how using explanations too frequently tends to turn them into excuses, because this too frequent use indicates the person is not working toward change. Also, review that explanations, though truthful and valid, don't negate consequences. Finally, discuss the fact that peers and adults tend to get angry when excuses rather than explanations are given.

"I'VE GOT WHAT?"

A Physician's Dialogue with Children Diagnosed with ADHD

Professionals are doing a better and better job of educating teachers and parents about what ADHD involves - from characteristics to what causes it and how to deal with it. However, we often fail to involve that essential ingredient of the child. For several years now, Dr. John Burnside, a psychiatrist practicing in San Antonio, has been doing a community service by taking his "Brain on Tour" talk to local elementary schools teaching fourth or fifth grade students about how the brain functions and the importance of avoiding drugs. For the past three years, he has willingly agreed to speak at a special session to our third, fourth, and fifth grade students on campus who are currently taking medication for ADHD and to answer whatever questions they might have about this condition and the treatment for it. Below is a synopsis of his talk with the students. He is also considering making a commercially available videotape directed toward children themselves.

"What is ADHD?"

ADHD stands for "Attention Deficit Hyperactivity Disorder." ADHD is a medical problem, like diabetes or asthma are medical conditions. ADHD kids are not bad kids - but they can look like kids who are not trying very hard or who are doing inappropriate things on purpose. Kids with ADHD are usually not noticed as having any differences until they start school and then may have a big problem with daydreaming instead of concentrating and staying on task.

"Does having ADHD mean you're dumb or retarded or sick or something?"

No! In fact, some of the smartest kids I've ever seen have had ADHD. They can be just as successful as they want to be! But sometimes they need help to reach their true potential.

"How come there's mostly boys here today?"

Well, fewer girls than boys have ADHD. Some people think it is about ten times more common in boys than in girls. But, doctors are finding that more and more girls have ADHD, especially the kind without hyperactivity. About 5% of all children have ADHD. Boys are more commonly diagnosed than girls.

"How can you tell if you have ADHD?"

Well, there are several things that ADHD kids usually have in common:
- ☆ a short attention span
- ☆ easily distracted
- ☆ very impulsive (like doing something first and thinking second), and sometimes, very hyperactive (though not everybody has this part).
- ☆ They may also be disorganized, forgetful, and hate writing!

There can be lots of reasons kids act in these ways, and it takes a doctor who knows a lot about ADHD to tell for sure if this is what kids have. Teachers and parents and kids can't tell just by looking.

"Is there something different about my brain if I have ADHD?"

Perhaps. There is a doctor in San Antonio, Dr. Steven Pliszka, who has done research in this area; and there are doctors all over the country doing brain research trying to see what the differences might be. All of the work is not completed yet, but scientists are working with the part of the brain whose job it is to help people pay attention and screen out other things happening around them and to sit still and to think before acting. Researchers think that in "ADHD brains," the part of the brain that acts like a "filter" may not be working as well as it should; that it is "under stimulated." It's almost like as it develops, this part of the brain is not growing as fast as we would like it to. For some kids, their brain will eventually "grow out" of this condition as a teenager or as a grownup. Other kids never seem to grow out of it but can learn ways to cope.

"What can a person do if they have ADHD to make it better, especially if they might not grow out of it?"

Well, that's for a doctor to help them and their folks to figure out. Doctors have learned that if we take a medicine that works as a "stimulant," it will help that part of the brain that controls attention, impulses, and activity level to do its job better. Some of you may take Ritalin, Dexedrine, or Cylert; and they are medicines that work this way. Other medicines work differently. There is a Dr. Edward Hallowell who has written a couple of books about ADHD who says that taking medicine for ADHD is like wearing glasses to correct nearsightedness.

"Do these medicines have any side effects?"

Sometimes they do, but some kids have no side effects at all. That's why you can't just walk into a drug store and pick them up "across the shelf." These medications need to be monitored by a doctor. The side effects that are reported by some people are lack of appetite, trouble getting to sleep at night, or maybe having headaches for the first few days you take the medicine. But, remember, many kids never have ANY side effects. If side effects do happen, the doctor can help by changing the amount of medicine. About 95% of the time, the doctor can find exactly the right kind of medicine to help. Sometimes, you hear on TV or read in the newspaper bad things about kids using Ritalin, but these bad things don't happen when a doctor is in control of the medicine. Doctors think that when Ritalin is being used properly, it is even safer than aspirin for kids!

"How do doctors figure out how much a kid should take?"

Usually doctors start by how much the person keeps the dose as small as possible. But as a kid grows, he or she usually needs more of the medicine. I knew a fifth grade boy once who had ADHD and his sisters in first grade had it too. He said he was confused because they took even more medication each day than he did and he was bigger! So, I explained to him that sometimes there is more involved in figuring out the dose than just what a person weighed, and that was why it was so important that a person with a doctor's training be in charge of how much medicine to take.

"How does the medicine work exactly? Does it make the brain develop faster?"

Now that's the hard part! Doctors know some medicines work, but they don't know exactly how. They know it helps to stimulate the part of the brain that helps us pay attention, but the medicine doesn't help the brain develop more quickly. Taking medicine does not "cure" the ADHD, it just helps the brain work better while the medicine is in the body. Scientists are even beginning to think that more than just one part of the brain may be involved. Our brains are so complicated that it is taking many years of medical research to figure out an exact answer. But since this is becoming known as the "Decade of the Brain," I bet we can find out soon.

"Does taking my pill make me behave? and How come people are always asking me if I've taken my medicine today?"

Wow, I wish a pill could make a person behave! But no, it doesn't work that way. Like we said before, the pill helps your brain to focus like a pair of glasses helps someone's eyes to see things more clearly. But just like a person who sees clearly with his glasses can choose to look out the window instead of reading his book, the ADHD person who is able to focus better with his pill still has the power to choose how he is going to act.

Now about the second part of your question, your mom, dad or teacher might sometimes ask you if you've taken your pill because they notice changes in your level of paying attention, sitting still, staying on task, or talking softly; and they are not sure if you are choosing to do these things or if you're having trouble controlling yourself because the medication has worn off. But, remember, it's really important not to use having ADHD or forgetting to take your medicine as an excuse for making poor choices.

"Is there anything besides medicine that helps?"

You bet! Sometimes, being in a smaller class helps or working in an area like CMC (Content Mastery Center) helps because it is very quiet there and has fewer distractions. Having reminder lists help kids and adults who have ADHD to be less forgetful; and learning how to structure their day and practicing hard to stick to the structure really helps. Sometimes it helps to have somebody "coach" them in learning new skills. Also, doing what you are doing today - learning more about ADHD - makes it easier to understand and live with.

"I have ADHD and sometimes I have a hard time reading. Does ADHD cause my reading problems?"

Good question! Actually, ADHD does not cause reading problems exactly. But if you aren't paying attention to details and taking time to read directions, reading work gets harder. Also, sometimes kids who have ADHD might have another medical condition called a "learning disability" or "dyslexia" that can cause them to have a hard time in a particular area like reading, spelling, writing, or doing math problems. Since the brain is kind of like a complicated computer, its wiring sometimes can get crossed up and make learning difficult. But, kids who have a learning disability are not dumb or stupid; they have a harder time learning exactly like other students. They may need different ways of learning, just like ADHD kids may need a different way of learning too. Many famous and "smart" people have even had a learning disability (like Winston Churchill, Albert Einstein, President Woodrow Wilson, or actors Tom Cruise and Dustin Hoffman).

"Well, exactly how do you get ADHD? Can you catch it?"

I'm glad you asked that question. Usually, a person is born with ADHD; they can't "catch" it from somebody else. It is - hold on now for a really big word - a "neurodevelopmental" difference in the brain. Like a lot of other medical conditions, you can have a little bit of ADHD or a whole lot of it. Often, if it is mild, that person will not need any medicine and will outgrow the ADHD or will learn to "compensate" or make up for the difficulties in paying attention and being active. If it is severe, that person usually does not outgrow the ADHD and can usually respond best to medicine. We have found that even people without ADHD can pay a little better attention on special medication because every brain responds a little bit to it. But, a person with a lot of ADHD notices a lot of difference in the ability to pay attention when they are on the medicine.

"Are kids with ADHD really just allergic to food coloring or sugar?"

Well, I know a lot of parents think that, but almost all of the scientific research says no. There may be a small percent of ADHD that is due to a severe allergy or diet, but that would be very, very rare. It is not proven in research, but most parents and teachers think that lots of sugar will cause kids to be hyper. Kids with ADHD may crave sugar, but they are not usually allergic to it and sugar does not cause ADHD.

"Is there anything good about having ADHD?"

Absolutely! Many people think that those who have ADHD tend to be more creative than the average person. Steven Spielberg and Robin Williams, are reported to have ADHD, and look how creative they are! People with ADHD learn to use the creative parts of their brain more and that part of the brain is not really affected by the ADHD. And, some doctors, like Dr. Edward Hallowell and Dr. John Ratey, the successful psychiatrists who have written books on ADHD and even have ADHD themselves, say that they think this whole thing is named all wrong! They think it's not a "deficit" (like, not something missing), but just a "difference" in how people learn, a difference in learning styles that is still based on a difference in people's brains. They even say that sometimes when people pay close attention, they have "ASD" or "Attention Surplus Disorder!" (Ha! Ha!) In addition to being very creative, many people with ADHD notice small details that other people miss and they usually are enthusiastic and energetic people! They can also "hyperfocus" on stuff they are really interested in (like Super NES games).

Dr. Hallowell gives a theory in one of his books about ADHD that explains how he thinks America was settled by people who had ADHD tendencies. These people were unhappy with the way things were in Europe and were willing to take a chance to find a better life. Thom Hartmann is a scientist who has a theory that people with ADHD used to have a great advantage during "caveman" days. Their ability to "hyperfocus" and notice small details in their environment probably helped them be better hunters! So you see, many people see lots of benefits to having some ADHD characteristics!

Thank you for giving me a chance to answer your questions today! You have all asked some really smart questions! If you think of other questions after I have gone, be sure to ask your counselor, your parents, or your own doctor the next time you go for a checkup.

© 2001, McDougall & Roper

Activity 13.2 - Famous Flops

GAME PLAN

1. Explain to students that for the final session today, they will have a last opportunity to participate together in a problem solving activity. Using the analogy of continuing to go the distance on this lifelong trek, tell the students: "Pretend that you are a group of space travelers who are stranded on a planet with no oxygen. After your space craft has landed because of mechanical difficulties, you realize that there is a remote outpost that will be able to help your group if you can travel across hazardous territory to get there. Your group has a "lifeline" and plenty of oxygen to make the trek. All of you must go, because there will not be enough air on your spaceship to keep any one person alive for long. Try to move as a group to the outpost without breaking your oxygen lifeline. Have students stand fairly close together and run a single, continuous piece of masking tape around the group, going in and out, over and around, up and down their arms, legs, shoulders, etc. in a random fashion. (Tape only on top of clothing to avoid painful removal of tape and/or body hair!)

2. Have students go from point A to point B without braking the tape. (You may decide to do this activity inside as opposed to outside. One year, a group actually worked so well together that they were able to crawl through a playground gym and survived intact!)

3. Ask discussion questions from below.

4. Have students return inside Using the "Famous Flops" handout that describes famous people who have experienced failure, but overcame these temporary setbacks to by their own persistence and determination, have students read situations and guess who the people are. You may choose to cut the boxes out and put them into a bag to draw from or just have students read directly from the sheet.

5. If you are planning a student-parent "Celebration" culminating group event (see "Parent Section" on pages 265- 278 for details), discuss details and distribute reservation forms..

DISCUSSION

☆ How difficult was it to move from one place to another as a totally connected group?
☆ Was there anyone in our group who really helped us to be successful in this activity? How?
☆ How do you think you would have done in this activity if we had done it the first week we met together? How has our group changed? Have we as individuals changed also?
☆ What five things have you learned from our group meetings?
☆ What were your most favorite activities?
☆ What could you change about the group to make it better?

HOME PRACTICE

Have students take home the reservation form for the family "Celebration" activity if you have not already sent it home.

Famous Flops

(Most of these "failure stories" are adapted from "Consider This" in A 3rd Helping of Chicken Soup for the Soul by Canfield & Hansen).

NEVER GIVE UP! Has anyone ever said that to you? Sometimes we think that our problems are so big that we can never be successful in solving or overcoming them. We are tempted to say, "Yeah, sure. What do they know about problems!" Well, test yourself by reading the following facts about famous people who faced "seemingly insurmountable" problems. Can you guess who they were or are?

1. Which soft drink company, during its first year of business, sold only 400 drinks?

2. Which NBA super-star was actually cut from his high school basketball team?

3. What was different about Rafer Johnson (a decathlon champion) when he was born?

4. Which major league hockey player (trying out for the pros) was told he didn't weigh enough & wouldn't survive on the rink?

5. Which famous world leader was unable to get into Oxford or Cambridge Universities because he was too weak a student?

6. What famous cartoonist, movie-maker and business-man was considered to be a failure for the first half of his life?

10. Which famous U.S. President was considered to be a failure by many people during his lifetime?

7. Which famous author & illustrator of childrens' books had his first book rejected by 27 publishers? (The 28th company published it & sold 6 million copies!)

8. Which young physics student had his doctoral dissertation turned down by his university "as being irrelevant & fanciful"?

9. Who failed at least 1,000 times to prove (in important experiments) that a now-common household item could work?

(The answers are given below in a secret code. After everyone has tried to guess the answers, look at the code to see if you are correct!)

ANSWERS: a. cola coca   b. jordan michael   c. feet club with born   d. gretsky wayne   e. churchill winston   f. disney walt   g. seuss doctor   h. einstein albert   i. edison alva thomas (bulb light)   j. lincoln abe

This week our Objectives included:

☆ Continuing to learn about how I think, feel & act is one way that I can maintain a healthy perspective.

☆ I have personal characteristics that can be positive or negative depending on how & within what situations I use these traits.

☆ It is important for me to know the difference between making an excuse for my behavior & understanding why I tend to behave in certain ways.

☆ Being persistent & believing in myself may be more important than any other abilities I have.

☆ I can learn to work with different & unique individuals to accomplish many tasks.

☆ Groups can benefit from my & others differing points of view.

"Coach," please be on the lookout for times when I have used these skills at school.

The Lifelong Trek - Going the Distance Understanding ADHD - Part 2

High 5's

This week I noticed _____ practicing the skills & ideas in the "Objectives." I've circled on the left the areas I've seen improvement in this week. Below are compliments that "celebrate" his or her good behavior.

_____   _____

Teacher's Signature   Date

This week our Objectives included:

☆ Continuing to learn about how I think, feel & act is one way that I can maintain a healthy perspec tive.

☆ I have personal characteristics that can be positive or negative depending on how & within what situations I use these traits.

☆ It is important for me to know the difference between making an excuse for my behavior & understanding why I tend to behave in certain ways.

☆ Being persistent & believing in myself may be more important than any other abilities I have.

☆ I can learn to work with different & unique individuals to accomplish many tasks.

☆ Groups can benefit from my & others differing points of view.

"Coach," please be on the lookout for times when I have used these skills at school.

The Lifelong Trek - Going the Distance Understanding ADHD - Part 2

High 5's

This week I noticed _____ practicing the skills & ideas in the "Objectives." I've circled on the left the areas I've seen improvement in this week. Below are compliments that "celebrate" his or her good behavior.

_____   _____

Teacher's Signature   Date

HOME PRACTICE

This week's **"Objectives"** for <u>The Lifelong Trek - Going the Distance Understanding ADHD - Part 2</u> are:

☆ Continuing to learn about how I think, feel & act is one way that I can maintain a healthy perspective.

☆ I have personal characteristics that can be positive or negative depending on how & within what situations I use these traits.

☆ It is important for me to know the difference between making an excuse for my behavior & understanding why I tend to behave in certain ways.

☆ Being persistent & believing in myself may be more important than any other abilities I have.

☆ I can learn to work with different & unique individuals to accomplish many tasks.

☆ Groups can benefit from my & others" differing points of view.

The home practice on the other side is to help your child apply these skills in "real-life" situations. Please help record your child's ideas. **<u>Your child will receive points in group for returning this completed & signed sheet.</u>**

High 5's

I noticed my child applying ideas from **"Objectives"** learned this week **or in previous weeks**.

Compliments & Comments:

_____

_____

_____

_____

_____   _____

Parent's Signature   Date Due Back

From Your Number ONE FAN

END-OF-GROUP CELEBRATION ACTIVITY

It is always difficult for children to face the end of a support group. Often, even for a week or two after group has ended, children will show up at the door expecting to meet again. One way to deal with this separation issue is to make a real celebration of the end of group. Sometimes having a "party" with snacks or meeting at lunch to share a pizza or having a special game session together is sufficient. However, if you have chosen to involve parents in supporting their child in this group each week through Home Practice activities and sending in High 5's, it really helps to cement the experience to have an ending that involves both parents and students (and even their teachers if they choose to come). Nancy and fellow counselors, Pat Eddy and Lois Bohl, held family celebration nights at the end of their divorce groups. These events have proven to be so successful that they were adapted as an ending for other groups. A sample celebration night might be set up in the following way:

Send invitations to parents at one of the last two group meetings. Siblings are usually not invited because children with ADHD will need a lot of supervision from and interaction with their parents. Parents who have participated have said that they really appreciated the opportunity to have this special time with their child. Some group leaders choose to work with their cafeteria managers to serve a simple snack meal and have parents pay. Other group leaders have parents sign-up and bring a covered dish and have the school provide dessert and drinks. Beginning with a meal sometimes allows families to get to school a little sooner after work and is a relaxed way to start. Consider starting the evening at 6:00, serving the meal until 7:00, doing center activities from 7:00 until about 8:00, and then taking about fifteen minutes to have parents complete evaluations before your closing remarks. Ask parents to help with clean up if you need assistance.

One focus during the meal is the "*Table Conversation*" cards. It is productive to have parents sit and experience dinner conversations other than "Why did you get in trouble at school today?" Rounding up colorful tablecloths and decorating with small centerpieces make the evening more festive. One year, we asked teachers to bring in table cloths and had more than we needed. And putting out an all-call "plea" over the intercom brought several potted plants and flower arrangements from teachers' desks to help decorate. If the session is held in a large cafeteria, then the dinner tables can be arranged in the center with tables for later activities set up in each corner.

After the families have had an opportunity to arrive, eat their meal and discuss topics, the group leader has a chance to make any comments about the group sessions in general, thank parents for their continued support, etc. Then the leader describes that several stations have been set up in the corners of the cafeteria for parents and their children to visit. Emphasize that the children are to serve as the "guides" for their parents for the evening. One option is to have everything extremely structured and divide families up equally and rotate every fifteen minutes when a timer rings. However, since children who have ADHD may have difficulties with short attention spans and with switching activities, it is probably preferable to ask families to distribute themselves and go from center to center pacing themselves as they choose (avoiding the most crowded centers). Following is a list of some types of activities that could be included that will give children a chance to show off the fun things they did in group or give them an opportunity to interact with parents.

☆ **Role playing center** - This center tends to be the hit of the evening! Place four shopping bags, each with various props and a (laminated) script for a *"Role Reversal"* role play attached to the bags. Following directions on the bags, parents play the child's role and children play the parent's role and then discuss feelings involved and how better to handle the situations.

☆ **Family traditions center** - This activity gives families an opportunity to remember special times that have been significant for them. Traditions can range from simple (having pancakes every Sunday night or having dad rub your head at bedtime) to seasonal (special holiday foods and activities), to playing cards and eating munchies instead of dinner once a month. When several families at a center get into the swing of generating and sharing ideas, parents are often surprised by what their children remember and find significant. Brainstorming a few new traditions allows family members to be creative together.

☆ **Goal setting center** - Parents and children work together to set a family goal using the same type of criteria that students have used earlier in group to set personal goals. This can be difficult for families to do. Encourage them to begin goal setting and follow up at home.

☆ **Game playing center** - This is a good place to lay out any commercial board games you used during group sessions. Let parents know if they are available for them to checkout.

☆ **Attention and memory center** - Include several activities from group (possibly items on a "covered" tray for parents to remember or a memory card game). Children will enjoy seeing their parents rise to these challenges.

☆ **Additional centers** - Make up additional centers to replace those above or to add to them to help your families have some special bonding time that will strengthen the parent-child relationship.

☆ **Closing** - Gather parents in a circle with children watching from behind. Explain that parenting involves "juggling" many responsibilities and that the task is made easier when shared with others. Involve parents in a group juggle of items representing their commitments.

It is probably best to have had students already give you feedback about what they did or didn't like about the group. Parents can choose to complete the brief evaluations before they leave, or may take them to return later. Generally, families enjoy pitching in to help clean up and organize materials in a centralized area for you. They also tend to recognize the extra effort you put in to organize the evening and appreciate the gift of your time as a validation of them and their child!

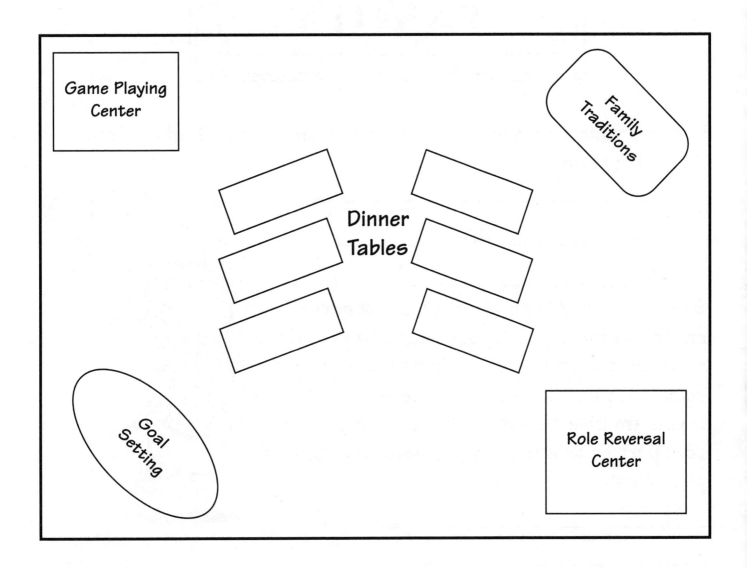

ADMIT ONE
1
FAMILY

You and your child are invited to be present at our "End of Group" Celebration! on

_____

from _____ **until** _____

at _____

Bring a covered dish for our meal together. After dinner, you & your child can participate in various center activities designed to celebrate what we've learned. Please let us know if you are able to attend by returning the bottom part of this note. If you have any questions, please call:

_____

_____ .

- -

Yes, we plan on coming! We will bring (circle one):
salad   or main dish   or dessert.

_____/_____/_____
Parent   Child   Phone

TABLE CONVERSATIONS

Mealtimes together for today's families are often rare because of numerous scheduling conflicts. When you are together, do you ever feel like the table talk consists of "pass the peas" comments, a time for touching base about coming events or a battleground for solving family conflicts? Below you'll find six clusters of ideas for discussion starters at meal times. You may decide to designate specific days of the week to dialogue together, but spending focused conversational time is a great way to get to know one another better and to explore and impart family values.

☆ Share the best thing that happened in your day.

☆ Tell about a big decision you are having a tough time making.

☆ Share three things you are good at.

☆ Tell about the happiest day of your life.

☆ Share one compliment or kindness you showed someone else today or one that you gave to another person.

☆ Complete the statement, "If I were king (or queen) for the day, I would change_____."

☆ Tell what your favorite toy, hobby or activity is and why.

☆ Tell about an important decision you made today.

☆ Share 1 new thing you learned today & how you'll use it in your life.

☆ On Sunday, have family members set a goal for the week & give a one-sentence update on their progress each night this week.

☆ Discuss how you think family arguments could best be settled.

☆ Tell about your best friends. How did you get to be close? How do you handle disagreements with them?

☆ Tell what your favorite animal is & why. Tell other family members what animal you think they are most like & why.

☆ Tell what you think your family motto or creed should be.

☆ Talk about trust. How do you earn it or lose it? Tell who you trust the most and why?

☆ Share the toughest part of the day for you.

☆ Discuss how your family could have more joy.

☆ Tell what recent current event upset you most. Which made you feel hopeful?

☆ Tell about the most favorite time you ever spent with your family.

☆ Share what spiritual values your family believes in.

☆ Tell who your hero or heroine is.

☆ Tell three words that describe your family. Do you like those words? What would you change if you could?

☆ Bring one short newspaper or magazine article to share at dinner.

☆ What is your most favorite holiday memory?

☆ Which is best to be - oldest, middle or youngest?

☆ What is most important to you in life?

☆ If your family has seen a movie lately, tell who was your favorite character and tell why.

☆ Have a backwards dinner - eating dessert before main meal. Tell what you *do* best in a "backwards" or different way.

☆ Tell about the scariest thing that ever happened to you.

☆ If you could be any age right now, what age would you be & why?

☆ What activity would you like to add to become part of your family's ongoing tradition?

☆ Share the funniest thing that happened to you last week.

☆ Share what you will be doing five years from now. In ten years?

☆ Eat a picnic dinner on the living room floor or outside in the backyard. Plan a weekend outing to a natural setting.

☆ Tell three things you appreciate most about each family member.

☆ Tell what your favorite board game is & about your most favorite memory of playing it. Play a game together after dinner.

☆ Discuss the best way to handle a bully and share an experience of when you had to.

☆ Share your favorite "childhood" memory.

☆ What was the hardest lesson you ever had to learn?

☆ Tell about your biggest hurt.

☆ Share what your favorite book is and tell why.

☆ Tell about what your most embarrassing moment was.

The above suggestions are only a starting point for creating deep, more meaningful relationships with your family members. Have your family brainstorm other topics they'd like to discuss. You will probably find that everyone will be willing to share more if common communication blocks are avoided (i.e., interrupting, judging, giving advice, dominating, putting down, etc.). Remember that modeling positive listening and making encouraging comments are powerful parenting tools!

Role Reversal Center

BREAKFAST TIME!

Directions:

Swap roles with parent(s) playing the child's role & the child playing the parent's role! Use props from the bag at the center to help you act! Decide what the child will say & how the parent will respond. Have fun!

Then discuss:
*How each of you felt in the role
*How things are handled in your home
*Suggestions for improvement

Parent Role

You are trying to get ready for work while your child is supposed to be getting ready for school.

* Time is running short.
* Your child has not yet gotten dressed.
* Your child hasn't eaten breakfast.
* You are getting upset because your child is going to miss the bus.
* You have to be at work at 8:00 am.
* Lately the boss has been complaining because you have been late a lot!
* Also, there is more traffic on the freeway when you leave home later.
* Now your child is asking you to sign some note!

Child Role

It is a weekday morning. Mom or Dad is trying to get ready for work while you are supposed to get ready for school.

* Time is running short and you have not yet gotten dressed for school.
* Your parent is becoming upset because you could miss the school bus .
* You want your folks to sign a note from school that needs to be returned today or you will have to miss recess or go to the office!
* You can't find your shoe; it's lost!
* You are upset!!!
* Your stomach is beginning to hurt!

 271

Role Reversal Center

TIME TO CLEAN YOUR ROOM!

Directions

Swap roles with parents playing the kid's role & kid playing the parent's role. Use props from the bag at the center to help you get into roles. What will the child say? How will the parent respond? Have fun & then discuss how things are handled at your house. Any suggestions for improvement?

Child Role

It is Saturday morning & Mom or Dad has told you to clean your room. You really want to watch cartoons & play outside. So, you go in your room and shove all of your dirty clothes under your bed, cram your toys in the closet and close the door. If anybody opens it, watch out! Then you come out and tell your parents that your room is clean.

Parent Role

It is Saturday morning & you have reminded your child several times to clean his or her room. Cartoons are on & when a commercial comes on, your child rushes to the bedroom to clean up a monumental mess. When the child comes & says the room is all clean, you go & take a look. It still looks pretty bad to you. An argument starts. What do you do & say?

272

Role Reversal Center
TELEPHONE TIME!

Directions

Swap roles with parents playing the child's role & child playing the parent's role. Use props from the bag at the center to help you get into roles. What will the child say and do? How does the parent react? Parents, act out the part of the child. What are you thinking, feeling, wanting? Talk about this together after you role-play the situation. Can you role-play an effective way to deal with the problem? Have fun!

Parent Role

You have had a long day at work and have just sat down to relax after fixing dinner. The phone rings and it is your boss with a question about an important meeting that will happen at work tomorrow. It is very important that you talk with your boss before you get to work in the morning. Important decisions need to be made over the phone. Your child continues to be a pest while you are trying to talk over the phone. How will you handle it when they won't stop making noises and trying to interrupt you?

Child Role

You have been at home for two hours before your parents get home from work. You have been a little lonesome around the house this afternoon. It is now after dinner & getting dark outside. There is nobody to play with. You really want some attention from your mom or dad, but they have been talking on the phone for what seems a long time. You keep bugging them while they are trying to talk on the phone. You ask several questions, play loudly with some of your toys and turn up the TV really loud to get their attention.

 273

Role Reversal Center

TIME FOR BED!

Directions

Swap roles with parents playing the child's role & the child playing the parent's role. Use props & clothes from the bag at the center to help you enjoy your roles. Decide what the child will say & how the parent will react. After you role-play the situation, discuss:
* How each of you felt in the role
* What the most effective solution to the problem was.

Child Role

Your parent tells you it is time to go to bed.
* You would really like to spend some more time with mom or dad.
* Last night they had a meeting and didn't get to spend much time with you.
* It would be fun to read more than just one book so you keep thinking of reasons to ask them to come back to your room.

Parent Role

It has been a busy day at work for you. You are very tired & would like a chance to sit & relax after you finish up some quick paperwork; BUT, your child ...
*Keeps bugging you
*Wants a drink of water
*Wants to go to the bathroom
*Wants another story read

You really just want him or her to go to bed so you can relax & have a few minutes alone.

⭐ 274 ⭐

FAMILY TRADITIONS

At this center, take some time to list some of your favorite family traditions–from hotcakes on Sunday evenings, to special holiday traditions, to bedtime rituals.

Setting & Reaching Goals
One Step at a Time!

OUR GOAL:

_____

_____

_____

Step #5: _____

Step #4: _____

Step #3: _____

Step #2: _____

Step #1: _____

Change wishes & dreams into reality by reaching goals one step at a time!

SETTING & REACHING GOALS
...one step at a time!

Goals will never become anything more than dreams unless you take that first step!
Setting goals effectively means that we have to make them:

Specific   Measurable   Accountable   Realistic   Totally ours

After we have set these goals, we have to get busy!
At this center, you will practice setting a family goal.
Next to each step, write a few words telling what you are going to do at that
step in the journey toward reaching your goal.

ALL-STARS GROUP EVALUATION

1. What feedback have you received from your child about the group?

2. What part of the program did you think your child benefited from the most?

3. Which part of the group did you find was least helpful for your child?

4. How beneficial was the introductory parent meeting about the program setup and ADHD characteristics discussed by our speaker?

5. Concerning our end-of-group "Celebration" event, rate each activity from 1 to 10 (with 10 being the best rating) as to how well you enjoyed participating in each.

   Having supper at school with your child _____
   Discussing specific dinner table conversation topics with your child _____
   Going to the game-playing center with your child _____
   Reviewing materials at the media table _____
   Setting a family goal with your child _____
   Doing role-reversal role plays with your child _____
   Noting family traditions or making a family shield with your child _____
   Please list below (or on the back of this sheet) any other additional comments or suggestions for improvement for our program. We appreciate you and your child working and learning with us. Thank you for taking the time to share your ideas, thoughts and feelings.

_____
Parent's Signature (Optional)

INVOLVING PARENTS & TEACHERS

IT TAKES A VILLAGE

In this section, we have attempted to provide a minimum of background information which will be helpful in working with the adults who are involved in the lives of children with ADHD. There are many current publications on the market which give more in depth treatment to understanding what attention deficit is, how it is diagnosed and treated, what the latest research says, and how best to adapt instructional settings or behavioral approaches for children diagnosed with ADHD. Our bibliographic references, though extensive, are limited to those items used most directly in planning or implementing this program. The publication, *Think Fast! The ADD Experience*, has about the most comprehensive and up-to-date list of resources that we are aware of and is worth checking out, especially if you want to provide a comprehensive list of support services for parents. Following are practical tips on using information from most of these sections.

CHARACTERISTICS - These pages describe the basic criteria physicians use in diagnosing ADHD. These two pages could be referenced for parent or teacher inservices.

THEORIES AND PERSPECTIVES - This section is an overview of the thinking of several professionals currently working in the field of attention difficulties. It is so easy for people to view ADHD in a totally negative light that it is important for teachers, family members and children themselves to be exposed to theories that may well create a paradigm shift in the way they view and approach individuals with ADHD. Being able to see ADHD as a difference rather than a disorder creates a more positive psychological climate of acceptance which can provide the empowerment necessary for the affected individuals to be successful. The "Dear Coach" letter allows adults to see through a child's eyes a little of what it is like to live with the everyday reality of ADHD.

WHAT THE RESEARCH SAYS - This is a brief summary of current scientific findings which would be useful to share with parents and teachers who express skepticism about "all this ADHD stuff." Scientific studies tend to legitimize and lend credibility to a condition all too often trivialized or sensationalized by the media.

BROACHING THE SUBJECT WITH PARENTS - The initial contact with parents is so critical that it is essential to recognize the emotional impact on parents that this issue evokes. Failure to proceed gently will result in unnecessary confrontation that may erect a barrier to providing timely help for the child. It is important to talk with parents at their comfort level without over intellectualizing. The conversational format needs to be adapted to one's particular situation.

DEVELOPING A PLAN OF ACTION - This section provides a conceptual framework that answers that ever-present question, "Besides medicine, what else do we do to help?" Few people stop to think how accurate identification and genuine understanding relieves the "fear of the unknown."

GIVING LEARNING DIFFERENCES A CHANCE - Again, volumes exist that describe specific techniques to support children with ADHD in the classroom. However, knowing all the techniques in the world is not helpful unless one's attitude is adjusted to see the need for individual modifications. It is helpful for parents and teachers to see specific examples of how dramatically medicines can affect performance (like handwriting). A special classroom lesson is offered to help elicit peer support and "A Parable" allows adults who need to "walk a mile" in ADHD moccasins to experience the pain of not being understood.

ISSUES WITH MEDICATIONS - While educators are not qualified to answer medical questions about ADHD, it is important to have a basic understanding of medications in order to give parents intelligent feedback and encouragement to maintain close contact with their physicians.

GETTING BEHAVIOR IN LINE - Suggestions are given for designing systems that allow adults to stay in close communication and to provide consistency in behavioral reinforcement for children with ADHD.

. . .characteristics

TIP!!

Reprinted with permission from the *Diagnostic and Statistical Manual of Mental Disorders, Fourth Edition.* Copyright 1994 American Psychiatric Association. There are three subtypes of ADHD:

314.01 Attention Deficit/Hyperactivity Disorder, Combined Type. This subtype should be used if six or more symptoms of inattention and six or more symptoms of hyperactivity-impulsivity have persisted for at least 6 months. Most children and adolescents with the disorder have the Combined Type. It is not known whether the same is true of adults with the disorder.

314.00 Attention Deficit/Hyperactivity Disorder, Predominantly Inattentive Type. This subtype should be used if six or more symptoms of inattention (but fewer than six symptoms of hyperactivity-impulsivity) have persisted for at least 6 months.

314.01 Attention-Deficit/Hyperactivity Disorder, Predominantly Hyperactive-Impulsive Type. This subtype should be used if six of more symptoms of hyperactivity-impulsivity (but fewer than six symptoms of inattention) have persisted for at least 6 months. Inattention may often still be a significant clinical feature in such cases.

A. Either (1) or (2):

(1) Six or more of the following symptoms of **inattention** have persisted for at least 6 months to a degree that is maladaptive and inconsistent with developmental level.

Inattention

☆ often fails to give close attention to details or makes careless mistakes in schoolwork, work or other activities

☆ often has difficulty sustaining attention in tasks or play activities

☆ often does not seem to listen when spoken to directly

☆ often does not follow through on instructions and fails to finish schoolwork, chores or duties in the work place (not due to oppositional behavior or failure to understand instructions)

☆ often has difficulty organizing tasks and activities

☆ often avoids, dislikes or is reluctant to engage in tasks that require sustained mental effort (such as schoolwork or homework)

☆ often loses things necessary for tasks or activities (e.g. toys, school assignments, pencils, book, or tools)

☆ is often easily distracted by extraneous stimuli

☆ is often forgetful in daily activities

---

2) Six or more of the following symptoms of **hyperactivity-impulsivity** have persisted for at least 6 months to a degree that is maladaptive and inconsistent with developmental level:

Hyperactivity

☆ often fidgets with hands or feet or squirms in seat
☆ often leaves seat in classroom or in other situations in which remaining seated is expected
☆ often runs about or climbs excessively in situations in which it is inappropriate (in adolescents or adults may be limited to subjective feelings of restlessness)
☆ often has difficulty playing or engaging in leisure activities quietly
☆ is often "on the go" or often acts as if "driven by a motor"
☆ often talks excessively

Impulsivity

☆ often blurts out answers before questions have been completed
☆ often has difficulty awaiting turn
☆ often interrupts or intrudes on others

B. Some hyperactive-impulsive or inattentive symptoms that caused impairment were present before age 7 years.

C. Some impairment from the symptoms is present in two or more settings. (e.g., at school or work, and at home)

D. There must be clear evidence of clinically significant impairment in social, academic or occupational functioning.

E. The symptoms do not occur exclusively during the course of a Pervasive Developmental Disorder, Schizophrenia or other Psychotic Disorders and are not better accounted for by another mental disorder (e.g., Mood Disorder, Anxiety Disorder, Dissociative Disorder or a Personality Disorder).

Note: **314.9 Attention-Deficit/Hyperactivity Disorder Not Otherwise Specified** is described as a category for disorders with prominent symptoms of inattention or hyperactivity-impulsivity that do not meet criteria for Attention-Deficit/Hyperactivity Disorder.

While clinical indicators are useful, a simple down-to-earth description goes a long way in establishing understanding acceptance. Working with a child to compose a letter like the one below can be a meaningful activity for parents and/or counselor and might help a teacher or "Coach" who receives it to be more insightful and empathetic.

Dear "Coach,"

At the first practice, you asked each of us to write you a letter telling you a few things about ourselves. Well, I sure do hate to write, and I reckon you're gonna figure this out soon enough anyway, but here goes!

Be patient with me - I just can't sit still very long.

Sometimes it doesn't look like I'm listening, but I really am.

I may not let you know when you hurt my feelings.

I hope you can teach me how to relax - inside, my mind is racing a thousand miles an hour.

Help me to figure out what's important & what's not. Sometimes I don't know the difference between what feels urgent & what's truly important!

My mind is often "in left field." (But please don't let me stay at that position all year!) Help me learn how to focus.

When I've done anything 10 times in a row, I may get distracted or bored & not finish. Please notice what I <u>have</u> done.

Sometimes I'm ashamed of all the mistakes I make and all the things I forget. Help me to see the good in myself.

Sometimes I'm "clueless" about small details. It's okay to point them out to me.

It may help me to calm down if you talk to me without yelling and put your hand on my shoulder.

I tell time two ways - "NOW" and "NOT NOW." Help me learn how to manage and use my time wisely.

No matter what, don't give up on me! I do learn to get better with lots of patience, understanding, limits and good coaching!!!

Love, Your loyal, energetic, determined, creative, fun-loving

. . .theories & perspectives

COACHING TIP:
It all depends on how you
look at it. Doesn't it always?

TIP!!

A book entitled *Think Fast! The ADD Experience*, edited in 1996 by Thom Hartmann and Janie Bowman with Susan Burgess is unique in that it includes a CD for readers to access to CompuServe's ADD Forum where members can exchange views about various topics and experiences relating to ADHD or to access files of important articles and physician's talks. This book has several sections ranging from what it is like to have ADD, how to choose the type of treatment that is best for you, issues that arise through the life span of a person with ADD and learning to live successfully with those issues, how to be an advocate for your child in school, "101 Ways to Help Children with ADD Learn", " Tips From Successful Teachers," and other timely topics. Of great interest to those who don't really understand just exactly WHAT ADD IS, there is a section describing the different perspectives and outlooks of various experts in the field.

Two psychiatrists who each have attention deficit themselves, Dr. Edward M. Hallowell and Dr. John J. Ratey, have written two highly acclaimed books recently, *Driven to Distraction* and *Answers to Distraction*, which are must additions to the library of anyone interested in ADHD. In an article for *Think Fast*, Hallowell encourages us to think of ADHD not as an abnormal state or disorder, but rather as a natural difference in brain functioning. He humorously suggests that there are no attention "deficit" people, only a lot of people with an "attention surplus disorder!"

Thom Hartmann, author of *Attention Deficit Disorder: A Different Perception*, explains attention deficit with a more anthropological approach as he theorizes that the ADHD person has always been with us - just called by a different name: Hunter! He examines the major traits associated with ADHD and suggests that each may represent an adaptation in certain cultures or historical time periods. For example, distractibility could have been equated with the "scanning skills" so essential within successful hunting societies. Impulsivity could be an asset when viewed within the context of making decisions quickly and inviting new challenges. Restlessness and risk-taking aspects of hyperactivity enabled men and women to conquer and "tame" many wildernesses.

Dr. Russell A. Barkley, the author of four books on ADHD and known as "the father of ADD," has extended the theories of Jacob Bronowski widely known for his book, *The Ascent of Man*. Bronowski's work in the area of language development has significant impact with respect to ADHD. Bronowski attributes human superiority to the ability to delay responding to a stimulus. It is this frontal lobe function that enables four distinct skills: the ability to separate neurologically separate signals into feeling and content (separation of affect), the "fixing" of the signal into working memory (prolongation), the use of internal language and reflection before responding (internalization), and the ability to draw from past experiences to analyze, synthesize and anticipate consequences of behavior (reconstitution). Barkley postulates that these tasks not only result in functional language development, but also seem to be closely related to the process which prevents impulsive behavior. In other words, attention deficit is really misnamed - it is much more of an "impulse control" or "output" disorder than it is one of inattention to "input."

Some wonderful analogies have been suggested that help adults and children alike create a global "mind picture" of what it's like to have ADHD. Consider them and develop some of your own! One favorite is a combination of descriptions from Hallowell and Patricia Quinn, author of *Putting on the Brakes: Young People's Guide to Understanding ADHD*: Imagine an intelligent, nearsighted motorist speeding headlong into a driving rainstorm in a car that has faulty windshield wipers, and brakes that don't work consistently. While life will move at a breathtaking speed for that person, lots of things will be a blur! There are bound to be some serious accidents, many near-misses and a few dull moments (like when forced to stop for repairs). Attempting to understand ADHD from the inside out will not only make us better therapists, counselors, teachers and parents, it will also help us to be effective, caring advocates and coaches.

. . .What the research says

TIP!!

A lot of research has been done over the years about different aspects of ADHD. The most comprehensive study to date began in 1992 when the National Institute of Mental Health and the Department of Education cosponsored the Multi modal Treatment Study of Children with ADHD (also known as the MTA study). This fourteen month, multi-site, multi-modal treatment study utilized randomized clinical trials involving 579 children ages 7 to 9.9 years with ADHD combined type. The study involved comparison of four treatment approaches.

Group I - Behavioral Treatment
- Parent training (eight individual family sessions & 27 group sessions)
- Child-focused treatment - Summer Treatment Program (day-long camp for 8 weeks with point systems tied to rewards, time outs, and social skills training)
- School-based intervention - biweekly teacher consultations for 10-16 weeks focused on behavior management strategies and paraprofessional support in the classroom to reinforce behaviors for 60 days with daily behavior report sent home.

Group II - Medication Management
- Doses titrated on an individual basis with half-hour monthly medication visits and practical advice or reading lists given as requested by parents.

Group III - Combined Treatment
- All treatments in Groups I & II were given.

Group IV - Community Care (control group)
- Parents of participants were provided a copy of the assessment completed on their child and were given referrals to local community mental health resources. Of this control group, 64% of children received primarily stimulant medication from their own provider during the study. The mean daily dose of this group was 22.6 mg at 2.3 doses per day as compared with 32 to 37 mg for 3 doses daily for those in Groups II or III.

The following results were documented in the article "A 14-Month Randomized Clinical Trial of Treatment Strategies for Attention-Deficit/Hyperactivity Disorder" by The MTA Cooperative Group in the Archives of General Psychiatry, Vol. 56 DEC 1999. (For more information see, www.archgenpsychiatry.com)

- Medication treatment was superior to behavioral treatment for ADHD. (This does not mean that behavioral treatment alone had no effect, since three-fourths of the participants were "maintained" throughout the study. However, this sort of intensive behavioral program would be difficult and costly to implement in most public and private educational settings.)
- During the fourteen month period of the study, there were few significant differences in results obtained from combined treatment (behavior plus medication) and medication alone, except that those receiving combined treatment showed improvement with a lower dosage. Further study is planned to determine if there are more positive long-term effects of combined treatment.
- Participants in the combined treatment strand improved significantly over those receiving only behavior support in the areas of reducing oppositional and aggressive behaviors and in reading achievement scores.
- Combined treatment and medication alone were both superior to the control group of standard community care, whereas behavioral treatment alone was not better.
- Participants who had anxiety and depression accompanying ADHD did show marked improvement when given combined treatment. Parents also reported less aggression and better parent-child relations, and teachers reported better social skills and improved reading scores.

The study suggested that children diagnosed with ADHD who receive carefully monitored doses of medication will probably not require intensive behavioral interventions.

"Combined treatment and medication management groups were clinically and statistically superior to behavior treatment and community care in reducing children's ADHD symptoms." Above all, the study emphasized the importance of remembering that ADHD is a chronic disorder in which the need for active treatment will "wax and wane" over the course of a lifetime. The type and intensity of treatment will be dictated by environmental stressors. For example, a child with ADHD may need less intensive treatment during a year when assigned to a highly understanding teacher and have optimal family functioning for support.

For those interested in a summary of other research completed prior to the MTA study, The Journal of the American Academy of Child and Adolescent Psychiatry in August 1995 offers an in depth review. Some pertinent studies are summarized below.

General Facts

1. Nationally 3-9% of children are affected by ADHD. (American Psychiatric Assn., 1994)
2. ADHD accounts for 33-50% of all referrals for childhood mental health services. (Popper, 1988)
3. Clinical features of ADHD are: Inappropriate activity levels, low frustration tolerance, impulsivity, poor organization, distractibility, inability to sustain attention and concentration. (Pelham, 1982)

Comorbidity

1. Since inattention, impulsivity and hyperactivity can interfere significantly with typical developmental tasks, academic, social and emotional impairments often exist and can result in comorbid disorders (Abikoff et al., 1980; Gozette et al.,1978; Milich & Landau, 1982; Whalen et al., 1978; Hinshaw, 1987; Klein & Mannuzza, 1990; Loney & Milich, 1982)
2. Biederman &Associates (1991) describe conduct and oppositional/defiant disorders, mood disorders, anxiety disorders and learning disorders among the most common comorbid conditions. (note: Some people believe that the populations used in his studies may be more extreme than the incidence rate reflected in the general population.)
3. More recent study estimates of the comorbidity of learning disabilities are within a range of 20-25%. (Hinshaw, 1992; Semrud-Clikeman et al., 1992)
4. An estimated 70% of children with ADHD continue to manifest some symptoms of ADHD in adolescence. Although by age 25, 20% will meet criteria for ADHD, a substantial number of them learn to accommodate successfully. (Gittelman et al., 1985; Klein & Mannuzza, 1991; Mannuzza et al., 1991; Barkley et al., 1990; Loney et al., 1971; Mendelson et al., 1971)
5. Up to 66% of teens with ADHD have serious discipline problems in school that result in low self esteem and high rates of suspension. (Mendelson et al., 1971; Weiss et al., 1971)
6. 50% of young adults with ADHD continue to exhibit symptoms of ADD (Mannuzza et al., 1991), antisocial disorder, and significantly higher levels of non-medical drug use, court referrals, incarceration and personality disorders. (Hechtman et al., 1979, 1984; Loney et al., 1983)

Short Term Effectiveness of Medical Treatment

1. An estimated two to two and one half percent of elementary age children in North America are medicated for ADHD. (Bosco & Robin, 1980)
2. The majority of one month prescriptions for ADHD are not renewed during a one year period. (Sherman & Hertzig, 1991)
3. Stimulant medications can produce dramatic reductions of ADHD symptoms including:
    *   Task-irrelevant activities (fidgets, off task, classroom disruption) (Abikoff & Gittelman, 1985; Jacobvitz et al., 1989; Kaplan et al., 1990; Whalen et al., 1979)
    *   Aggressive behavior (Gadow et al., 1990; Hinshaw, 1991; Hinshaw et al., 1989; Kaplan et al., 1990; Whalen et al., 1979)
    *   Covert antisocial behavior, such as stealing (Hinshaw et al., 1992)
4. Use of stimulant medication also produces positive effects in areas of :
    *   Compliance and sustained attention (Abikoff & Gittelman, 1985; Jacobvitz et al., 1990; Pelham, 1982)
    *   Parent-child relationships (Barkley & Cunningham, 1979)
    *   Problem solving with peers (Whalen et al., 1979)
    *   Auditory and reading comprehension, spelling recall and math computation (Pelham, 1982; Peril et al., 1991; Stevens et al., 1984)
    *   Improved (but not normalized) status with peers (Whalen et al., 1989)

5. Stimulants alone don't tend to produce significant enough change to move peer perceptions into the normal range. (Whalen et al., 1989)

6. Long-term effectiveness has NOT been demonstrated. (Jacobitz et al., 1990; Weiss & Hechtman, 1986)

7. A range of 10-40% of children who have ADHD do not respond to meds. (Barkley, 1977; Swanson, 1989; Swanson & Kinsbourne, 1979)

8. Some researchers believe that the efficacy of stimulants can be increased if:
   * use of more than one stimulant drug is considered (Elia et al., 1991)
   * doses are titrated on an individual basis (Pliszka, 1989)
   * subgroups (composed of children with a comorbid condition) are more carefully examined regarding their response to medications (Pliszka, 1989)

9. Although inadequately studied, it is possible that stimulants are less reliable in their longterm benefits. (Schachar & Tannock, 1993)

10. While stimulants are effective in stabilizing hyperactivity, learning and behavior problems must still be addressed. (Pelham & Bender, 1982; Sprague & Sleator, 1977)

Combined Treatment Plans

1. Combining approaches of psycho-social (social skills training, cognitive training, home-based interventions, summer treatment programs) and medication may be more effective than single treatment modalities alone. (Hollon & Beck, 1978; Pelham & Murphy, 1986)

2. Cognitive-behavioral interventions have been shown to produce improvement in the areas of increased self-control and use of specific coping strategies. (Hinshaw et al., 1984)

3. Token reinforcement systems have had a positive impact on aggressive and off-task behaviors in the classroom. (Abikoff & Gittelman, 1984)

4. A critical problem common to most studies is the failure to demonstrate long-term generalization of behavioral gains into other settings. (Abikoff, 1987; Abikoff & Gittelman, 1985)

5. Barkley (1990) found that parent involvement in home-based interventions seemed to facilitate generalization of positive behavioral effects.

6. Parent training in behavior modification with medication has been shown to reduce impulsivity and inattention as well as improvement of overall behavior at home and school. (Firestone et al., 1981; Horn et al., 1983)

7. Work by Horn, et al. (1991), suggests that combination of parent training, child self-control training in conjunction with school intervention allowed the optimal dosage of Ritalin to be reduced.

8. "There is promising evidence for clinical utility of a variety of psychosocial interventions in treatment of hyperactive children." (Richters et al., 1995)

9. Speculative or discredited treatments not utilized in the current NIMH study include: modified diets (NIH, 1982; Chiel & Wurtman, 1981; Conners et al., 1987; Rapaport, 1982) vitamin, mineral, amino acid supplements (Arnold, 1984; Coleman et al., 1979; Nemzer et al., 1986; Reimherr et al., 1987), and sensory-motor integration training. (Ayres, 1973; Bauer 1977)

"On the basis of existing research findings, there is little reason to expect isolated treatments of any type (psychopharmacological or psychosocial) to produce lasting, clinically significant, broad-spectrum therapeutic effects..." (Richters, et al., 1995). Instead, current thinking supports the idea of "tailoring" a combination of treatments to the individual needs of the child and his or her family. Satterfield and associates (1979, 1981, 1987) are recognized pioneers of the approach and have conducted both one and three year follow-up studies that indicate sustained improvements when such individualized, multi-modal intervention occurred.

. . .broaching the subject with parents

COACHING TIP:

To paraphrase Faber & Mazlish, the trick is to learn how to talk so parents will listen and listen so parents will talk!

TIP!!

In the last few years, has it sometimes seemed to you that every educator who walks through your door is going to ask for help with a student they think might have ADHD? Information about attention deficit has become more widely known in the past few years as evidenced by recent articles in the local media and in national magazines like *Time* (July, 1994) and *Newsweek* (March, 1996). If the reader can get past the somewhat inflammatory headlines ("mother's little helper" or "Are we over medicating our children?"), one can manage to find some very accurate information about this condition. However, that old adage about a little information being a dangerous thing often comes into play at this point whenever educators and parents rapidly latch onto ADHD as the answer for many of our children's inappropriate educational and behavioral problems. What the general public and even the professional educator often fail to understand is that not every child with attention, impulsivity or activity level problems will have ADHD. When this trend occurs, schools begin having more like 10-15% of their children on medication for ADHD instead of the 5-6% closer to the average that physicians expect to find. Educators and parents alike are often under the mistaken impression that medication is the only treatment for ADHD.

There are a number of different physical and emotional problems that initially evidence themselves through similar symptoms. Diagnosis of ADHD can be a very complicated matter, requiring an in-depth clinical interview by a specialized physician who is experienced in the field. This doesn't mean that families can't begin with their pediatrician or family doctor, but parents must understand that among these doctors there are vast levels of expertise concerning this condition. And, since ADHD is rarely "pure," and is often accompanied by features of anxiety, depression, oppositionality or learning disabilities, the diagnosis and treatment become even more difficult. Sometimes even professional territoriality comes into play with district diagnosticians and family physicians disagreeing as to whether educational evaluations are necessary in addition to the medical one, which should be done first and by whom. There are some school districts who claim to "diagnose" ADHD for purposes of school programming, whereas others adamantly refuse to consider qualifying children for special programs until after the family has completed (and paid for) the medical evaluation. Some school districts serving impoverished communities have gotten to the point where they keep a psychiatrist on retainer for the purpose of doing such evaluations for families who have no medical coverage or who can't afford a private evaluation.

Couple the difficulties in diagnosis with the cost of a good medical evaluation and the often irrational, knee-jerk reaction that some parents tend to have if they perceive that someone is trying to get them to "put my kid on drugs or in special ed just so he'll behave in your room," and you have a volatile mix that must be handled very carefully. For that reason, we are including the most frequently asked questions and comments by parents with suggestions for successfully responding to them in the least inflammatory way. But, one must remember, there are no guarantees! It is also important to realize that we may unwittingly "hit a nerve" and cause one or both parents to recall their own painful childhood experiences.

As our director of guidance, Carol Churchill, has said to us before, one must proceed with the premise that some parents are basically irrational when it comes to discussing their own child, but almost all want what they perceive is best for that child. If you happen to be a parent yourself and think this sounds silly, just remember how you felt when you headed for your baby's first parent-teacher conference. Did you have a rapid heart beat and sweaty hands? It becomes our job to deal with parents' fears and concerns and to convince them that we want the same thing they do!

Some teachers are even asked to refrain from specifically discussing "attention deficit disorder, ADD or ADHD" at a parent conference without a counselor or administrator present. In fact, some principals have been known to "forbid" their teachers even to mention the issue after having received numerous parent complaints that "their staff wants to put every kid on medicine!" Obviously, a lot of misunderstanding can arise between what is stated by the educator and what is perceived by the parent. That's one reason why, in order to preserve the teacher-parent relationship, the teacher can stick to describing specific classroom behaviors and discussing what modifications have already been tried, and let the counselor or administrator be the one to bring up suggestions for what could possibly cause such behaviors and the role a medical evaluation can play in helping adults find answers to what is happening.

It is also helpful if the teacher is the type who has made early initial contact with parents during the school year, has taken the time to mention the positive characteristics of the child (energetic, lively, enthusiastic, creative, vivacious, etc.), has encouraged parents to call if they have any questions, and has then welcomed their calls. Then, when difficulties are discussed, a groundwork for trust exists upon which problem solving can begin. The parent is more likely to believe that the teacher is trying her hardest for their child when specific behaviors are listed along with the accommodations that have already been attempted. At this point, most parents (some of whom have read enough on their own to ask if ADD might be the problem) are generally receptive to the teacher's suggestion that an additional support person be brought in to see if there are any additional ideas about what can be done. It is a good idea for this other educator to have had an opportunity to observe the child's on and off task behaviors and to have previewed the child's cumulative record before the conference. One way to begin is by asking questions of the parents about the child's previous educational background and about how the child handles directions with chores and tasks to be completed at home. Parents will usually ask most of the following questions, which can also be addressed in a didactic way to resolve the sometimes unspoken fears and questions that parents tend to have.

"What causes Scotty to keep doing this? He promises he'll do better, but he just keeps getting in trouble. He gets along fine with the kids in the neighborhood."

One response might be, "Whenever children display these kinds of behaviors in the classroom, it can be several different things that could be causing them to have these difficulties. Sometimes, children have a hard time paying attention or acting impulsively and being over active because of some underlying emotional upset such as being very anxious about something in their lives. But, I do not think that your child is experiencing any undue stress emotionally from what you have been able to share with us so far, unless there is something else you are aware of . . .?"

"Children might show these behaviors in one class or with one particular teacher perhaps because of a teacher's style of teaching or method of discipline. But, in talking with you about what your child is like at home and looking at the comments from teachers in years past, it looks like your child has been experiencing these difficulties to some degree for longer than just this year."

"Well, I think if he really tried hard enough, he could be in control. Last year, we told him he couldn't have his birthday party if he got any marks that week, and he did just fine! We're just going to have to toughen up on him some more!"

Sometimes adults in the child's life think that if the child REALLY wanted to badly enough and tried, he or she could always control the inappropriate behaviors. Often parents believe that if they just discipline the child more stringently and work with them more at home, that the problem will go away. It is very confusing when a child can perform appropriately for a short while but then not be able to do it all the time. And sometimes, a child who can't seem to focus well in the classroom will be able to "hyperfocus" when sitting in front of the Nintendo screen. One good way to check out this theory that "we're just dealing with a behavior problem" is to develop and implement a three to four week individual behavior plan (which includes a step process and consequences as well as positive rewards) and will address from one to three or four targeted behaviors. If indeed, the child can control the behavior, you would expect to see consistent, sustained improvement which will plateau within the acceptable range. Even if the problem is not primarily behavioral in origin, you can expect some degree of improvement initially because almost all children want to please their parents and teachers and will respond positively to the increased attention and novelty of the plan. However, if the problem is not just behavioral, they will not be able to maintain consistent, sustained improvement and will dip erratically between acceptable and unacceptable.

"We've tried those behavior charts last year when he was in second grade, and they didn't work for long. We've also done chore charts and lists and stars at home, but we don't always follow through and he gets tired of them and they don't work any more."

The professional educator might respond, "Well, I was going to suggest we try one if you hadn't yet done so. But, if you have tried some carefully designed behavioral interventions and they haven't worked well by themselves, there could be other causes of these behaviors that have a physical basis that could be considered. For example, a child might have a chemical imbalance in the body. Sometimes, children have a physical condition that makes it very difficult for them to pay attention, to stay on task with boring or demanding written tasks, and to stop and read directions before working or to act deliberately instead of impulsively. This condition is called Attention Deficit Disorder and is often, but not always, used to describe children who can be hyperactive. Attention deficit can occur without hyperactivity, in which case the person with ADD is often described as a space cadet, out-to-lunch, day dreamer, etc. Attention deficit is considered a medical condition, and even though we as educators can help parents identify behaviors, we are not qualified to diagnose this condition. Diagnosis requires an evaluation by a qualified physician. Whenever parents decide they want to have an evaluation done, the school can help by sending information in the form of behavioral checklists or narrative descriptions of how the child is acting in school."

"I've heard about this ADD stuff before. I think it's just an excuse. Everybody's got their kid on that Ritalin medicine, and I don't want my kid on drugs." Or parents may respond with "What kind of doctor?"

There are a number of things involved in treating ADHD, but that is for a family and their physician to discuss if and when ADHD is diagnosed. Not all kids with ADHD may need medication. Physicians who most often are called on to diagnose ADHD are developmental pediatricians, psychiatrists and sometimes even neurologists. One place to start is with your family doctor or pediatrician. Some pediatricians and family doctors are very comfortable diagnosing ADHD, whereas others are not as up-to-date and think that if a child can sit quietly in the waiting room for an hour and can sit quietly in an office during an interview, that the child must not have ADHD. Some parents feel that going to a neurologist is more costly than what they want to start with; and since there is not a specific EEG measure for ADHD, think that a neurologist is not the first route to go unless there is some specific indication of a neurological problem.

Many experts think that psychiatrists are the best trained doctors to diagnose ADHD because there is no "blood test" and determination requires an in-depth look at the child's background and environment through a detailed clinical interview. Just because a psychiatrist is doing the evaluation doesn't mean to imply the child is "crazy" or "mentally deranged" either! Physicians have found that the primary characteristics of ADHD (inattentiveness, impulsivity and sometimes hyperactivity), if left undiagnosed or untreated, can lead to secondary characteristics such as difficulties in social interaction, in dealing with anger, in responding appropriately to authority figures and in academics. Many children who have attention deficit may also have some types of learning disabilities whereas other children may have fine academic skills. Many physicians believed that children outgrew ADHD by adolescence. Now, however, many doctors believe that about sixty percent of children with ADHD carry this condition with them to adulthood.

"Why do doctors say this is a physical problem if there is not a physical test they can do to figure out if somebody has it?"

People wish there were a simple chemical test that could be done to let them know definitively whether someone has ADHD or not. Recent brain research in the early nineties by Zametkin and others have shown with brain scanning techniques that there are actual physical differences in the brains of people with ADHD and of those without the condition. Zametkin showed that the brain's rate of absorbing glucose (an excellent "marker" of metabolic activity) in the frontal lobes of people with ADHD was slower than that in other brains. Dr. Edward Hallowell and Dr. John Ratey's recently published book, *Driven to Distraction*, devotes an entire chapter to summarizing recent ADHD research. This book is particularly interesting in that the two psychiatrists who wrote it have attention deficits themselves.

"Well, if there isn't a "test" for ADHD, exactly how do doctors 'diagnose' it?"

Physicians have parents complete very thorough behavioral rating scales and family medical histories. If a person has ADHD, they will exhibit the characteristics to some degree throughout their life - not only at school, but also at home, and at extra-curricular activities. Depending on the environment, the symptoms may look different but actually be differing expressions of the same thing. Also, these behaviors will have been present for a long time - perhaps not having as major an impact as at the present time, but present never-the-less. For example, if an ADHD child is bright (which is often the case) he or she may make fine grades for the first few years of school. However, teachers from kindergarten through second grade may have recorded comments like:

- ☆ "He has a hard time completing his center work."
- ☆ "I often have to remind him to get back to work."
- ☆ "He can sit at his desk and do nothing but put his name on his paper in 30 minutes if I don't go over and redirect him."
- ☆ "He is out of his seat all the time. But, if I sit next to him, he knows the work and can get it done if I'm right there."
- ☆ "She just day dreams so much!"
- ☆ "He can never find his papers. His stuff is everywhere!"

Bright ADHD kids can sometimes make up work quickly if kept in at recess and they really want to go play, or if an adult gives them one-on-one attention and assists them with increased structure, logical sequencing and assistance with pacing. However, the VOLUME of independent work they are expected to produce increases dramatically by the third or fourth grade; and all of a sudden, the child is not able to "pull it out" at the last minute any more. He or she can't keep up with the volume of work expected, and the assignments are so long that he or she can't "whip it out" with a few minutes of concentrated effort. The child falls farther and farther behind, gets discouraged and the discouragement spreads to teacher and parents alike.

"You know, this sounds an awful lot like my brother Joe. He had a horrible time in school, yet he was really smart."

An educator might share, "I'm not surprised that some of what we are talking about sounds familiar to you as parents. Often parents mention that they, or another relative in their family, has had a similar educational experience growing up. Since it has a physical basis in different brain chemical compositions, it is likely to be inherited.

"Well, we can probably have this checked out. We need to think about it." (Or if only one parent is there), "I'll have to talk to my husband (or wife) about this."

Often when a parent says something like this, educators get excited and expect the parent to follow through in a timely manner. However, when the parent is contacted several weeks later, it becomes clear that nothing has been done. Parents may offer several excuses for not making an appointment or will say that the other parent was adamantly opposed to such a notion. I know that many of us educators are just assured of our own diagnostic skills. In fact some teachers say they've seen enough kids with ADHD that they'd "bet their bottom dollar that this one is too!" While many educators identify these children with an impressive degree of accuracy, we cannot be content with this "unofficial diagnosis!"

Asking a parent to take their child to a physician to diagnose their child with a lifelong medical impairment or handicap may seem like an easy or at least a necessary thing to you; but recognizing and accepting this news is difficult for all parents and devastating to some. Educators have a difficult time understanding what seems to be an overwhelming denial on the part of parents in the face of the obviously recognizable problems of their child. Denial is, of course, the first stage in the process of grieving and parents often experience grief at the idea of the loss of a "perfectly normal" child. Understanding this concept often makes it easier to accept parents' hesitations and to refrain from getting angry at them. It is not unusual for the process of accepting input from the school and of finally going for an evaluation to take two to three years from the time that the issue is first discussed with parents. Furthermore, even if an evaluation is completed and the physician recommends placing the child on a trial of medication, parents cannot be blamed for refusing to turn a deaf ear to potential side effects. No matter how slight the chance, would you be readily willing to ignore the possibility of liver damage just because it only happens to 3% of the population taking one type of drug?

It is of absolute importance that the initial contact with parents be nondefensive, nonconfrontational, gentle and caring, and private. If the parents perceive negativity at this first discussion, or if they think that the school is already convinced that the child "needs to be labeled," they are likely to refuse to cooperate at any time in the future. One such parent was turned off to the idea of attention deficit being her child's problem when she perceived the teacher as telling her "Your kid needs to be on medicine for ADD" during the open house with other parents present in the room. It's doubtful the teacher said exactly those words; but the parent was so mortified that the issue would even be discussed in a room with other parents present, that her perception of what was said was enough to block any referral for the next five years! At last report, this extremely bright child was experiencing great difficulties adjusting to middle school behavioral expectations and spending a great deal of time in the hall, in detention, and in the office.

Don't ever feel that a conference is wasted just because parents do not take action on the school's suggestion to have an ADHD evaluation done. Planting the seeds in a caring way and waiting for next year's teacher to share the same type of specific behavioral observations and similar extensive modifications to help the child accommodate to the learning environment will often bear fruit after several years. Whenever a medical evaluation on a child does show the presence of ADHD, the next step will be serving as part of a team to develop a treatment plan of successful interventions.

. . .developing a plan of action

COACHING TIP:
Remember the KISS principle
-Keep It Simple, Stupid!

TIP!!

ADHD TREATMENT PLAN

DIAGNOSIS

EDUCATION

STRUCTURING

COACHING

MEDICATION

Psychiatrist Dr. Edward Hallowell has had a lot of experience working with patients who have ADHD and with Dr. John Ratey has written *Driven to Distraction: Recognizing and Coping with Attention Deficit Disorder from Childhood through Adulthood* (see bibliography). In this book, the authors recommend a five-part treatment or intervention plan for people diagnosed with ADHD.

DIAGNOSIS

The first step in treatment is to contact a credible, experienced psychologist or physician who can render an accurate diagnosis. Many pediatricians feel comfortable making this diagnosis; others refer to specialists (psychiatrists or neurologists). The diagnosis requires an in-depth clinical interview and review of family history, gathering data not only from parents but also from people who work with the child outside the home environment (like the school). There is no one medical "test" that can show a person has ADHD, and even though several computer-based tests exist that measure reaction times of people and claim to diagnose ADHD, most credible physicians do not believe that ADHD can be diagnosed in a single office-based exam. Doctors can use information from these measures along with their clinical interview to determine if ADHD exists. In an extensive research project, Dr. Steven Pliszka determined that diagnoses could be made with thorough clinical interviews without relying on computerized measures of attention span. Once an accurate diagnosis is made, parents, teachers and even the child usually experience considerable relief when an actual name can be used to explain many of the behaviors and "personality traits" that have been causing problems.

EDUCATION

It seems too basic to even mention, but after diagnosis, education in the aspects of ADHD is critical for a child and his or her parents. The more a family can learn about ADHD, the more successful therapeutic intervention will be. A thorough understanding of what ADHD is, allows them to realize more fully how this condition affects their lives and often provides the motivation to want to learn what to do about it. A genuine understanding of the disorder can bolster a growing sense of confidence and increase the likelihood of sharing information with others. Part of the education process for children can be participating in curriculum-based support groups such as the one described in this curriculum. Parents can gather information from many books and tapes currently available on the market. For those who are already "online" and technologically literate, there is the ADD Forum on CompuServe which provides opportunities to interact through a bulletin board format and to access articles about ADHD. Finally, for parents who learn best by interacting face-to-face with others, many schools and communities provide parent support groups that meet regularly to listen to speakers and discuss issues relevant to living with ADHD. Local chapters of national support groups, such as CH.A.D.D. (Children and Adults with Attention Deficit Disorders, 1-800-233-4050) are available in many areas.

STRUCTURING

Hallowell uses this term to refer to the external limits and organized support that people with ADHD so urgently need. They need assistance in structuring time, space and the "stuff" that fills it, work tasks, and behavior. Practical strategies and tools such as lists, organizing work on a page, reminder notes ("sticky" notes must have been invented for them!), simple filing systems, appointment books, daily planning, and setting of short and long range goals greatly reduce the inner and outer chaos and improve productivity of a person who has ADHD. Gradually, individuals with ADHD begin to structure themselves when it's essential! However, long before they reach this point of being able to bring order to their environment, they must learn as children how to circumnavigate the educational world. Providing educational accommodations is

essential to helping some children with ADHD survive classroom demands. Modifications may include adaptations in the presentation of information, in the expectations of responses required, in the environmental surroundings, or in behavioral expectations. Students whose ADHD significantly impacts their learning can be considered legally handicapped and qualify for special services.

COACHING

The person with ADHD will greatly benefit from having a "coach" - someone to stand on the sidelines calling out encouragement, instructions, reminders, and generally helping to keep things going in the right direction. People with ADHD thrive with this sort of structured encouragement, and they feel lost without it. That is why coaching from parents and teachers has been stressed throughout this curriculum. Such coaching is an integral part of successful group and individual therapy. Traditional forms of therapy may also be indicated if depression, anxiety, problems with self-esteem, or other comorbid conditions exist along with the ADHD.

MEDICATION

Several medications can help correct many of the symptoms of ADHD. In a sense, medications act like "internal eyeglasses," increasing the brain's ability to focus and sustain attention on a task while filtering out competing stimuli or distractions. Medicine can also reduce the sense of inner turmoil and anxiety that is so common with ADHD. The medication works by correcting a chemical imbalance of neurotransmitters that exists in ADHD in the parts of the brain that regulate attention, impulse control, and mood. While medication is not the whole answer, it can provide profound relief, and make it more likely that other interventions will be successful.

. . . giving learning differences a chance

COACHING TIP:

As principal Ruth Fowler has said many times, if a child arrived at your classroom in a full body cast, you can bet you'd treat that child differently without worrying about fairness!

TIP!!

There are many publications on the market that describe numerous strategies and educational accommodations that teachers can use in working with children who have ADHD (see bibliography). In this section is a very brief overview of some important modifications and the justification for them, a sample of how educational performance (in handwriting) can be dramatically affected by medication, an example fo a classroom lesson explaining ADHD behavior to peers and finally, a parable which provides "food for thought" concerning our attitudes as professionals.

The foundation upon which all educational and behavioral accommodations are built is structure. To create structure where there often is none, is to provide a framework within which a child can harness the creative energy necessary to succeed at his or her life's work. Just as the most effective architectural plans call for subtle, unobtrusive supports that don't interfere with the esthetics of a building, so the structure we are speaking of needs to be a discreet, inherent underpinning of support for all students in a class. Philosophically, it is often difficult to accept what seems to be preferential "pampering" of a difficult child when the "good" student seems to be overlooked for doing what is expected. But providing the types of structure that children with ADHD require is just like making a building accessible to those who are handicapped. It doesn't hurt those who are not physically challenged, but is a necessity for those who are. Just as federal guidelines ensure equal access to buildings, so laws have been passed to guarantee that necessary educational accommodations must be provided for children and adults with ADHD in the classroom and in the workplace. Special education laws such as IDEA (Individuals with Disabilities Education Act) and Section 504 of the Rehabilitation Act of 1973 are two such regulations that have had a significant impact on services provided for individuals with handicapping conditions.

Structured classes and modifications that meet the "average daily requirement" for children with ADHD may not be needed by the majority of students in the class everyday. But, when Suzy's parents are in the middle of a messy custody case, she is likely to be more inattentive and forgetful about following through on assignments and need this very same "extra" support. When Jake breaks his arm, his assignments will need to be modified accordingly to compensate for his very real, but temporary, limitation. Each year, our students, whether from normal or dysfunctional families, experience numerous life changes - births and deaths, illnesses and accidents, moves and changes in family's economic status, etc. Additionally, providing appropriate, supportive accommodations for all on an "as needed" basis keeps teachers and classmates from focusing on the label or the handicap rather than the child as a whole.

The successful classroom incorporates structure within both the instructional and behavioral arenas. Before a child can succeed academically, he or she must have certain classroom learning behaviors in place. And, even though recess and unstructured times are a small part of the school day, these can be critical times during which a child's social skills can be developed and his or her acceptance among peers established. The chart on the following page briefly summarizes some basic strategies fundamental to providing appropriate boundaries within the classroom, during less structured transition times, and during times of increased social interaction or group work.

Learning involves not only being receptive to the teaching that is going on (getting the input) but being able to manage time and organize clutter in order to produce concrete evidence of learning (output). Page 304 outlines a few instructional strategies. Because of their inherent (chronic) inattentiveness, children with ADHD will often be the ones to appear at a teacher's desk the moment after instructions have been given and utter the most dreaded and infuriating words, "I don't get it. What am I supposed to do?" It would be easy at this point for a teacher to respond sarcastically, abruptly, or judgmentally - laboring under the assumption that the child didn't listen, wants attention, is too lazy to figure it out for him or herself, delights in making one's life miserable, or all of the above. The reality may be none of the above, but rather a reflection of the child's internal chaos and uncertainty about where to start and how to unscramble all the pieces need-ed to begin the project. Sequencing, prioritizing, and discernment, all essential skills in reading the blueprint of a design and completing a task, often become obstacles for a child who has ADHD. Once a teacher con-firms a child's understanding of directions, monitoring and facilitating time on task are probably the most important adaptations that a teacher can provide to ensure a child's output. Over all, any modification will usually be more effective for children with ADHD who have a positive response to medical intervention (as evi-denced by the handwriting samples on pages 305 - 308.) As educators, our overriding concern must always be to maintain the delicate balance between the esthetics of a comfortable learning environment charac-terized by effective modifications and intact relationships with the actual edifice of learning, founded upon a structure that enhances personal accountability and measurable achievement.

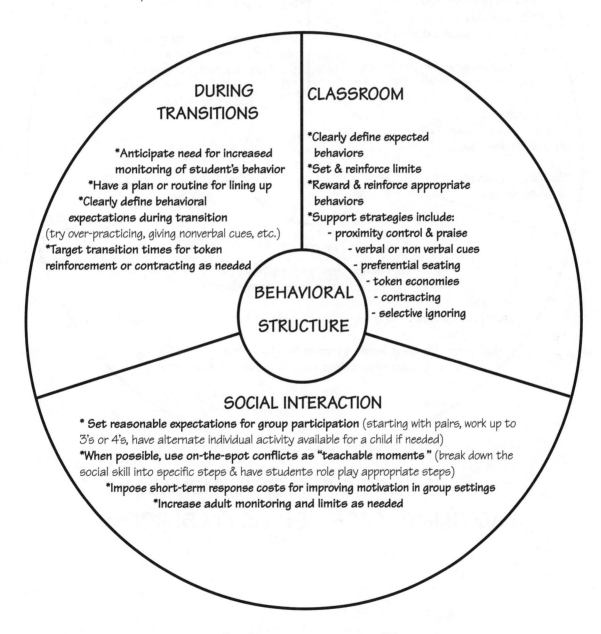

DURING TRANSITIONS

*Anticipate need for increased monitoring of student's behavior
*Have a plan or routine for lining up
*Clearly define behavioral expectations during transition
(try over-practicing, giving nonverbal cues, etc.)
*Target transition times for token reinforcement or contracting as needed

CLASSROOM

*Clearly define expected behaviors
*Set & reinforce limits
*Reward & reinforce appropriate behaviors
*Support strategies include:
  - proximity control & praise
  - verbal or non verbal cues
  - preferential seating
  - token economies
  - contracting
  - selective ignoring

BEHAVIORAL STRUCTURE

SOCIAL INTERACTION

* Set reasonable expectations for group participation (starting with pairs, work up to 3's or 4's, have alternate individual activity available for a child if needed)
*When possible, use on-the-spot conflicts as "teachable moments" (break down the social skill into specific steps & have students role play appropriate steps)
*Impose short-term response costs for improving motivation in group settings
*Increase adult monitoring and limits as needed

STRATEGIES FOR BEHAVIORAL
ACCOMMODATIONS IN THE CLASSROOM

ORGANIZATION
*Well-structured daily classroom routine
*Daily agendas on board
*Individual assignment sheet for work to be completed
*Study buddy assigned
*Specified & frequent time for filing & clearing desks
*Coordinating support from parent (who provide appropriate materials, daily checking and signing of assignment sheets, remov ing old papers)
*Uncluttered work space & give more space as needed (tubs, empty desk beside)
*Facilitate easy access to materials with colo coding, etc.

INPUT
*Creative, motivational pre-sentation of material ("hooked" with a concrete focus to previous les-sons and multi-sensory in approach)
*Increase attentive behaviors (with cues, eye contact, calling name, proximity control)
*Check for understanding of directions (repeat, rephrase directions & check for under-standing and accuracy shortly after assignment begins, highlight key words in written directions, put written directions of board)

EDUCATIONAL STRUCTURE

OUTPUT
* Facilitate time-on-task (pacing, timer, frequent checks with teacher, have student set time goals for completing sections of paper, encourage self-checking before turning in)
*Modify assignment (extended time, shortened, oral or other alternative to a written assignment)
*Recognize effort, set & expect reasonable quality (esp. with handwriting)
*Good environmental balance of stimulation & distractions

STRATEGIES FOR EDUCATIONAL ACCOMMODATIONS IN THE CLASSROOM

HANDWRITING SAMPLE OF A CHILD DIAGNOSED WITH ADHD
(work sample done at school when medication is wearing off)

> Sean   Jan. by 1992
> What is climate? I think that
> do.
> What is the climate like where ya
> Live? Hot.

Written by a child with ADHD who has a high average to superior range IQ. This sample was written in class, probably near the end of a medication dose's effectiveness. (There were multiple erasures and extemely short answers.)

HANDWRITING SAMPLE OF A CHILD DIAGNOSED WITH ADHD
(work done for evening homework - before medication was given)

> The magic Schoolbus
> by joanna
> This Book is about the
> human body, a magic bus
> is inside arnold's body.

These two sentences were written by the same child at the end of the day without the advantage of medication. In order to get the child to compose these sentences, the parent gave one-on-one assistance in this manner: the child dictated information out of sequence and verbal questions or prompts were given to put things in proper order. The adult "scribed" as the child dictated. Then the child was asked to copy the sentences. This last step took over 10 minutes due to the child's extreme frustration and avoidance.

HANDWRITING SAMPLE OF A CHILD DIAGNOSED WITH ADHD
(evening homework - after medication has been administered)

An evening dose of Ritalin was administered. Thirty minutes later, the child was able and willing to complete the copying work. The report was copied in it's entirety in approximately twenty minutes without the child exhibiting frustration or anger.

.The Magic Schoolbus
insiDe The human body
by Joanna cole   2pts.

This book is about the human body
and a magic school bus ride inside
Arnold's body. Ms. Frizzle is
the craziest teacher in School.
She takes the children on a crazy
ride through the body and they learn
about the human body.
Her clothes were "out of this world!"
I love this book; it was funny
and I think other children would
learn a lot about the body if they
read it. too.

HANDWRITING SAMPLE OF A CHILD DIAGNOSED WITH ADHD
(before medication has been administered)

Matthew, a second grade child, produced this work sample when near the end of his morning medication cycle. The teacher reported that he was also getting angry about having to write his spelling sentences.

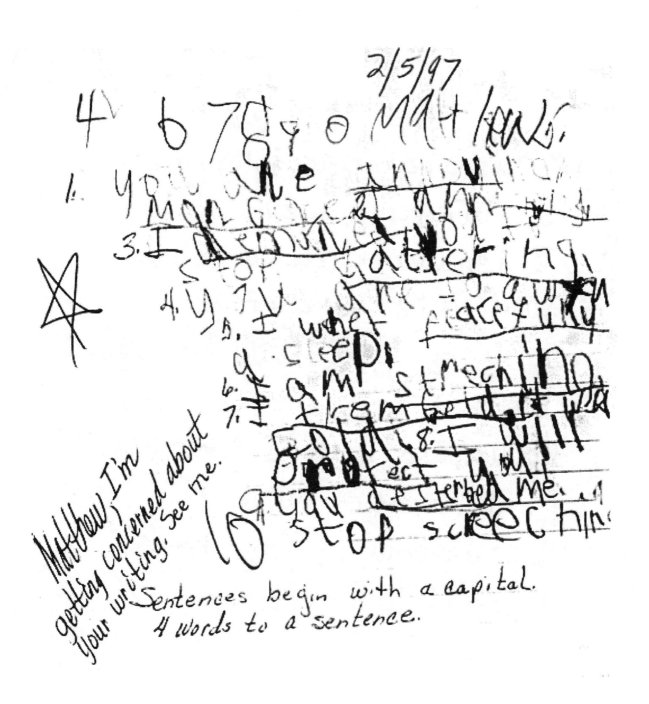

HANDWRITING SAMPLE OF A CHILD DIAGNOSED WITH ADHD
(after medication has been administered)

This page, completed on the same day by Matthew was done st school in the afternoon, after a dose of medication for ADHD had taken effect. Note the dramatic difference in handwriting "before and after" medications.

2/5/97

Matthew S.   Excellent Work !!

1 You are annoying me.

2 I am very angry.

3 I demand you to stop.

4 You are so awful.

5 I went peacefully to sleep.

6 I am streching the yarn.

7 It was so cold I trembled.

8 I will protect you.

9 Your destrubing me now.

10 The owl is screeching.

Understanding Differences

A Guidance Lesson to Enlist Peer Support for the Child with Severe ADHD

Many times a child with a <u>severe</u> case of ADHD suffers most when socially rejected by peers. Depending on the maturity and anxiety levels of the child, it may be appropriate to discuss with the child the advantages of talking to the classmates about ADHD. It is imperative to obtain the parents' and teacher's consent ahead of time. Dialoguing with classmates usually works best if the child is out of the room during the discussion and if participants agree to keep the talk confidential. Professionals who have used this method report that classmates almost always respect confidentiality.

1. Begin by reading an excerpt from or summarizing a children's book about ADHD (see bibliography). Suggest that the description you shared may remind them about a sibling, fellow student, or even themselves. Then ask how many have heard of ADHD or ADD and identify the child in their class that you wish to speak about. Mention specific behaviors of the child that sets him or her up for ridicule or rejection by peers and ask if the kids have noticed those behaviors. Then explain that many of these behaviors are often associated with ADHD, a medical condition that results in people having different characteristics or ways of being.

   ☆ A. **Hyperactivity** - "You may have noticed the _____ fidgets in his seat or gets out of his seat a lot. This is because his body is very energetic and he almost always feels the need to be moving. When you talk about people's energy levels, it helps to think about the 'Energizer Bunny®', who just keeps going and going and going, long after other batteries run out. People like _____ who have a lot of energy have a hard time keeping their body still."

   ☆ B. **Impulsivity** - "You may have noticed that _____ often says or does things without thinking about the consequences of what will happen next and is then often sorry later. We all do this sometimes. But with people who are very impulsive, it means that as soon as an idea pops into their head, they are likely to say or do something BEFORE they stop to think, kind of like 'OMOM' - meaning 'on the mind, out the mouth!' If what they said or did hurts someone's feelings or gets them into trouble, they realized then how inappropriate they were being, but it is already too late. Learning to think before they speak or act takes longer than for most kids."

   ☆ C. **Disorganized and forgetful** - "You may have noticed that _____ 's desk is often a mess and that _____ sometimes forgets things or loses papers. Part of having ADHD means that so many signals come into your brain at the same time that it is difficult to sort through everything. Let's demonstrate this now." Have two students come up one at a time. The first student is in Mrs. McGillicutty's class and receives directions for two papers at a time and is told to do them and file them. Briefly role play. Then have the next student come up. This child is in Mr. White's class. Role play handing back ten graded papers and five new assignments with brief directions one right after the other. This child should feel "snowed under!" Explain that we have all felt overwhelmed at times, but that some people get overwhelmed more easily than others.

☆ D. **Distractibility** - "You may have noticed that _____ looks around the room a lot and has a hard time following along in the book or in discussions. He may even daydream. I Explain that we are going to do an activity that illustrates how difficult it is for a person with ADHD to pay attention.

2. Ask for a volunteer who thinks they pay attention really well. Have the volunteer sit in a central location. Gather five other students, hand each of them a sandwich baggie filled with marshmallows, and quietly instruct them to throw all the contents at the seated volunteer whenever you give them a "thumbs up" signal. (One marshmallow in one bag only will have been previously marked with a large colored dot.) Tell the student who is seated to pay close attention to what is going to happen. Give the "thumbs up" signal. When the bombardment is over, ask the volunteer if they were paying close attention. Then ask, "Who threw the marshmallow with the dot?" When they are unable to answer accurately, ask them why they weren't paying attention. Make the point that kids with ADHD often believe they ARE paying attention, but are noticing too many things at one time or don't know which thing of many happenings is most important to focus upon.

3. Other key points to make during the discussion are that children with ADHD:
   ☆ are often smarter than average.
   ☆ have trouble organizing "stuff", finishing work and writing neatly.
   ☆ find it difficult to pay attention to things around them.
   ☆ are not always aware of their own behaviors (especially things that excite them).
   ☆ often look like kids who aren't trying or who are doing inappropriate things on purpose.
   ☆ emphasize that there is always a reason when a kid behaves a lot differently than others.
   ☆ People with ADHD are not to be pitied, just understood.

4. Consider doing role plays that illustrate appropriate ways to react to impulsive or annoying behaviors of people with ADHD. Take a specific example that children mention of inappropriate behavior and model a low-key or caring way to respond.

5. Conclude by focusing on the positive sides of ADHD. Daydreaming at appropriate times leads to great creativity like that of movie maker Steven Speilberg or inventor Thomas Edison. Impulsivity at its best leads to a fun and spontanous personality like comedian Robin Williams. Hyperactivity gives a person a fantastic energy level that when tapped appropriately allows a person to be involved in lots of projects and activities at one time!

A PARABLE

Once upon a time, there was an efficient principal, Mr. N. Flexible, of Triple A Elementary School who was highly esteemed by his central office superiors. He always got results! His school-wide standardized test scores were consistently high; his reports were always on time; his student and staff attendance was 96%! However, the central administration was baffled by the high number of transfer requests that came in from teachers each year. So an official observer, Mr. R.E. Spect, was sent out for a short time every day for a week to assess the situation and solve the mystery. Mr. R.E. Spect, being an astute judge of human nature, decided to spend his time eating lunch in the teachers' lounge. The following are excerpts from his personal notes:

Monday - Ms. E. Mergency came in with tears in her eyes and shared with the others at her table that she had asked to leave early on Friday to take her husband to physical therapy treatments for a back injury. But Mr. N. Flexible had said that if he made an exception for her, he'd have everybody in his office asking to leave early for one reason or another and how fair would that be? Discouraged, but being resourceful, she then asked the principal if she could turn in her weekly lesson plans on the following Monday in order to leave as soon as school was out. Mr. N. Flexible rejected that request too, for the same reasons. Mrs. M.E. Too murmured sympathetically that she also had been denied additional time to complete her lengthy committee report even though her arthritis made it painful to write. Mr. N. Flexible told her that if she had planned ahead, started earlier, and budgeted her time more wisely, she could have been finished on time like the other committee chairs.

Tuesday - Mr. R. Brain came into lunch dejectedly. The other teachers on his grade level asked if his students had misbehaved that morning. "No, but on my desk this morning, I found one of those infamous sticky notes telling me how messy and unprofessional my room looked. Doesn't he realize that sometimes when the kids are in the middle of a big project, everything's not going to be neat as a pin!" Mrs. O. Fended piped in, "And rooms aren't the only thing he's picky about. Why, just last week he walked by my room and said that I looked really frazzled and unprofessional with those runs in my pantyhose!" A heavy silence fell upon the group.

Wednesday - Miss Gnu Here came in to lunch angrily. When her team asked what was wrong, she replied, "Well, you know that idea we discussed at grade level meeting about revising our grading policy? I got nowhere with Mr. N. Flexible. He was adamant about 'doing it the way we've always done it' and told me that change almost always leads to chaos. I say, better to have temporary chaos and be innovative than to stagnate." Mr. Onn Edge, her team member, said, "Speaking of chaos, a lawyer called me today! Before I took the call, I got confused about the district's policy on talking to legal counsel. I felt like this was enough of an emergency to interrupt him when he was in conference with a teacher. Mr. N. Flexible said that he didn't have the time to talk with me, without even knowing what I needed! So, I talked with the guy. I hope that was ok."

Thursday - Wednesday faculty meeting was the topic of discussion over lunch. Ms. Sochelle Butterfly was still humiliated as friends attempted to comfort her. "We've all whispered during faculty meetings before; your voice just carries farther than most. I can't believe he asked you to share that with everyone!" At this point, I realized the only smiles I'd seen all week were in response to a private joke among the staff about what the three "A's" stood for in the school's name - Anger, Animosity, and Anxiety. I'm beginning to understand the morale problem here.

Friday - On this day, I noticed that the teachers seemed inordinately relieved to have the week over with, and all were planning to clear the building by 3:31 pm. I stopped by the office to let Mr. N. Flexible know that our conference with him and his supervisor would be held first thing Monday morning. The principal barely acknowledged me, since he was busy making telephone calls regarding some lawsuit involving the parents of a child in Mr. Onn Edge's classroom.

The Next Monday - During Monday's meeting, Mr. N. Flexible was appalled when Mr. R.E. Spect suggested that teachers on his campus wondered if they could do anything right to please their principal. He listened skeptically as R.E. explained that some of the staff doubted whether they would ever be "good enough for him." Hence, the "mass migration" from the campus. Mr. N. Flexible just couldn't see how the situations Mr. R.E. Spect described affected teacher morale. He secretly thought that the teachers were just lazy and didn't like being held accountable. Mr. R.E.Spect had anticipated this type of response from the principal and entered the following evaluative comment into the personnel file:

" Mr. N. Flexible never lets an opportunity go by in which he can share his experience about how particular staff members could improve any number of imperfections in their professional and personal lives. Suggested Growth Plan objectives are:

1. Use best judgment in determining degree of flexibility necessary in extending time requirements or making other reasonable accommodations for ANY staff member when necessary.
2. Be tolerant and realize that some limitations (i.e., arthritis) are life-long conditions which make some types of work difficult and perhaps even painful.
3. Recognize that one negative comment from someone in authority over you greatly outweighs several positive remarks.
4. Acknowledge and respect individual differences. Do all you can to encourage teachers to develop their unique approaches to learning and teaching."

THE REST OF THE STORY: Mr. N. Flexible did not make any noticeable improvement during that semester; in fact, he seemed more uncompromising than ever since being written up by his superiors. However, the following summer, he experienced a lengthy illness related to high blood pressure and was relieved when allowed to start back to work at his own pace. His fear that he would not be accepted or respected due to his physical limitations proved to be entirely unfounded. He was amazed that his teachers went out of their way to make allowances for his adjusted work schedule. Instead of complaining because he wasn't as able to meet deadlines, they seemed to overlook his liabilities and sent written notes of encouragement each day. Over the next few months, he began to see the wisdom of Mr. R.E. Spect's evaluation and with the help of supportive colleagues experienced an amazing metamorphosis in his approach to educational leadership. Central office noted a distinct decline in requests for transfers from the newly-named school. You see, the school has grown so much that it is now Five A Elementary. The "A's" now stand for Acceptance, Affirmation, Affiliation, Accommodation, and Achievement.

Counselors, in sharing this parable with teachers or parents, consider asking:

☆ Could you identify with any of the people or situations in the story?
☆ How might the story be viewed differently if the parable had been told from a child's point of view about his or her teacher for the year? How are children as well as adults impacted by positive learning and working environments?
☆ Privately and individually, consider the impact of your comments and accommodations (or lack of them) upon children's willingness to perform.
☆ Discuss the fine lines in both school and home environments between flexibility and inconsistency and between offering accommodations and failing to demand accountability.

Since attention deficit has definite physical or neurobiological components, but is not readily "visible" as a "handicap," it is easy for parents and teachers to forget, in the urgency of the moment, and resort to negative or sarcastic comments that may serve to relieve the adult's stress but are experienced as hurtful and remembered for years by the child.

. . .issues with medication

COACHING TIP:

Keep reminding yourself,
"If this were my child…"

TIP!!

Common Pharmological Interventions
for ADHD
(and accompanying disorders)

Stimulant Medications

☆ Ritalin   Short acting (or time release)

☆ Dexedrine   Takes effect within 30 minutes

☆ Adderall   Does not build up in bloodstream

☆ Cylert   Takes up to 3 weeks to take effect while building up in the bloodstream

Antidepressant Medications

(for the most part, all of these need to build up
blood levels for maximum effectiveness)

☆ Imiprimine (Tofranil)   Targets impulsivity most

☆ Desipramine   Targets impulsivity most

☆ Well Butrin   Targets oppositional defiant & depressive behaviors

☆ Clonodine   Targets oppositional defiant & aggressive behaviors

☆ BuSpar   Targets overanxious behaviors with ADHD

☆ All may have side effects in certain individuals

☆ All must be monitored by a physician

Parents and teachers have many questions about medication issues.

☆ *"What type of medication is my child on and just how does it work?"*

☆ *"What are the potential side effects and how can I know if my child is on the right dosage?"*

☆ *"Which is better, generic or name brands?"*

☆ *"Are timed released forms as effective as the short acting kind?"*

☆ *"What kind of feedback should I give the doctor about my child's behavior on medicine?"*

☆ *"What if my child doesn't want to take the medication?"*

☆ *"How long does my child have to be on the medicine? When will I know to take him off?"*

☆ *"Why do I have a hard time getting Ritalin refilled? The pharmacy's always out!"*

Yes, there are a lot of questions. It is imperative that families, schools and physicians work closely together in order for the child to gain the most benefit from this type of intervention. Educators do not have the medical knowledge to prescribe, physicians are not present in the classrooms to see the child's level of daily functioning, and the poor parents often have the child only in an unmedicated state in the evenings. Sometimes parents are desperate for reassurance on a medical issue and haven't been able or haven't tried to reach their doctor. While educators can speak in general terms to reassure parents, they must always emphasize that parents stay in close contact with their physician who is the only one with the training and background necessary to meet their child's medical needs.

Parents may find it hard to get specific prescriptions refilled. Many of the medications used to treat ADHD are classified as controlled substances (like Ritalin) and as such, have manufacturing limitations. As more people are receiving treatment for ADHD, pharmacists may have difficulty keeping certain medications in stock. Even though this can be a hassle, most professionals agree that the chance for abuse of this drug is too great for it not to be a controlled substance.

As to whether generic or name brands are best, parents give varied reports. Some parents swear that their child did best on a generic form of a specific medicine whereas others claim much better results from the name brand of the same kind. It really seems to be an individual's specific biochemical response that is unique for each person. Again, encourage parents to keep in close communication with the classroom teacher so that the physician will be getting accurate information. The same holds true for determining whether the short or long acting forms of a medication are most effective and for deciding when a child might have outgrown the need for medication. Most physicians do not recommend taking a child off medication for ADHD at the beginning of the school year, but rather to do a trial of a few weeks off medication in the middle of the year if academic and behavioral feedback have been good up to that time. Then, if a child starts having increased difficulty, the teacher will have a baseline of behaviors with which to compare. Reliable and accurate behavioral feedback (for example, through use of a standardized behavioral checklist) is a must!

Communicating with the child about how this medicine will help them is an essential step with this treatment option. How often have kids been told that "drugs" are bad for you? Even though they know that "medicines" given by parents are safe, there is often an underlying fear of "drugs that alter my mind," especially if the parents have communicated their fears along this line. When children are told up front that they might experience "the following side effects," they very generally do. One fifth-grade girl, upon being given her "hyper medicine," began turning around in circles and acting very silly. When asked what was going on, she told her mom, "Well, the medicine must be working because it is making me hyper."

Whereas some parents wholeheartedly embrace medication as a cure-all and neglect to explore additional treatment modalities, other parents may lack confidence in medication for treatment of ADHD and thus may have a pervasive sense of distrust in using medication for the treatment of ADHD at all. They may often want to discontinue medication at the first sign of problems instead of being willing to work with physicians to help find the exact dosage. It can be very frustrating for educators who find it difficult to understand parents' hesitancies when they see such positive results in the classroom. It is important to remember that often the parent does not actually see these improved behaviors; they only hear reports of them. And, what educators as parents themselves would be willing to welcome their children being placed on a medicine that would help them at school but would also carry a "slight" chance of producing serious side effects? Suppose a specific serious side effect is reported in "only" three out of a 1000 cases. Would you accept the risk if the child were your own?

The charts on the following two pages contain brief information about several medications that are currently being used to treat ADHD. The information has been reviewed for accuracy by several physicians. It is often helpful for educators to have access to this type of information in case they are surprised by unexpected parent questions. Remember, parents should always be referred to their own personal physician to get reliable answers to their specific medical questions!

Recently, two other brands of methylphenidate have been released in addition to Ritalin. Concerta is an extended release tablet swallowed whole in 18 to 36 mg levels that can be administered once in the mornings. Dosage may be adjusted in 18 mg increments up to 54 mg per day. Metadate ER is a similar methylphenidate available in 10 to 20 mg tablets. Since both of these medications are active for about eight hours, patients who do not want to bother with a midday dose now have additional options. As new medications are developed, you may learn of a student taking something that you have never heard of. If you are unable to get information from your school nurse or from the parent about the new medicine, you can always ask a pharmacist to give you a sample insert that will give you information about the newest treatments.

HELPFUL INFORMATION ABOUT MEDICATIONS COMMONLY USED TO TREAT ATTENTION DEFICIT DISORDER

MEDICATION	DOSAGE RANGE	BENEFITS OF MEDICATION	COMMON SIDE EFFECTS	ADDITIONAL INFORMATION
(Stimulant) Methylphenidate (known as Ritalin)	**Tablet form-** 5,10,20 mg Takes effect within 1/2-1 hour & lasts 3-4 hours.	Works quickly to address most symptoms of ADHD (distractiblity, impulsivity, hyperactivity, memory & motor skills) and is effective in about 70% of patients. About the safest of all medications for ADHD.	Loss of appetite, headaches, difficulty sleeping, stomach ache, irritability or mood swings, possible rebounding.	Since this is a stimulant medication, persons who have a great deal of anxiety or a history of muscle tics or Tourette's should not use this drug since it would probably aggravate these conditions.
	Sustained release- Only in 20 mg SR May take 1-2 hours to take effect, but lasts 6-10 hours.	Same as above but, also good for older children who do not want to have to take a mid-day dose.	Same as above	Same as above
(Stimulant) Dextroamphetamine (known at Dexedrine)	**Tablet form-** 5, 10 mg short acting Takes effect within 1/2-1 hour & lasts 3-4 hours	Same as Ritalin tablets	Same as Ritalin tablets	Same as Ritalin tablets
	Spansules- 5,10,15 mg long acting. Takes effect within 1/2-1 hour & lasts 6-10 hours.	Same as Ritalin-SR	Same as Ritalin-SR	Same as Ritalin-SR
(Stimulant) Pemoline (known at Cylert)	**Tablet-long acting** lasts 12-24 hours 18.75, 37.5,75 mg (37.5 mg available in chewable tablets)	Same as Ritalin-SR	Same as Ritalin-SR (plus abnormal liver functions have been reported in rare cases)	Same as above, plus may take 2-4 wks for clinical response. Also, slight potential for liver damage calls for regular blood test.
(Stimulant) Adderall	**Tablet form-** 10,20 mg; lasts 4-6 hours	Same as for other stimulants	Same as for above stimulants plus elevation in blood pressure, heart palpitations or tachycardia	Same as for Ritalin

*Reviewed by physicians for accuracy of information and checked against the *Physicians'Desk Reference* (49th edition)

HELPFUL INFORMATION ABOUT MEDICATIONS COMMONLY USED TO TREAT ATTENTION DEFICIT DISORDER

MEDICATION	DOSAGE RANGE	BENEFITS OF MEDICATION	COMMON SIDE EFFECTS	ADDITIONAL INFORMATION
(Anti-depressant) Imipramine (known as Tofranil)	**Tablet form-** 10, 25, 50, 75 mg long acting & given in various combinations (depending on age & size). Given 2-3 times daily (50-150 mg/day) & lasts 12-24 hours	Seems to target impulsivity more than other symptoms. Is especially effective for ADHD patients who have depression, anxiety or separation fears, or panic or obsessive compulsive disorders.	Decreased appetite, dry mouth, headache, stomach ache, blurred vision, dizziness or lightheadedness from decreased blood pressure, constipation, rash, tiredness, or racing heart (tachycardia).	May take 2-4 weeks for clinical response. Therefore, a baseline ECG may be taken to detect pre-existing heart problems. Medication should be discontinued gradually.
(Anti-depressant) Desipramine (known as Norpramin)	**Tablet form-** 10, 25, 50, 75, 100, 150 mg long acting & effect lasts 12-24 hours. Given in sgl or div. doses-am/pm (25-150 mg/day)	Same as for Imipramine	Same as for Imipramine but reportedly fewer and less intense.	Same as for Imipramine
(Anti-depressant) Buproprion (known as Well Butrin)	**Tablet form-** 75, 100 mg - given up to 300 mg/day	Seems to work best with depressive features and oppositional defiant symptoms.	Same as for Imipramine and Desipramine	Contraindicated in patients with seizure disorders.
(Anti-hypertensive) Clonidine (known as Catapres)	**Tablet form-** .1, .2, .3 mg given 3-4 times per day & lasts 3-6 hours. (0.15-0.3 mg/day)	Not as effective for attention span but works better than stimulants to decrease hyperactivity. Works best with highly aggressive, oppositional defiant or comorbid ADHD	Sleepiness, change in blood pressure & pulse, headache, dizziness, stomach ache or nausea & vomiting, dry mouth, & uncommon depression.	Several weeks to judge full effect. Discontinue gradually to avoid possible rebound hypertension. Starting dose can be given at night & increase slowly.
	Dermal patch (lasts for 5 days)	Same as for tablet form of Clonidine	Possible skin reactions to patch plus same as for tablets.	Same as for tablet form of Clonidine
(Anti-anxiety) Buspirone (known as BuSpar)	**Tablet form-** 5, 10 mg - given up to 60 mg/day, 3 times daily	Seems to work best with overanxious patients.	Dizziness, nausea, nervousness, headache, lightheadedness, nonspecific chest pain.	Less sedating than other anxiety meds; withdraw gradually.

*Reviewed by physicians for accuracy of information and checked against the *Physicians' Desk Reference* (49th edition)

318

. . .getting behavior in line

TIP!!

Behavioral contracting is designed to help students develop a beginning awareness of the benefits and basics of taking control of and making changes in their lives. Students are able to build a positive mind set and to develop a sense of control related to the process of changing behavior when they participate in developing a personal contract and when they experience success as a result. If the student is able to voice a desire to change habits to make his or her life more pleasant or less hassled, then he or she will see contracting as a tool to help reach personal goals and not as a punishment imposed by adults. Adults need to avoid the temptation of playing "gotcha" each time a child "messes up." It is important to emphasize concrete ways for children to be able to redeem themselves and reverse inevitable setbacks. Behavioral contracts may need to be periodically adjusted for the child's optimal success. For example, some children may need a "fail safe" system of earning rewards. That is, whenever they have had five successful (not successive) days at school, they will earn a reward. Otherwise, some children may be successful 4 out of 5 days forever, may never achieve the set award, and feel like a failure for achieving only 80%! Some children tend to set themselves up for failure to prove to others how accurate their miserable self image really is! A sample contract for an intermediate student who earns a reward after accumulating a certain point total (i.e., a video rental when 50 points have been accumulated) is shown on page 325.

Frequent and consistent verbal and written encouragement greatly facilitate the process of change and can counterbalance the ongoing negative feedback that's bound to occur when others evaluate the child's behavior. This need for reinforcement is pronounced in children with ADHD and must become an inherent part of all interactions (parent-child, teacher-child, counselor-child, child-child). In addition, it is essential to help children with ADHD analyze feedback from others because of their impaired ability to self evaluate. Contracting helps children to be aware of the impact of their behavior on themselves and others. Ultimately, adults help children to internalize the concept that greater personal freedom results from consistent follow-through on personal responsibilities.

The process of individual contracting with weekly monitoring by an educator falls beyond the scope of the All-Stars group described in this curriculum. A counselor or teacher serving as a behavior manager might decide to work with students individually or add these students to a contracting group. In her book *Charting Through Troubled Waters*, Lynn Lavelle, behavioral specialist for NEISD in San Antonio, recommends the following steps as essential to sound contract development:

The educator:

☆ Meets with teacher and parents to pinpoint the problem and prioritize behavioral goals.

☆ Meets privately with each student and assists him or her in developing ownership of these goals. Often a student will identify the same category of needs that adults have and then it becomes a matter of rephrasing and prioritizing the goals.

☆ Works with the student to see the existing negative consequences of behavior, and uses a rewards inventory (formal or informal) to identify extrinsic rewards to be earned as behavioral progress occurs. (Lavelle believes that it is difficult to identify intrinsic rewards as they are usually recognized after they occur; but such things as affirmation, more positive responses from others, a feeling of acceptance or pride, increased self-esteem, etc. are the ultimate goals of any contract.)

☆ Develops a trial contract which is used for one week to establish a baseline of behaviors. The counselor, teacher and student should mutually agree upon the contract which clearly explains behavioral expectations, type and frequency of reinforcers, consequences, and the mechanics of recording data. This trial allows for development of reasonable expectations for improvement and for working out any "kinks" in the system.

☆ Follows up with the student after the first week to help set a realistic goal for improvement in the following week (80% mastery, three or four days out of five, fewer conduct marks each week, increase positive points earned, etc.). The educator also spends time helping the student analyze what went right and what didn't. Then, options for improvement can be discussed and written down.

☆ Has periodic contact with parents and all school staff members who are involved to evaluate the effectiveness and practicality of the current agreement and to make modifications accordingly. Whenever possible, changes should be made to reduce the degree of external monitoring and control.

After initial contracts are firmly established, individuals working on different goals can be combined into a single group. By doing this, the educator creates a powerful opportunity for positive reinforcement among peers. Because, after all, there are few things more motivating than experiencing positive peer pressure. The effect is further enhanced when the group can work together to accumulate points for a group reward. Although traditional rewards of food and goodies may be used, group members seem to enjoy and benefit from activity-based rewards which are also opportunities for practicing social interaction. For example, the group could work to earn a twenty minute basketball game, board game, etc. Group members can serve as encouragers and engage in problem solving with each other. Peers can be notoriously yet constructively relentless in giving feedback, because they rarely accept one another's lame excuses.

A participant in such a contracting group who sustains progress toward his or her personal goal for several consecutive weeks can "graduate" from daily use of the contract to more infrequent and informal monitoring. "Alumni" may then choose whether to start work on another goal within the group setting or to choose not to attend subsequent group sessions. The group establishes its own traditions for celebrating these accomplishments. For example, the successful student could wear a distinctive hat and impart words of wisdom to the group. Such a system implies a fluctuating group membership. As openings arise, older members can initiate new inductees regarding the purpose and procedures of the group.

One of the inherent difficulties with self-reporting of successes and difficulties is that some students may wish to avoid recognizing problems they are encountering and may minimize the obstacles faced during the week. Other students may have a limited self-awareness of their interactions with others. Therefore, the group leader must be prepared to serve as a "reality check," especially if he or she has received specific feedback from other sources that problems have arisen during the week. The group leader provides a delicate balance between reality and ensuring that other students within the group remain in the positive, encourager role.

Remember, following the process outlined above will help to increase the effectiveness of the results. Do not be discouraged when teachers and parents say they have "already tried" contracting and it hasn't worked. Often, many poorly designed systems have led people to believe that behavioral management doesn't work with a particular child; when in fact, a team approach to contracting could prove to be very beneficial. If parents and teachers are willing to accept assistance via the group monitoring, great! But, realistically, some teachers or parents are unable or unwilling to be observant and consistent in giving accurate feedback. In such cases, the group leader will probably be most effective if he or she helps the teacher to modify the environment or assignments and attempts to affect behavior indirectly.

On the next few pages, there are several sample contracts for primary and intermediate students. Several sample behaviors are also listed which can be cut out and pasted onto the blank contract forms. Since most students seem to sprout law degrees when it comes to interpreting loopholes for contracts, make sure that all details about rewards, consequences, frequencies of reporting, length of time system is to be used, and anything else you can think of are spelled out in writing and clearly understood by all parties. Then, it is always good to check back with everyone after a few days to clear up any residual misunderstandings. For example, with the contracts on pages 323 and 324, parents have set consequences for each type of day. Children earn a small reward when they have all smiley or straight faces (green); no consequences if they have a frown on any one behavior (yellow), and a consequence if they earn two or more frowns in one day (red). Greens may be totaled for a larger periodic reward. Each day the primary aged child gets to "start over." Don't be afraid to try any system that seems to be effective. Harvey Parker's book, *The ADD Hyperactivity Workbook for Parents, Teachers, and Kids* (see bibliography), has many additional samples of behavioral contracts that can be tried at home or in the classroom.

Name:

Day of: _____

Go for it! You are making good choices!

Slow down! Watch what choices you are making!

STOP! You need to make better choices!

Teacher Signature: Parent Signature:

_____   _____

Today, _____
earned: (Red, Yellow or Green)

© 2001, McDougall & Roper   323

Name:

Day of:_____

◠‿◠   Treats other people with respect.

◠‿◠   Controls anger

Hit pillows...
not people!

◠‿◠   Behaves in PE and Music

◠‿◠   Goes to "I'm angry" spot when mad-PM

◠‿◠   Work all done! Yeah!!

Teacher Signature: Parent Signature:

_____   _____

🙂 Go for it! You are making good choices!

😐 Slow down! Watch what choices you are making!

🙁 STOP! You need to make better choices!

Today, _____
earned: (Red, Yellow or Green)   ◯

⭐ 324 ⭐

Contract for the week of _____

(_____ is responsible for obtaining signature & points at the end of the day.)	Monday	Tuesday	Wednesday	Thursday	Friday
BONUS POINTS					
Daily Total / Teacher Signature					
Parent Signature					

Code: 3 pts = acceptable 1 pt = marginal 0 pt = unacceptable	If _____ falls below ____ points daily, the following consequences apply: _____	Weekly Total

_____ total points = _____ (privilege)

Points carried forward from previous week(s) = _____

⭐ 325 ⭐

SAMPLE BEHAVIORS FOR CONTRACTS

Controls talking

Raises hand to speak

Has travel folder daily

Has no missing homework assignments

Pays attention in class

Stays on task

Uses humor appropriately

Successful day in PE and Music

Follows all bus rules

Respects others without disturbing them

Follows directions

Completes classwork neatly

Does quality paperwork

Accepts redirections without arguing

Behaves appropriately in the cafeteria

Shows respect to peers

Walks on water
(just kidding!)

. . .a final word for creative coaches...

COACHING TIP:

The trek is a long and arduous one for us all!

TIP!!

It's probably fairly obvious by now that the conscious decision to practice "creative coaching" represents a major commitment in terms of both the personal time involved and the emotional energy you'll expend. In order to achieve excellence in helping children to reach their potential, you will encounter and overcome significant challenges that will come in the forms of ignorance, the unconscious prejudices we find in ourselves and in others, impatience, rigidity, and disappointment.

Overcoming these obstacles requires vigilance and the willingness to adopt the following strategies:

- ☆ Focus more on the diversity and differences of those with ADHD than on their deficiencies.
- ☆ Walk the fine line between making excuses for behavior and offering explanations that encourage acceptance of personal responsibility.
- ☆ Understand the "nature of the beast" while creating plans that support adaptation in a world that prizes focused concentration, attention to detail, and consistent productivity.
- ☆ Help children who have ADHD, and their families and teachers, to create a structured framework within which their creative chaos can be most productive.
- ☆ Model patience and acceptance and encourage others to teach and reteach the basic skills that many children find automatic.
- ☆ And maintain the balance between striving for goal attainment and acknowledging successive approximations over time.

Creativity and flexibility are important to remember when you are implementing the ideas in this curriculum. Hopefully, you will become so comfortable with what you are doing, that you will begin to see new combinations of activities and metaphors that can be tailored to address each of your groups' unique needs. If *Creative Coaching* can be thought of as a blueprint for building a successful team, then the more seasons you have spent with it, the more confident and adventurous you'll become. When you begin to have fun and revisit the world of play, you will relate to children on a whole new level; and they, with you.

Yes, professionals must not lose sight of who they will be coaching - not only the children with attention deficit, but also the teachers who work with them daily and the parents who will live with them for many years to come. You have an awesome opportunity to impact lives!

BIBLIOGRAPHY
RESOURCES FOR CHILDREN AND TEENAGERS

BOOKS or NEWSLETTERS

Aborn, Allyson. *Everything I Do You Blame On Me: A Self-Esteem Book to Help Children Control Their Anger.* The Center for Applied Psychology, Inc. 1994. (1-800-962-1141)

Brandenberg, Aliki. *Feelings.* Mulbery Paperback Books, 1984.

Cannon, Janell. *Stellaluna.* Scholastic Inc., 1993.

Copeland, Lori. *Hunter and His Amazing Remote Control.* Youthlight, Inc. 1998. (1-800-209-9774)

Dwyer, Kathleen. *What Do You Mean I Have a Learning Disability?* Walker and Company, 1991.

Galvin, Matthew. *Otto Learns About His Medicine: A Story about Medication for Hyperactive Children.* Magination Press, 1988.

Gehret, Jeanne. *Eagle Eyes: A Child's Guide to Paying Attention,* Verbal Images Press, 1991.

Gehret, Jeanne. *The Don't Give Up Kid.* Verbal Image Press, 1991.

Gordon, Michael. *My Brother's a World-class Pain: A Sibling's Guide to ADHD/Hyperactivity.* GSI Pub., 1992.

Gordon, Michael. *I Would if I Could: A Teenager's Guide to ADHD/Hyperactivity.* GSI Publications, 1993.

Gordon, Michael. *Jumpin' Johnny Get Back to Work! A Child's Guide to ADHD/Hyperactivity.* GSI Pub., 1991.

Lachner, Dorothea. *Andrew's Angry Words.* North-South Books. 1995.

Levine, Mel. *All Kinds of Minds.* Educator's Publishing Service, 1993.

Moss, Deborah. *Shelley, The Hyperactive Turtle.* Woodbine House, 1989.

Nadeau, Kathleen and Dixon, Ellen. *Learning to Slow Down and Pay Attention,* Revised Edition, Chesapeake Psychological Services, 1991.

Parker, Harvey. *Pay More Attention - Listen, Look and Think: A Self-Regulation Program for Children.* Impact Publications, 1995.

Parker, Roberta. *Slam Dunk: A Young Boy's Struggle with Attention Deficit Disorder.* Impact Publications, 1993.

Quinn, Patricia. *Adolescents and ADD: Gaining the Advantage.* Magination Press, 1995.

Quinn, Patricia and Stern, Judith. *Putting on the Brakes: Young People's Guide to Understanding Attention Deficit Hyperactive Disorder.* Magination Press, 1991.

Quinn, Patricia and Stern, Judith. *The "Putting on the Brakes" Activity Book for Young People with ADHD.* Magination Press, 1993.

Quinn, Patricia and Stern, Judith. *BRAKES: The Interactive Newsletter for Kids with ADHD.* Magination Press. (1-800-825-3089 for subscription)

Shapiro, Lawrence. *Sometimes I Drive My Mom Crazy, But I Know She's Crazy About Me.* The Center for Applied Psychology, Inc. 1993.

Wood, Audrey. *Quick as a Cricket.* Child's Play International Ltd. 1982.

GAMES and VIDEOS

Dealing With Feelings Cards. Feelings Factory, Inc. (919-828-2264)

Mind Your Manners. At Ease, Inc. (513-241-5216)

Stop, Think, Relax. Childswork/Childsplay. (1-800-962-1141)

The Family Happenings Game or *My Game, Your Game, Our Game* from Kids in Progress, Inc.

The Great Feelings Chase. Childswork/Childsplay.

The Social Skills Game. Childswork/Childsplay.

The Talking, Feeling & Doing Game. Childswork/Childsplay.

Sunburst Communication (1-800-431-1934) has several excellent videos that are affordable for your school librarian to order. Some that we have found to be good include:

All About Anger (grades one - four)   Conflict Resolution (grades two - four)

I'm So Mad! (grades one - four)   Respecting Others (grades two - five)

Be Cool Series. James Stanfield Co. inc. (1-800-421-6534 or www.stanfield.com).

Order catalog to preview lower, middle & upper elementary and middle or high school modules.

PARENT RESOURCES

BOOKS and ARTICLES

Barkley, Russell A. *Taking Charge of ADHD: The Complete, Authoritative Guide for Parents.* Guilford Press, 1995.

Flick, Grad. *Power Parenting for Children with ADD/ADHD: A Practical Parent's Guide for Managing Difficult Behaviors.* The Center for Applied Research in Education. 1996.

Dendy, Chris. *Father to Father: The ADD Experience.* Clark/Hill/Communications. 1997 (770-962-0828)

Dendy, Chris. *Teen to Teen: The ADD Experience.* Clark R. hill, Inc.. 199. 9 www..chrisdendy.com

Grant, Wilson. *Strategies for Success: How to Help Your Child with ADHD or Learning Disability.* Health Resources, 1988.

Hartmann, Thom. *ADD Success Stories: A Guide to Fulfillment for Families with Attention Deficit Disorder.* Underwood Books, 1995.

Hartmann, Thom and Bowman, Janie with Burgess, Susan. *Think Fast! The ADD Experience.* Underwood Books. 1996.

Kelly, Kate and Ramundo, Peggy. *You Mean I'm Not Lazy, Stupid or Crazy?! A Self-Help Book for Adults with Attention Deficit Disorder.* Scribner, 1995.

"Life in Overdrive," Claudia Wallis, *Time,* Vol. 144. Nol 3 (July 18, 1994), p.42-50.

McNamara, Barry and McNamara, Francine. *Keys to Parenting a Child with Attention Deficit Disorder.* Barron's Educational Series, 1993.

"Mother's Little Helper," Lyn Nell Hancock, *Newsweek,* Vol. 127, Nol 12 (March 18, 1996), p. 51-56,59.

Parker, Harvey. *The ADD Hyperactivity Workbook for Parents, Teachers, and Kids,* second edition. Speciality Press, 1994.

Silver, Larry. *The Misunderstood Child. A Guide for Parents of Children with Learning Disabilities,* Second Edition. McGraw-Hill, 1994.

Silver, Larry. *Dr. Larry Silver's Advice to Parents on ADHD.* American Psychiatric Press, 1993.

Taylor, John. *Helping Your Hyperactive/Attention Deficit Child.* Prima Publishing, 1994.

VIDEOS

Goldstein, Sam. *Why Won't My Child Pay Attention?* Neurology Learning & Behavior Center. 1989. (76 mins.)

Phelan, Thomas. *1-2-3 Magic: Training Your Preschooler and Preteen to Do What You Want Them to Do.* Child Management, Inc. 1990. (120 mins.)

NATIONAL ORGANIZATIONS

Attention Deficit Information Network (AD-IN), 475 Hillside Avenue, Needham, MA 02194. (617) 455-9895.

Attention Deficit Disorder Association (ADDA), 1-800-487-2282. Support Group Referral & Info.

Attention Deficit Resource Center, Suite 14, 1344 East Cobb Drive, Marietta, GA 30068.

ADD Warehouse (ADDW), 1-800-233-9273. Call to order free catalog of published materials.

Children and Adults with Attention Deficit Disorders (CH.A.D.D.), 1-800-233-4050.

Call for additional information on local chapters.

CompuServe's ADD Forum. Call 1-800-487-0453 for information on joining CompuServe.
(ADD Forum is the world's largest interactive ADD Support Group.)

ERIC Clearinghouse for Handicapped and Gifted Children, Council for Exceptional Children,
1920 Association Drive, Reston, VA 22091, 1-703-264-9474 for numerous articles.

Office of Civil Rights, U.S. Department of Education, 400 Maryland Ave., SW, Washington, DC
20202-4135, 1-202-401-3020. Call for information on Section 504 and Public Law 94-142.

PROFESSIONAL RESOURCES

BOOKS and ARTICLES

American Psychiatric Association: *Diagnostic and Statistical Manual of Mental Disorders, Fourth Edition*,
Washington, DC, American Psychiatric Association, 1994.

Armstrong, Thomas. *In Their Own Way: Discovering and Encouraging Your Child's Personal Learning Style*.
Jeremy P. Archer, Inc. 1987.

Barkley, Russell. *Attention Deficit Hyperactivity Disorder: A Handbook for Diagnosis and Treatment*.
The Guilford Press, 1990.

Canfield, Jack and Wells, Harold. *100 Ways to Enhance Self-Concept in the Classroom: A Handbook for
Parents and Teachers*. Prentice-Hall. 1976.

Canfield, Jack and Hansen, Mark Victor. *Chicken Soup for the Soul*. Health Communications, Inc. 1993.

Canfield, Jack and Hansen, Mark Victor. *A 2nd Helping of Chicken Soup for the Soul*. Health
Communications, Inc. 1995.

Canfield, Jack and Hansen, Mark Victor. *A 3rd Serving of Chicken Soup for the Soul*. Health
Communications, Inc. 1996.

Cihak, Mary and Heron, Barbara. *Games Children Should Play: Sequential Lessons for Teaching
Communications Skills*. Goodyear Publishing Co. 1980.

*Comprehensive Guidance Program for Texas Public Schools - A Guide for Program Development (PreK-12th
Grade)*, Texas Education Agency, 1990.

Copeland, Edna and Love, Valerie. *Attention Without Tension*. Resurgens Press.

Fluegelman, Andrew, ed. *The New Games Book*. Doubleday & Company, Inc. 1976.

Hallowell, Edward and Ratey, John. *Driven to Distraction: Recognizing and Coping with Attention Deficit
Disorder from Childhood through Adulthood*.Touchstone, 1994.

Hallowell, Edward and Ratey, John. *Answers to Distraction*. Pantheon, 1994.
Kids Connection Program, Rainbow Days, Inc. 1989.

Learned, Charles. *Adventure Based Resources Index System (ABRIS)*. Learned Enterprises Publication, 1991.
(1-800-462-0411 for information)

Lavelle, Lynn. *Charting Through Troubled Waters*. Pro-Ed., Inc. 1998.

LeFevre, Dale. *New Games for the Whole Family*. The Putnam Publishing Group, 1988.

Levine, Mel. *Educational Care: A System for Understanding and Helping Children with Learning Problems at
Home and in School*. Educators Publishing Service, Inc. 1994.

McCarney, Stephen B. *The Attention Deficit Disorders Intervention Manual, Revised & Updated Edition*.
Hawthorne Educational Services, Inc. 1994.

McGinnis, Ellen and Goldstein, Arnold. *Skill-Streaming in Early Childhood*. Research Press, 1990.

McGinnis, Ellen and Goldstein, Arnold. *Skills Streaming the Elementary School Child*. Revised Edition, 1997.
Research Press.

Moe, Jerry and Ways, Peter. *Conducting Support Groups for Elementary Children K-6: A Guide for
Educators and Other Professionals*. Johnston Institute, 1991.

Moe, Jerry. *Discovery: Finding the Buried Treasure: A Prevention/Intervention Program for Youth from High Stress Families*. Sierra Tucson Educational Materials Publications, 1993.

"NIMH Collaborative Multisite Multimodal Treatment Study of Children with ADHD: I. Background and Rationale," Richters, John et al. *Journal of the American Academy of Child and Adolescent Psychiatry*, 1995, 34, 8:987-1000.

Nowicki Jr., Stephen and Duke, Marshall P. *Helping the Child Who Doesn't Fit In*. Peachtree Publishers, 1992.

Parker, Harvey. *The ADD Hyperactivity Handbook for Schools: Effective Strategies for Identifying and Teaching Students with Attention Deficit Disorders in Elementary and Secondary Schools*. Impact Publications, Inc. 1992.

Physicians' Desk Reference, 49th Edition. Medical Economics. 1995.

Rief, Sandra. *How to Reach and Teach ADD/ADHD Children: Practical Techniques, Strategies, and Interventions for Helping Children with Attention Problems and Hyperactivity*. The Center for Applied Research in Education, 1993.

Rohnke, Karl. *Silver Bullets: A Guide to Initiative Problems, Adventure Games, Stunts and Trust Activities*. Project Adventure, Inc. 1984.

Rohnke, Karl. *Cowstails and Cobras II: A Guide to Games, Initiatives, Ropes Courses, & Adventure Curriculum*. Project Adventure, Inc. 1989.

Senn, Diane & Sitsch, Gwen. *Coping With Conflict: An "Elementary" Approach*. Youthlight, Inc. 1996.

Shapiro, Lawrence E. ed., *The Book of Psychotherapeutic Games*. Center for Applied Psychology, Inc. 1993.

Trower, Terry. *Stories For Elementary and Middle School Students Who Are Dealing With Anger (Grades 3-6)*. Affective Enterprises, 1989.

Wenc, Charlene. *Cooperation: Learning Through Laughter, Second Edition: 51 Brief Activities for Groups of All Ages*. Educational Media Corporations, 1993.

"To Your Health," in *The Magazine of Human Health Care Plan*, Spring 1996.

Wender, Paul. *The Hyperactive Child, Adolescent, and Adult: Attention Deficit Disorder Through the Lifespan*. Oxford University Press, 1987.

THE
CREATIVE COACHING
TEAM

As a team, Nancy McDougall and Janet Roper offer a unique blend of personal and professional experiences that have contributed to their development of the award-winning **Creative Coaching** curriculum. Both began teaching science at the secondary level to general and special education populations. Having separately arrived at the belief that affective interventions were as important as those in the cognitive domain, and recognizing that earlier interventions held greater promise of success, they each entered the field of elementary school counseling.

With a combined experience of 47 years in the field of education, 29 of which have been in school counseling, Nancy and Janet have been actively engaged in writing guidance curriculum for the last five years. They have also enjoyed presenting professional development workshops and inservices for teachers, counselors and parents at the local, state, national and international levels.

As they relate their personal experiences with ADHD and involve workshop participants in activities designed to teach specific, practical intervention strategies, Nancy and Janet provide a dynamic and fast-paced alternative to traditional inservices. And, although their presentations focus on the needs of children with ADHD, most of what they share has relevance for all children. Professionals leave their workshops with valuable, down-to-earth, creative methods for making significant differences in the lives of children and their families.

Nancy and Janet are available for a limited number of workshops each year. If you are interested in talking with them about opportunities for professional development in your area, they can be contacted through YouthLight, Inc. at 1-800-209-9774.